FRONTIER FIDDLER

The Life of a Northern

Arizona Pioneer

Kenner Casteel Kartchner

Larry V. Shumway, Editor

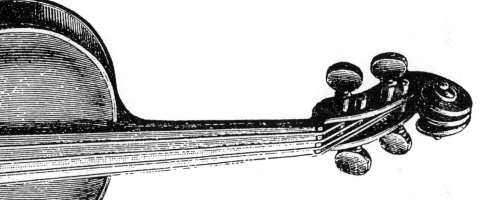

Frontier

Fiddler

The University of Arizona Press   Tucson

The University of Arizona Press

Copyright © 1990

All Rights Reserved

This book was set in Century Expanded.

Manufactured in the United States of America.

♾ This book is printed on acid-free, archival-quality paper.

95 94 93 92 91   5 4 3 2 1

Library of Congress Cataloging-in-Publication Data

Kartchner, Kenner Casteel, 1886-1970.
    Frontier fiddler : the life of a northern Arizona pioneer / Kenner
Casteel Kartchner ; Larry V. Shumway, editor.
        p.   cm.
    ISBN 0-8165-1153-5 (alk. paper)
    1. Kartchner, Kenner Casteel, 1886-1970.   2. Pioneers—Arizona-
-Biography.   3. Fiddlers—Arizona—Biography.   4. Fiddle tunes-
-Arizona.   5. Frontier and pioneer life—Arizona.   6. Arizona-
-Social life and customs.   I. Shumway, Larry V.   II. Title.
F811.K37A3   1990
979.1'05'092—dc20
    [B]   89-27085
                                                                          CIP

To my parents, James Carroll
and Merle Kartchner Shumway.
To Dad for his foresight in
recording for posterity;
to Mom for her dedication in
preserving pioneer music and
culture in the schools, church,
and community.

CONTENTS

Acknowledgments ix

Introduction xi

Map of Arizona xv

ONE   Beginnings 1

TWO   Adolescence 37

THREE   On My Own 59

FOUR   Country Fiddler: Dancing and Other Sports 82

FIVE   Work Away from the Farm 107

SIX   Punching Cows for the Long H Ranch 130

SEVEN   Selling Horses: The Globe Venture 171

EIGHT   Time to Settle Down 185

NINE   Seventeen Years in the Forest Service 205

TEN   The Violin and Public Relations 231

Appendix A:
Principal Fiddle Tunes Played by Kenner C.
Kartchner 253

Appendix B:
Brief Analysis of Kartchner's Playing Style 258

Appendix C:
Dance Descriptions 262

Appendix D:
Seventeen Fiddle-Tune Transcriptions 265

Index 273

ACKNOWLEDGMENTS

Much of the credit for the original memoirs goes to Kartchner's eldest daughter, Merle Kartchner Shumway, whose persistent encouragement and goading helped him to see the value of his life's experiences and how beneficial a record of them would be to later generations. She also did the first typescript from the original longhand manuscript. Through the years she accompanied his fiddling on the piano, having learned this art at an early age. She was in a position, therefore, to provide valuable stories and other information about the music and its role in early times. I would like to thank her for her considerable encouragement and help in this project. I would also like to thank Kartchner's other children—Stanley, Kenner, Jr., Jene, and Afton Kartchner Shreeve—for their help.

I also wish to acknowledge the help I received from Kartchner's three musical sisters—Thalia Butler, Jenny Morris, and Leone Decker—before they passed on, especially for their cooperation in providing background information.

I am indebted as well to the College of Humanities at Brigham Young University for research support in gathering and collating these materials, and particularly to the Humanities Research Center for computer-related help.

L.V.S.

INTRODUCTION

It is very difficult for us in this day and age to understand the hunger people of pioneer times felt for music or to comprehend the vitalizing role it played in their lives in relieving the harshness of their living conditions. This role is especially apparent during frontier times in northeastern Arizona. In personal journals, in reminiscences of oldsters, or in family traditions, we find people speaking with great warmth of the music or of their delight in finding someone who could sing or play an instrument. Fiddle music was in particular demand because dancing was the most important and widespread community social activity. Held at the church, schoolhouses, county courthouse, or even at outlying ranch houses, dances were frequent affairs and required a certain supply of musicians. While many people were but amateurs, other individuals and families excelled in music. One such person was Kenner Casteel Kartchner, who lived from 1886 to 1970 and was widely known in his day for his fine old-time fiddling.

Born in Snowflake, a mountain community in northern Arizona, Kartchner led a varied and colorful life as farmer, cowpuncher, fiddler, store clerk, forest ranger, forest supervisor, state game warden and federal fish and wildlife official. He was well known and highly respected in professional circles because of his knowledge of wildlife and range management, but it was his reputation as a fine, old-time fiddler that he is best remembered by the population at large. His music filled many dance halls in northern Arizona from about 1902 until the early 1920s when a marked shift of musical and dancing tastes led to a decline in fiddle music in favor of ensembles playing the popular music of the larger American culture.

Snowflake was established in 1878 by Mormon pioneers who came in from Utah. During Kartchner's childhood it was still very much a frontier community and reflected the life led by the pioneers. His childhood was conventional in many ways, typical of those growing up on a farm. His adolescence was somewhat out of the ordinary, however, for by age fifteen he was a fiddler of some repute and was playing regularly for dances at towns and ranches within a radius of about thirty miles. He was, therefore, more traveled, with a wider social acquaintance than his contemporaries, and as a result his view of the outside world was broader as compared to that held by those living the rather restricted life of an agrarian, homogeneous, and somewhat isolated community. This view was enlarged considerably after his marriage in 1908, when he moved to Salt Lake City and worked for almost three years in a men's clothing store, interspersed every spring with several weeks on the sheep-shearing circuit.

Returning to Arizona in 1911, Kartchner passed the Forest Service examination, which led to an appointment in January 1913 as assistant forest ranger, attached to the Sitgreaves National Forest. He spent the next seventeen years with the Forest Service, serving in five forests in Arizona and New Mexico and rising to the position of forest supervisor.

Kartchner left the Forest Service in 1930 and worked at several jobs in the private sector. He also did contract work for the Arizona Game Commission. He was appointed as Arizona state game warden in early 1940, a post he held until October 1943, when he accepted a position with the Federal Fish and Wildlife Service in region two, with headquarters at Albuquerque, New Mexico. Soon thereafter, he was promoted to assistant regional director, a post he held until retirement in 1956.

An astute observer of the times, Kartchner recorded his memoirs in his retirement years, aided by a phenomenal memory for events, names, dates, and places, and by journals kept over the years. Taken as a whole, his writings give us a perceptive, firsthand view of life in frontier Arizona, not only of the work-a-day world and its often attendant excitement and dangers, but also of the entertainments and other activities people pursued to find relief from the hardships of pioneer life. His writings are organized more or less chronologically, though he will occasionally break to follow an idea into later times. I have tried to preserve as much as possible the original form and flavor of the material, with only occasional shifting of material for clarity. I have annotated the text in places and added material from other sources to fill in gaps or make smoother transitions.

Fiddling was one of Kartchner's lifelong interests, and since he devoted a fair number of pages specifically to it, it seemed fitting to begin his memoirs with an introductory essay on music and dance in frontier Arizona and a synopsis of his role in it. Four appendices deal with the music itself in more detail, including music transcriptions of a number of his fiddle tunes.

Fiddle Music on the Arizona Frontier

At the turn of the twentieth century, Arizona was still a territory while most of its neighbors had already gained statehood. During the previous thirty-five years, permanent settlements had appeared—farming communities, sheep and cattle ranches, lumber and mining camps. In 1881 a railroad was completed across the northern part of the territory, which slowly brought added settlement and development. By the standards of more settled areas, however, life in the early 1900s still reflected many of the conditions under which pioneers had struggled, in spite of the fact that by then many settlements had been in existence for more than twenty years. Nevertheless, the permanent settlements were stable entities, and this made them focal points for community interaction. This was particularly important in the development of musical life, where music was performed primarily in connection with dancing.

There were three distinct groups of settlers in northeastern Arizona, each of which provided its own particular context for dancing: Mormon pioneer groups sent in from Utah and other places, numbers of assorted cowhands and ranchers, the majority from Texas, and Mexican Americans from New Mexico.

The most cohesive group was the Mormons. Pioneering and

colonizing groups were sent to Arizona from various parts of Utah beginning in 1876. They created a number of small settlements along the upper reaches of the Little Colorado River and its tributaries in both northeastern and central-eastern Arizona. The most prominent of the northeastern settlements became the towns of Snowflake and St. Johns. Differing from other conservative Christian churches that prohibited dancing, the Mormon church not only encouraged it but also lent its organization and facilities. For example, in less than a year after arriving in Snowflake in 1879, the Mormon pioneers had built a log schoolhouse that was used also as a hall for worship, civic meetings, and dancing. In 1881, a frame building was erected for the Relief Society, a church women's organization, to be used, among other things, for dancing. In 1893, a local store run by the Flake brothers, who were active in church affairs, moved into a new two-story brick building. The top floor was an open hall for dances, other socials, and theatricals. Thus in a period of fourteen years, three places for dancing and other social get-togethers had been built, two of which continued to be used well into the twentieth century.

Many cowhands came to Arizona in the 1880s, lured by the prospects of new opportunities in the large, open cattle-grazing ranges. While some came as individual cowhands or as small-time ranchers, others came as part of large ranching operations, one of which was the Aztec Land and Cattle Company (1884), known throughout Arizona as the Hash Knife outfit. These non-Mormon ranchers located in the same general areas as the Mormons. Except for the Hash Knife outfit, perhaps, the non-Morman ranchers were a less cohesive group than the Mormons. Nevertheless, they were bound by many common cultural traditions and musical preferences. Dances were held regularly in their areas, sometimes out at a ranch house, but also at the courthouse, the local schoolhouse, or some other public building.

Most Mexican and Spanish Americans in northeastern Arizona had come from New Mexico. The majority were originally connected with sheep-ranching operations, though many left that pursuit to take up farming. Three such communities were located at St.

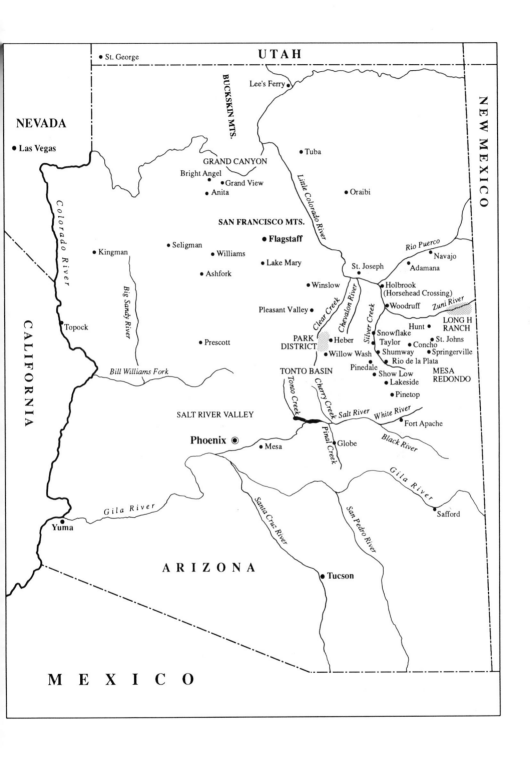

Johns, at Concho, a town about halfway between St. Johns and Snowflake, and at Rio de la Plata [Silver Creek], some ten miles south of Snowflake. Concho, a fertile grazing area, was by the mid-1880s a bustling farming and sheep town with many prosperous citizens. Though these people remained somewhat apart from the other two groups because of a different language and cultural background, their community life was full of music and entertainment connected with fiestas, weddings, and other festive occasions. They often called on Anglo musicians from the other groups to furnish the music for their dances.

The dance was the most important, frequent, and widespread form of community recreation. It might be held on any occasion but certainly would be part of any number of local or national celebrations, election day, harvest time, Fourth of July, and athletic events. While most came from miles around to dance, many also came just to listen to the music. Out-of-towners would often camp nearby. After the evening meal, when the children had been bedded down, the adults would gather for the dance. The usual pattern was to dance until about midnight when there would be an intermission with a big meal ("feed"), followed by an entertaining program. Then there would be more dancing until the wee hours of the morning, after which people would gradually drift home. In the outlying areas, following a similar pattern, dances were held in someone's ranch house, where furniture was moved out of the rooms to provide floor space for dancing.

Music was most commonly supplied by the fiddle, drawing from a large body of tunes basically of Scottish-Irish origin. Accompanying instruments were usually the guitar, which had come into general use by this time, the banjo, and occasionally the reed organ. Resonance, rather sturdy structure, and sheer toteability of the guitar made it an ideal accompanying instrument for the fiddle. Banjos were found less often, though Kartchner mentions them being used occasionally. In addition to these there were growing numbers of reed organs in the more settled areas. There were also a few pianos around, but it was not until the teens and on into the twenties that the piano came into general use as an accompanying instrument.

Of the early settlers moving into Snowflake from Utah in the 1870s, the William Decatur Kartchner family were among the most musical. Coming from Panguitch, Utah, they settled at Snowflake in 1878, bringing with them two guitars, harmonicas, and at least two violins. Two of the sons, John and Nowlin, played the fiddle, and two daughters, Prudence and Minda, played the guitar. The whole family were singers, and, while little is known about their fiddle music, many of their songs and guitar tunes have come down to us. They had both a strumming and a finger-picking solo style on the guitar.

Another musical family was that of John Hunt, who arrived not long after the Kartchners. His daughters—Ida, Lois, Annella, and Belle—became locally famous for their singing. While many people could sing parts, the singing of the Hunt sisters was of such a sweet and harmonious quality that they were in great demand.

Two other musical families were the Hamiltons and the Lindseys, who had converted to the Mormon faith in Banner, Mississippi, and had moved directly to Arizona in 1890. Among them were fiddlers and singers who added greatly to the musical scene and brought with them their own body of southern songs and fiddle tunes. One who was to become an important figure in the fiddling tradition was a grandson of the Hamiltons, Claude Youngblood. A boy of eleven when the family arrived, he had already been playing for some time. By the late 1890s he was considered to be one of the best dance fiddlers around and was in demand for dances in the Snowflake area and in communities east and west of Holbrook along the railroad.

The Hunt and Kartchner families came together in the marriage of Annella to the youngest Kartchner boy, Orin, in 1883, and to this union was born Kenner Casteel Kartchner, who was to become perhaps the most important figure in the fiddling tradition of the area. Kartchner's musical inclinations manifested themselves at an early age. He learned to accompany singing on the guitar at age seven, and at age twelve his father fixed up an old, undersized violin for him, which he immediately began learning to play, more or less on his own. Using local fiddlers, particularly Youngblood, as models, Kartchner apparently applied himself with some diligence, as he describes in the following words:

> By age 14 [1900] I was playing on church recreational programs and for kids' dances in Flake brothers' hall atop their general store. Within a year I was playing with Claude T. Youngblood, seven years my senior and considered the best dance fiddler in the area. No opportunity to hear him play had been overlooked and a teenager learns fast that which he loves to do most. . . . Before long we were playing together and very much alike.

A new ingredient was added somewhere at this point in the person of Frank Pruitt, a Texas cowboy fiddler who in Kartchner's estimation had "the touch of an artist on cattle country hoedowns (which were well suited for square dances, or quadrilles)." Pruitt had worked for a while for the Hash Knife outfit while his family lived in Snowflake. He later worked for the Bar W, ten miles south of Snowflake. Pruitt seldom played for dances, but his playing style was extraordinarily fine. Kartchner and Youngblood followed him around, as they were able, learning his tunes and copying his style, which enlarged their repertoire considerably.

Dancing, particularly in the conservative Mormon settlements, was usually restricted to quadrilles and partner dances that involved little body contact, except for hands and arms. In the late 1890s, the waltz began making its appearance in western rural areas, and soon news of it filtered into Snowflake. It is said to have been first brought there by Solan Marker of Holbrook, who with his father, Pete, was a popular dance fiddler. The older folks condemned the waltz as scandalous since it put male and female face to face and in too close quarters to be decent. On the contrary, it appealed greatly to the younger set, and frequently teenagers would sneak over to a large cement slab in front of the Co-op Store (the town "square") and dance the waltz surreptitiously to the accompaniment of Kartchner's fiddle. The waltz tune that started all this is known as the "Pete Marker Waltz."

The waltz became more acceptable around the turn of the century, and soon it and other types of "round" dances—among them the two-step, the circle two-step, the rye waltz, the varsovienne, and the Chicago glide—came into style. Many of the tunes for these dances lent themselves to harmonizing parts, and Kartchner, drawing on his family's musical background, began to specialize in playing harmony parts to Youngblood's melody, creating a duet style. This new violin harmony achieved such popularity throughout the territory that it put the musical team of Kartchner and Youngblood in constant demand. Their playing circuit included the towns of Holbrook, Winslow, Adamana, and Navajo along the railroad, and farther south the Mormon communities of Woodruff, Snowflake, Taylor, and St. Johns, and finally the Mexican-American communities in St. Johns and at Concho. It also included playing for dances at a number of ranch houses in between.

The "breakdown" tunes learned from Pruitt came in handy as they played for the regular Saturday night "jubilee dances" along the railroad to the north, where a large percentage of the population were former Texans. Playing much alike, Kartchner and Youngblood were able to spell each other and thus cope with the rigors of playing fast breakdowns for long periods of time. Together they could outlast any caller, and this added to their popularity, because most of the dances were all-night affairs, and their music was as good and strong at the end as at the beginning.

Kartchner and Youngblood began playing for dances in the Mexican-American communities at Concho and St. Johns in 1902. Though usually associated with church fiestas, these dances were also held in connection with weddings, which were very elaborate affairs. People sometimes requested Anglo dances such as the two-step, schottische, or rye waltz, but the predominant dances were the waltz, Spanish polka, and Spanish quadrille, a dance somewhat similar to the square dance but without a caller. The tempo for these dances was faster. With their large repertoire, Kartchner and Youngblood had no particular problems in coming up with the proper music, especially under the guidance of Antolino Tafoya, a local, blind guitar player who not only backed them up on the guitar but also gave them cultural advice and recommended appropriate tunes.

Violin harmony was especially fitting to waltz music and strongly appealed to Mexican Americans. As a result, Kartchner had many opportunities to polish up his harmonizing ability. Preceding the dance there was frequently a "grand marche" (sometimes found also at the Anglo dances). On the afternoon before the dance, they rode around town in a wagon playing to advertise the dance that evening. For weddings, they accompanied the bridal procession to and from the church.

During this period, Kartchner was running the family farm while his father was away on a church mission, and at the same time playing for dances up to three times a week. In February 1903, soon after his father's return, Kartchner, now sixteen, left home and spent a year in the Flagstaff-Williams-Grand Canyon area. He worked at several temporary jobs, but between jobs or on week-ends he found work evenings playing fiddle at saloons. Here he picked up a number of new tunes from people hailing from a variety of places and added substantially to his repertoire.

Almost a year to the day after leaving home, Kartchner returned. Jobs and money were scarce in Snowflake in 1904, so he and Young-blood, who had attained some popularity as musicians the year before, decided to go into music full-time. Word got around, and soon they became hard pressed to keep up with the demand for their services, particularly on Friday and Saturday nights. They traveled to their playing engagements by horseback, buggy, or railroad, sometimes using all three modes of transportation to get to a scheduled dance.

This was something of a formative period for Kartchner, who was only seventeen. The constant playing solidified his style and at the same time brought him in contact with a variety of musical demands that kept his full repertoire active and occasionally added new tunes. Over the next few years, he perfected his playing technique and became a well-known musical figure in northeastern Arizona. Much of his popularity was due to his gracious personality as well as his fiddling ability. He was willing to play whenever asked, no matter what the occasion. One story is told that shows how the people hankered for his music. He arrived for a playing engagement on the same train as a whistle-stopping politician, who was mystified but certainly gratified at a large crowd gathered around the rear-car platform in this out-of-the-way place. The politician headed for the platform to greet what he thought were people who had come to hear him speak. A cheer went up as he came out the door. Raising his arms grandly to quiet them as they pressed forward he began his speech, only to stop in mid-sentence as the crowd went right on past him to surround a curly headed young man carrying a violin who had just alighted from the same platform. The bewilderment and chagrin on this politician's face were of such proportions that the story made good telling for years afterwards.

On March 24, 1908, Kartchner married Adlee Electa Lindsey, and shortly thereafter moved to Salt Lake City, Utah, where they lived for three years. In that urban setting there was very little demand for his kind of music, but having been taught since childhood about the necessity to improve oneself, he decided to take formal music training on the violin. He approached a Professor Nebeker who consented to give him lessons. When asked to play for the professor to give him some idea of his ability, Kartchner played an old fiddle tune, "Leather Britches," with great gusto. In a solemn silence afterwards, the Professor's only words were, "That's vulgar." Though Kartchner always told this story in later years with a chuckle, he freely admitted that the training received from Professor Nebeker was invaluable in improving his technique. Besides broadening his musical horizons, it gave his hoedown playing a crisp clarity that added to the beauty of his music.

The Kartchners returned to Arizona in 1911 to a reunion with family and old friends. It was particularly heart-warming to be once again in an atmosphere where his music was esteemed. Playing for dances became a sideline as he pursued permanent employment to provide for his family. In January 1913, after passing extensive written and field exams, he was appointed to a post as U.S. forest ranger at Willow Wash Station of the Park district of the Sitgreaves National Forest, twenty-five miles southwest of Snowflake. This marked the beginning of seventeen years with the Forest Service.

Kartchner was at his musical prime during these years. Though living at various ranger stations, he found ample opportunity for fiddling. Every evening he played for family entertainment, accompanied on the guitar by his wife. Frequently, people from nearby homesteads and ranches dropped by and the evening was spent around a huge bonfire, singing or listening to the fiddle. Kartchner played also for dances at neighboring ranches and occasionally for one in Snowflake or other nearby towns. With the telephone party-line system, requests to play for listeners over the telephone were frequent, and he always graciously complied.

Besides its entertainment value, Kartchner's fiddling also had important practical value in helping him carry out his duties as a forest ranger. As a student of forest resource conservation, he was totally committed to the goals of the Forest Service. However, at the time, the Forest Service was still new, and the local people resented having it now dictate terms as to how they could use the forest and adjacent grazing lands, when in former times they had had a free run of it. With some justification, perhaps, they were very suspicious of Forest Service people, "guv'ment men," most of whom they regarded as outsiders (city people) with a lot of book learning but who lacked the common-sense know-how and cultural values typical of frontier life. The suspicion and resentment manifested itself in foot dragging relative to conforming to service regulations, and sometimes in outright hostility. In his work, Kartchner ran into this all the time, particularly in the areas he later transferred to in New Mexico and eastern Arizona where people did not know him.

As noted above, it had always been his practice to play for people when asked, and even to volunteer to play for them. Whenever possible, he took his fiddle with him on field trips, stashing it behind the buggy seat. He had discovered that when hostile ranchers, farmers, or lumberjacks, heard him fiddle, their image of him as a "guv'ment" man changed: "You couldn't be a guv'ment' man and fiddle like that." This led to an immediate rapport, and in the course of the conversations that followed, the people discovered he was indeed one of them. Having thus gained their respect, he was listened to as he spelled out the benefits to be derived from following the Forest Service regulations and guidelines for land usage. In most cases the people came to a new understanding of the Forest Service, and this went a long way toward implementing Forest Service policies.

Kartchner became known in his New Mexico areas as the "Fiddlin' Forest Ranger," and people always wanted to know when he would be coming their way again. His supervisors often remarked, only half in jest, that if they could send him and his fiddle to all the problem spots, they would "have this thing licked," "this thing" being negative responses to Forest Service policies.

During later years, beginning in the 1930s, Kartchner played the fiddle less and less. While the press of duties was part of it, much of it was attributable to the passing of the cultural milieu that supported and esteemed fiddle music. Life in northern Arizona before World War I had not differed much for twenty years. After the war, however, things changed rapidly. The musical preferences of a once isolated area changed, too, with the younger generations becoming interested in the jazz and popular music coming to them via radio and phonograph. The fiddle as the main instrument for dancing was replaced by dance orchestras playing in ensemble from sheet music. This went hand in hand with a change in preference for dances, such as the fox-trot, which were replacing the old quadrille and other formation dances. To be sure, the older generations still loved the old-time fiddle music, and never really gave it up. Because of them, fiddling was a part of the musical scene during the thirties and forties, but its status gradually changed from one of a vital, integrated role in community life to something of a museum art, to be trotted out for special occasions, the fourth or twenty-fourth of July or for a program at an old-folks party or reunion.

At the urging of family members, Kartchner still played from time to time. In 1943, accompanied on the piano by his daughter, Merle, he made some recordings of favorite tunes for his family, at least two sets of which are still extant. Even in their poor condition, and given the neglect that was hampering his playing style, the recordings show a superb technique and an artistry which leaves little doubt as to why his music was so universally esteemed.

Upon retirement in Phoenix, Kartchner took a renewed interest in the music of his youth, much of it a result of family encouragement and the prospect of recording for them on home recording machines, as well as a growing interest in participating in fiddling contests that were becoming popular, and of being asked to play at any number of reunions of people from northern Arizona who were now retired and living in the Phoenix area. His old partner, Claude Youngblood, was also living in the valley, and they often played together at these functions.

Fiddling style as it converged in the persons of Kenner Kartchner and Claude Youngblood can only be called eclectic. The music that came in with the settlers from Utah was itself eclectic, the Mormons having gathered from a variety of places. The coming of the Hamiltons and Lindseys to Snowflake brought a style and a body of tunes from the Deep South that formed a significant part of their repertoire. The hoedowns (breakdowns) and articulate Texas style of Frank Pruitt were other significant additions.

Kartchner and Youngblood became the most important exponents of northeastern Arizona fiddle music. Of the two, Kartchner excelled in his musical versatility in harmonizing parts and his articulate observations on tune origins, fiddling, and its role in community life, which are found interspersed among his personal writings.

In later life Youngblood made at least one commercial recording, which is no longer available. Kartchner, on the other hand, besides the three private records made for family in 1943, recorded in later years on home wire and tape recorders. A number of his tunes were thus documented and have come down to us.

Kartchner mentions in chapter 4 that in 1904 he and Youngblood played for a dance at the trading post of Charlie and Sam Day at Navajo, fifty miles east of Holbrook. Charlie had just acquired an Edison cylinder phonograph with a recording attachment, and he got them to play some of their tunes into it. They returned to Holbrook by train the following morning, and before leaving for Snow-flake they gave the cylinders to Frank Wattron, who ran the local drugstore, since he owned one of the two Edison machines in town. The cylinders have since been lost. How regrettable that the itinerant recording vans sent throughout the East and South by commercial recording companies during the twenties and thirties never made it out to Arizona. Some wonderful cow-country hoedown music has been lost to us all.

CHAPTER ONE

Beginnings

What do the experiences of one lowly human being, privileged to live out a life span on the planet we call Earth, really amount to when we consider that 150 billion other people down through the ages have had the same privilege? Perhaps nothing. But look at the billions whose accomplishments have meant as much or more to human progress, but who have left not a scratch of the pen by which to be remembered, or by which to profit. In the hope that some goodwill may come of it, I am impelled to jot down my life's story as memory permits. At least my own posterity may benefit from both its good and bad features, the former to emulate, the latter to avoid. If others find it of interest, the greater will be my reward.

Born of goodly parents, I first saw the light of day October 15, 1886, in the little Mormon town of Snowflake, Apache County (now Navajo), Territory of Arizona. As if in prophecy of my somewhat turbulent career, a violent off-season snowstorm raged outside our two-room log home in the north-central part of town, where Dad and Mother took up house-keeping in 1883. Since volumes of genealogy have been written by other family members on all sides, I shall make no attempt along that line except briefly to outline my lineage.

Orin Kartchner, my father, was the youngest son in the large family of Grandfather William Decatur and Margaret Jane Casteel Kartchner. Father was born in Beaver City, Utah, February 20,

1864. The family later settled in Panguitch, Utah, from which place they answered a call by Brigham Young, president of the Church of Jesus Christ of Latter-Day Saints, and migrated by oxteam to northern Arizona.

Leaving Panguitch in November 1877, the Kartchners came to Arizona by way of Lee's Ferry over the Colorado River, south to and up the Little Colorado. They arrived in January 1878 at a site later called Old Taylor on the south bank of the Little Colorado River, opposite the present Joseph City. In July they moved south to the new town of Snowflake on Silver Creek. Grandfather Kartchner had been the first postmaster of Panguitch, and he held this distinction at Snowflake as well. For years he was also Sunday School superintendent at the latter, sidelighting his vocations as farmer, expert blacksmith, wheelwright and millwright.

My mother was Annella Hunt, third in a family of six girls and two boys. She was born in San Bernardino, California, on February 15, 1862. Her parents were John Hunt, son of Jefferson Hunt of Mormon battalion fame, and Lois Pratt, daughter of Addison and Louisa Barnes Pratt. Grandfather John Hunt was sheriff for twelve years of Beaver County, Utah, prior to deciding to head south with the other Mormon colonists, finally settling at Savoia, New Mexico, in 1877, when Mother was 15. However, after being called by the church to take charge of Snowflake Ward as bishop in 1878, Grandfather Hunt moved there with his family that fall. He fulfilled the duties of that high office, may we say rigidly by present standards, for a period of thirty-one years.

At age seventeen, Mother taught the first school in Snowflake, and later the first one in Taylor, three miles south. Dad took his first job away from home in 1879 when he was sixteen, working on the Atlantic and Pacific Railroad grade, now the Santa Fe. Trains were running through the town of Holbrook twenty-eight miles north of Snowflake by the following year. One can be proud of such ancestry, its leadership and untiring efforts at taming a wild frontier.

Our oldest sister, Celia, died at one year. Following her, I became the oldest of two boys and three girls, all born in the original log

cabin. Jennie, born September 2, 1888, became Mrs. William Ammon Morris. Thalia came next, August 16, 1891. She taught school
some thirty-nine years until retirement in 1957. She finally married
in 1965 the fine gentleman, David A. Butler. Our deepest gratitude
is extended her for her devotion to and care of both our parents in
their declining years, until their deaths. Lafayette Shephard (Lafe)
was born December 17, 1893. He married Alice Smith of Snowflake.
Leone, the youngest, born October 12, 1895, became the wife of
Jack Fulton. Later, on their separation, she married the late Silas
Decker. She, too, made a career of teaching school.

It is doubtful that anyone ever enjoyed better relations with his
parents, brother, and sisters than I always have. My wandering nature, later added upon by frequent transfers in government service,
has kept me apart from my family circle to a greater extent than the
others. This fact has served to increase our mutual pleasure
whenever visiting back and forth has been possible.

Childhood

An attempt to describe the glorious feelings of a child entering upon this earthly scene is most difficult. No matter how humble his surroundings, mother love and constant care to a normal
babe keep him in a state of heavenly bliss. This is true perhaps
throughout the biological world and I was no exception. Between
two and three years of age memories of such paradise began sticking to my mind for permanent retention. The log home was a magnificent mansion around which I operated large freight outfits and
buggy rides, using worn-out horseshoes, according to size, for draft
stock and trotters. A long stick was my favorite saddle horse, having no peer in speed and beauty!

Weighing twelve pounds at birth, I grew like a weed under the
loving care of a devoted mother, which laid the groundwork for a
long life of excellent health and vigor. Rarely have I ever been ill,
but for kid diseases and occasional hangovers. It has been so commonplace, in fact, as to be taken for granted, and I sometimes

wonder if it is possible for me to appreciate the blessing as fully as
might those not so fortunate. Inheriting Dad's physique is a good
part of the story, coupled with a high longevity average on both
sides of the house. For these I am grateful. Of course, open-air
living and the hard physical exertion of frontier farm life had no
equal in the development of robust specimens of humanity.

Our quarter of a block, as the town was laid out, contained a fine
vegetable garden in season, with fruit trees, currants, and
gooseberries. Produce from these sources made up a good part of
our family larder, after providing breadstuff from wheat and corn
raised on a five-acre farm "across the creek." Silver Creek trickles
down through Snowflake Valley from its source at Silver Spring,
which gushes out from under a malpais (basalt) ledge, some fifteen
miles to the southeast. It never varies the year round and furnishes
irrigation for several thousand acres of tillable land at Snowflake,
Taylor—three miles south upstream—and the smaller Shumway,
another four miles on upstream. A water-powered gristmill at
Shumway (put in by early settler Charles Shumway, also called by
Brigham Young to settle in northern Arizona) manufactured flour,
graham, bran, shorts, cornmeal, and so forth, from wheat and corn
grown in Silver Creek basin, including Woodruff some twenty miles
downstream to the north.

To supplement an agricultural economy, there had to be a certain
amount of cash money with which to pay taxes and buy clothing,
farm implements, and many other articles not available to barter or
produce. Freighting U.S. government supplies from the railroad at
Holbrook ninety miles south to Fort Apache, where several companies of soldiers were garrisoned, went a long way toward meeting
this need. All farmers had from one to several teams and wagons
suitable for hauling freight after spring planting and fall harvest
seasons were over. Huge contracts were let to the lowest competent
bidder for all such haulage on a fiscal year basis, and the farmers
dealt directly with the contractor. The latter was usually a large
mercantile firm in Holbrook, either A. & B. Schuster, or the
A.C.M.I. (Arizona Cooperative Mercantile Institution), who looked
to the farmers to move the freight within time-limit guarantees.

Often emergencies arose where farming was carried on by the youngsters or hired hands, while those with teams moved the freight. As could be expected, a good part of the freighter's pay was taken in merchandise, over and above mandatory cash for taxes.

Another source of income to the farmers was the U.S. mail, carried over the same route. This, too, was handled by contract. Relay stations were located at Holbrook, Snowflake, Pinetop, and Fort Apache. Two sets of drivers operated between points, using trotting teams on buckboard vehicles. Dad was thus employed by Willis Brothers, contractors of Snowflake, at the time I was born, and for several years following. He drove daily between that point and Holbrook, spending every night at home.

As nature decreed, the mind of a normal child gradually evolves into comprehension of his surroundings. Later his play is based upon current pursuits of his fathers. In those days the automobile was unknown, and everything depended upon ox- or horse-power transportation. At less than a year old, they say, I learned to listen for the stage as Dad dropped by en route to the post office and stage headquarters, and would yell a series of "Whoas" as it approached. Also, a child mimics his parents and thereby learns to walk and talk. Eventually, the talk makes sense as he pieces it together from permanent memories. The name Geronimo was one of my first scare words. That notorious Apache outlaw was still the subject of frequent discussion, and I gathered he was some sort of demon to be feared. He had surrendered to General Miles at Skeleton Canyon on the Mexican border six weeks before I was born in 1886. Lying but thirty miles from the north boundary of Fort Apache Reservation, Snowflake, following its founding in 1878, had often been alerted to Indian uprisings and placed under guard.

Reports of murder and pillage by the Apache Kid were still rife as late as 1894, when in my eighth year Dad and I camped overnight with "Foul" (spelling not guaranteed—perhaps a nickname for File) Burk near the present village of Clay Springs, then called Perkins Farm. He was chasing wild horses; we were cutting a load of juniper fence posts. During the evening Burk confided that Apache Kid had been at his camp shortly before for food and rest for himself and horse. It seems they had met years earlier when the Kid was a trusted scout under the famous Chief of Scouts Al Seiber. Burk lived much like an Indian and was on speaking terms with many a back-country character whose record was not altogether clean. Incidentally, that night at Burk's camp it started to rain, accompanied by terrific thunder and lightning. Never shall I forget the man's yelling at the top of his raspy voice, "Let 'er come! We wuz here first. We're neither sugar nor salt, and nobody's honey!" And thus were conditions, still primitive, wherein law and order had yet to catch up with white outlaws and bad Indians. Burk will be mentioned in later paragraphs, as will famous sheriffs and outlaws of the period.

December 8, 1892, was a sad day in the history of Snowflake. It brought tragedy and grief to the whole community and left a permanent imprint of horror upon my six-year-old mind. On an errand for Mother, I was escorting my sister, Jennie, age four, down the street south three blocks to Aunt Sarah Miller's. She was my dad's oldest sister. As we reached the tithing office, two blocks away, on the west side of the street, I noticed cousin Marion L. Flake, three months my senior, on the opposite corner across the street east. He was crying. I left Jennie and ran over to see what was the matter, and there before my eyes, as I peeked through the board fence, was a most terrifying sight. The bodies of two freshly killed men lay there on the cold ground in pools of their own blood. One was Charles L. Flake, age thirty, Marion's father (Uncle Charlie to me), the other Billy Mason, the outlaw. Whether I had previously heard the four shots, as it seems I did, or whether it was the imagination of a young and tender mind, I cannot be sure. No doubt Marion had been attracted by them and went running to the scene.

Scared stiff, I ran back to Jennie, grabbed her by the hand, and ran as fast as she could stay on her feet, another block to Aunt Sarah's. She and children were shocked at my great excitement and could hardly believe my story. The errand accomplished, Jennie and I ran for home, promising Aunt Sarah we would go directly there and stay on the west side of the street. In a situation of this kind, youngsters want nothing as much as their mother, and we ran all the way. Whether she had gotten the word before our arrival, I cannot remember. But I do recall her donning an old-fashioned sunbonnet and running up the sidewalk, south a block and across the street, to the home of her next younger sister, Belle Hunt Flake, Marion's mother and the bereaved widow of his father who had fallen less than an hour before, victim of an outlaw's bullet through the neck.

Charlie Flake and his elder brother, James M., constituted the firm of Flake Brothers. Jim, an expert cowboy, took care of the outside ranching interests, and Charlie ran their thriving general store. Both were highly respected, honorable men, not only successful in business, but active in all civic affairs of the town of five hundred population. They were widely known in northern Arizona, and it was only natural, in the absence of local law officers, that they be contacted in the apprehension of criminals believed to be hiding in the vicinity.

Here is a brief résumé of events surrounding the two killings, erroneous perhaps, but only as to minor details. Billy Mason, of whom little was known, robbed a bank in Magdalena, New Mexico, escaping on horseback to Arizona. He put up for a time at a small rooming house in Woodruff, then a village of two hundred people fifteen miles southeast of Holbrook. Later he moved twenty miles south to Snowflake, where he obtained room and board with "Sister Hall," as she was known, and found hay and grain for his horse. A telegram received by Flake Brothers told of the robber—perhaps other crimes committed by Mason—that he was a dangerous man who shot a revolver with either hand, that a $1,000 reward had been posted for his capture, dead or alive, and that he was thought to be in that general area. Knowing no fear, as was typical of the Flake family, Jim and Charlie walked over that morning to Sister Hall's, where a man of Mason's description was known to be staying. Billy Mason was seated on the front steps cleaning a six-shooter. While Jim engaged him in conversation, Charlie went around to the back and told Mrs. Hall of their mission, and that she need not be alarmed. He came through the house to the front door, where Mason was sitting, which placed Mason between the two brothers.

On being told he was under arrest, Mason leaped to his feet with catlike speed, drew a second revolver all in one motion, and shot Jim through the left ear, burning his face with powder. In a flash he turned the gun back over his shoulder and shot Charlie through the neck, killing him instantly. By this time Jim had his own gun in action, shooting Mason in the mouth—tearing out most of his teeth— and again in the head before he fell to the ground dead.

It must have been after the shooting, while Jim was gone for help, that we came upon the scene, as no one was there at that time but Marion and the two dead men. Later in the day, there was a large gathering of relatives and friends at Aunt Belle's, where Uncle Charlie's body had been taken. My own curiosity centered on the hole in the upper portion of Jim's left ear. Seated in a chair, he never flinched as I watched his mother, Lucy, doctor the wound. No doubt this was the first medical attention given it or the nasty powder-burn lacerations over the left face. Longfellow's exhortation in his masterpiece, "The Psalm of Life," that we have a "heart for any fate," was fulfilled on that occasion by James M. Flake. He came literally within an inch of being killed himself, but with cold steel nerve and instant action, he was the victor over a deadly killer, menace to any society he came near. A boy my age must inherit an admiration for such nerve and heroism. I was deeply impressed.

Early Days on the Farm

In the early spring of 1896 we moved two miles up the creek to the Palmer farm, which Dad had rented for that crop year. Jennie and I walked the distance to school at ages seven and nine. Like other boys that age, my daily routine included "doing the chores," milking cows at night and morning, chopping and carrying in wood for heating and cooking, feeding the livestock, and many other tasks, dreaded for their interference with swimming or other play. Within a stone's throw, east of the house, ran Silver Creek, a constant temptation to a water-loving youngster.

As school closed in May, numerous farm duties took over. There were three cuttings of alfalfa to mow, rake, cock by pitchforks, and haul to the barn for winter feed. "Tromping" hay on a wide rack as huge loads of cured hay were built up on the wagon by two pitchers on the ground was the scourge of my young life, not to mention throwing the hay back in a hot barn as unloaders pitched it through a window. "Boy-like!" Dad would say when I proposed changing jobs with the men. "You hate the work you can do, but want to do what you can't!"

There were always weeds to hoe in corn, bean, and potato patches as well as a small garden of fresh vegetables for the table. All crops required irrigation, also, the turn for which might fall at any time, day or night, according to schedule for the district. Young boys soon caught on to that mode of life and, but for feeling sorely persecuted at times, could perform all but the heaviest tasks about a small farm. Times were hard and farmers took advantage of young help as fast as it could be developed. Such was my environment, and nothing could have been better for a young growing physique.

Dad purchased, or traded for, the Webb farm at the extreme west edge of Snowflake. At various times that summer we worked on the house located there, and also the well, to make the place livable. After lunch one day, while thus employed, Dad took a short nap. Rummaging in a box of bolts, nuts, and nails, I found an old .44-caliber cartridge loaded with black powder and a lead bullet. I wondered if it would still fire. Nothing short of a miracle saved my life to tell the story. Using a steel wire bent in the shape of a hammer, I squeezed the shell into a crack in the floor, pointed downward, and began pounding at the primer. The ensuing explosion in that empty room was worthy of a Civil War cannon. Being lighter than the bullet, naturally, the case shot up through the ceiling with terrific velocity, missing my head by inches. Imagine, too, the wild look of terror on Dad's face as he leaped to his feet and yelled, "What in thunder is going on here!" Some recovery from shock was necessary before I could explain. Almost totally deaf for a day or two, with eyesight temporarily impaired and permanent small specks of powder burn about the face, I thank my lucky stars for being permitted to live long after that never-to-be-forgotten occasion. It was my first good lesson in gun safety, as it were, that would serve me well in later years of frequent gun use.

On my tenth birthday, October 15, 1896, we moved from Palmer farm to the Webb place. School was now a short half mile distant as compared with the two miles from the ranch, and once more all community activities were within walking range. This was an important item half a century prior to our present custom of stepping in and out of cars, with no physical effort between. The land was good, and with the grazing of a small herd of livestock on open range to the west, we "prospered" by local standards for an extended period.

School Days

"Extra smart," for a child in school is often a misnomer, fraught with disadvantages that outweigh the honor. Mother had a brilliant mind, a good education for her time, and spoke faultless English. Her breadth of vocabulary and general knowledge were quite the exception in a frontier community with limited "book larnin'." She patiently answered my thousands of questions on any and every subject and taught me to read, write, and foot up simple addition a year or more ahead of entering school in 1893 at age seven. It was a quasi-public school, financed locally, no county system having yet been organized. The town social hall was used for the purpose, a huge log affair built by public subscription—mostly labor—on the site of the present building and movie theater by the same name. Wood-burning stoves provided ample heat as needed, and many a pupil received his "three R's" there.

My first teacher was Basha Smith, a model young lady, whose pay was less in cash than in farm produce, negotiable at the three local stores. Butter and eggs were common items of exchange at varying prices according to season and abundance. My own tuition and books were thus financed during at least the first term. The usual first-grade curricula were so familiar to me under Mother's tutoring, and being of a mischievous nature as well, I at once became a problem for Miss Basha. So little time was necessary for lesson preparation, she was hard put to keep me occupied and out of trouble. Throwing spitballs or setting crooked pins in the empty seats of little girls at class were sources of annoyance. Her most frequent punishment was to take a firm grip on the unbarbered hair at the back of my neck and tiptoe me up front where I must stand for a given time, face to the wall. Not exactly incorrigible, but always full of prunes, I was due for similar punishment through the higher elementary grades.

Miss Basha Smith was also my second-grade teacher in 1894–95. She finally got fed up with my idleness and mischief to the point of placing me in the third grade, which took more of my time to keep up with the lessons and thus partially solved the problem. But as the years went by, my tendency was to work ahead of the class, despite the fact that jumping a grade had thrown me with older boys who gave me a bad time. They were less studious in most cases but resented my being with them. Their ridicule was often hard to take. To make matters worse, halfway through the seventh grade, in 1898–99, teacher, Mrs. George Bailey, complained to Principal Joseph Peterson that I was ahead of my class and should be given something to do by promotion to his eighth grade. He called me in for an interview and decided it was the proper thing to do. My class relationship troubles were just beginning. Being singled out for midterm promotion, to a class membership from two to five years older than my twelve years, was more than some could stand. Pleading that I had not asked for the change made no difference with several of the older boys suffering from inferiority complexes in varying degrees. The only thing, I had for a long time admired at a small-boy distance one beautiful girl, Adlee Lindsey, whose family had converted to Mormonism in Mississippi and come to Snowflake to be with the Saints. The first time I saw her I went home and told my mother about that "prettiest black-eyed girl" in school. She was in the eighth grade, and now I was up with her. I had no idea I would one day marry her—she was three-and-a-half years older than I—but now I could watch her daily, though she seemed entirely unreachable.

But the older boys' on- and off-campus abuse, mental and physical, was the bitterest ordeal I had ever faced and left me in a killer frame of mind, not good for any youngster. Happily enough, grudges wore off to a degree, and for the first time I was up against studies that demanded every bit and more of my time and ability. Professor Peterson did right in expressing some doubt that I could pass graduation exams, which doubt, in itself, was a challenge sufficient to fire my determination. To flunk a test was unthinkable and I set to work. Mother was of great assistance except in mathematics. In that field we were beyond the limits of both her and Dad. In fact, the whole class was on its own with respect to help at home.

It was something new to rise at 5 A.M., light a wood fire in the fireplace, and study by coal-oil lamp. By only such studious application could I hope to stay up with the grade and qualify for graduation. Late in the term, we encountered tough problems in algebra, which Professor Pete insisted we solve with no outside help. There were no answers in the back of the textbook, contrary to those in lower grades, so it was impossible to take an answer and work back from there. One particular problem was a stunner, and we all came to class without its solution. Professor Pete made it plain he was getting tired of our apathy and sheer laziness, that he had no intention of working it for us, and if we did not get down to work it could mean denial of eighth grade certificates for another year! These were harsh words and the problem was held over. But the second morning found us still without an answer, and this time we got a real going-over.

After several hours of hard study that evening, I despaired of ever finding a solution on my own and went to bed disappointed in the extreme. Unable to sleep, I pondered every angle of the problem for a possible oversight in my thinking and resolved to give it another try next morning. By daybreak the fire was going and I determined to give that thing all I had. The challenge had a certain fascination, even in defeat. With a clear head I began ruling out false leads and looking for anything worth trying that had not already been explored time and again, only to get an answer that could not be proven and was therefore incorrect. Then came one of the happiest moments of a lifetime. As a ray of sunshine after storm, the correct procedure shot through my mind. I followed it through with X's, Y's, and figures to the right answer and proved it on paper. My delight was shared by Dad and Mother, who had watched helplessly the three-day struggle with sympathetic interest.

At class the third morning, Professor Pete sternly looked us over. He broke the silence slowly: "How many have the problem?" I waited for other hands. There were none. I timidly raised mine. It caused quite a stir, yet there was doubt that I, the youngest, had solved it in fact. The professor rebuked the others by saying he was tempted not to give them the benefit of my solution, if I had a correct one, but to have me work it for him privately. However, since it had been such a stumbling block to the whole class, he would have me work it out on the blackboard. This I did, followed by the necessary proof at the bottom. Professor Pete then questioned me with regard to any possible help I might have had. On learning there was none, and about the long hours, evening and early morning, spent in finally solving the problem, he held me up as an example of what can be attained by application and hard work. It was the principle he had been trying to instill in classes throughout the grades, ours in particular. Instead of stressing the fact, it would have been better for my well-being that he omit reference to my status as the youngest of the class. It tended to renew the jibes from the older boys and a certain amount of feminine scorn. However, my spirits were lifted that Adlee Lindsey was not one of these, but instead seemed to look at me with admiration. But, the fact remains, the class of '99 went on to graduate with appropriate ceremonies, and my resentment of the youthful ridicule wore off in time.

More detail is given here than such an incident would ordinarily call for. But it was to have quite a bearing on my general attitude toward life. It proved, for instance, that practically nothing is impossible when one has the desire and ambition to attain a certain goal. Strangely enough, it reduced my ego, knowing full well it was desire and hard work that put me over rather than any superior intelligence. Even the interclass derision served as an obstacle to be overcome without bloodshed, and finally, it taught me the value of thought—using your head. Only a small fraction of human beings use their brains to anything like full capacity. More than from natural talent, brilliance of mind comes from hard study. Professor Peterson had this in mind when asked years later who he would say was his most brilliant scholar over a long teaching career. After some thought he gave me the honor, but with certain qualifications involving specialist students.

Naturally, I thrilled when friends wrote me at Albuquerque, New Mexico, concerning the professor's statement, but it caused me to reflect upon our association and the tremendous influence for good he had been during my formative years. It all started soon after he came from Utah to teach his first term as principal of Snowflake's grade school, believed to have been in the fall of 1897. I was then in the sixth grade, and eleven years old that October. During a recess, just to be cussed, I wrote in white crayon on the steps of the main east entrance of the red brick building: "Peterson Old Socks." The bell rang ahead of schedule for reassembly. With all students in the "big room," the professor inquired as to who was responsible for the writing. I raised my hand, whereupon he ordered me to get my books and go home. Knowing the cooperative attitude of my parents toward teachers and school authorities, I was scared. Instead of going straight home, I loitered around a brick addition to the nearby Smith D. Rogers home being built by Joe Ramsey. The latter razzed me about not being in school, but I put him off until nearly time for it to let out, and arrived home at about the usual hour. If the folks were suspicious they said nothing, although it was breaking custom to bring all my books home except on Fridays for the weekend. But somehow I felt a storm brewing and was not to be disappointed. Sometime after supper, Professor Pete came to the house and I knew this was it. With the bearing of a perfect gentleman, which he was in truth, he related the day's events. Right off, a total lack of parental sympathy for my cause permeated the household. I sheepishly complied with their decision that I ask the professor's forgiveness, which he granted in all good grace. Humiliating indeed, but it opened the way for an enduring wholesome relationship that I fondly cherish.

In the fall of 1899 Professor Pete took over the Snowflake Stake Academy—now the Union High School—coincident with my entry there as a freshman. [A stake is a large geographical unit of the Mormon church and is composed of several wards or congregations.] Venerable and efficient, he remained as principal for many years, having made Snowflake his permanent home. He was my only "Prof" through high school, which for lack of common sense, I left just short of graduation in February 1903. With all my regrets for not finishing high school and going on to college, I am indebted to Professor Joseph Peterson for his assistance and guidance in laying a solid groundwork for basic education. And his influence did not stop there. He was a builder of character by precept and shining example that never failed to impress his students or fellowmen. Attributed largely to his studious leadership, I was eventually to occupy positions in government, federal and state, not ordinarily achieved with less than a college degree.

Religion

Settling Snowflake and vicinity was religiously inspired as part of the Latter-Day Saints program of colonizing the West. Fertile valleys everywhere were scouted for that purpose and church leaders acted upon recommendations of the explorers. Permanent water for irrigation was of primary importance, and when scouts Alma Z. Palmer (son-in-law of William Decatur Kartchner, and therefore my uncle) and William Jordan Flake came upon Snowflake Valley in the spring of 1878, there was no doubt in their minds that a prosperous colony could be established there.

The original church call was for settlement of the Little Colorado River basin, including Silver Creek, Show Low Creek, and other tributaries. Apostle Erastus Snow, then in charge of Arizona colonization for the church made trips from Salt Lake City to consult with the settlers on ways and means. Snowflake, the name for the community, was a combination of surnames, Snow and Flake, in honor of the apostle and William J. Flake.

A call from the church to colonize new sites had the same force and effect as did those for filling two-to-four year missions throughout the world, and was just as dutifully complied with. And thus it was when Grandfather William Decatur Kartchner, of Panguitch, Utah, received his call to settle in Arizona with his two large families. Some members complained of the hardships involved, pointing out, among other things, that he might not reach there in his poor state of health, brought on by years of suffering rheumatism and incident complications [as a result of being a guard of the Nauvoo Temple during bitter cold weather]. His reply was to become famous in family tradition, an epitome of his devotion to the religion of his choice. He said, in effect, "On the day that they start for Arizona, I shall arise from my bed. I may fall, but I'll fall with my face toward Arizona!"

On the other side of my family it is said that, while John Hunt (my maternal grandfather) was not actually called to settle in Arizona or New Mexico, he did consult church authorities before making the move. Tiring of the constant tension attendant upon his duties as sheriff of Beaver County, Utah, he refused to run for a seventh term and in 1875 moved the family to a farm he had purchased on the Sevier River. But it was not for long. Many of the Saints were moving to Arizona, and he grew anxious to follow suit. He traded the farm for teams and wagons and on February 15, 1877, Mother Annella's fifteenth birthday, he and family started south, their route previously described.

These frontier communities, founded and organized by church decree, naturally were comprised of staunch and sturdy members of the faith, people who could be depended upon to set up and execute standard church programs and discipline. There was something for everyone to do, from small children to adults, a pattern for which the Mormons are noted. Strict obedience to authority in all affairs, spiritual and temporal, was fundamental doctrine, only by which their leaders were able to cope with myriad problems of frontier life. For lack of any other law of consequence up to the nineties, they were a law unto themselves and ruled with a firm hand.

By the turn of the century, older leaders were having difficulty holding on to the strict discipline that had been so effective in the migration and settlement of the Rocky Mountains. A new generation was emerging which often resented the constant direction of their private lives. So-called "Gentile" towns had sprung up with their saloons and other enticements for the adventurously inclined. It was a critical period wherein peremptory orders of church authorities must gradually give way to more tactful persuasion of their young people to follow the paths of righteousness.

During this transitional era, Dad was called to fill a two-year mission for the church. So, following the harvest of 1900, he sold the work team, several head of cattle and other livestock, wagons, machinery, and equipment in order to finance the project as well as partially support Mother and her five husky children during that time. William J. Flake proposed that the family occupy, free of charge, an old adobe house near his own, and his offer was accepted. We could then lease the Webb Place to better advantage where the house went with it, and would be more centrally located in town.

As preparations were thus completed, Dad took leave for his mission in the state of Texas, September 3, 1900, six weeks short of my fourteenth birthday. So far as possible he was to travel "without purse or script" as did the prophets of old. We still owned seven acres of alfalfa land across the creek to the northeast, for which Dad had traded five acres he was allotted from the William D. Kartchner holdings farther south when he was married October 11, 1883. This would also be nearer to home. The plan was for me to operate the alfalfa farm as our main source of family income, and it worked out very well. Helping missionaries' families was a basic tenet of the church under which I was furnished the necessary machinery and equipment to handle three cuttings of hay when they were ready. Irrigation came on regular turn, which I could handle day or night without help. I could also work out the ditch tax, receiving credit at the rate of two dollars per day for hand labor. But at harvest time, a team and mowing machine were necessary for cutting and a horse-drawn rake for wind-rowing and piling when the hay was dry enough. In those days, boys were trained early for such tasks, and I needed no help to operate teams and equipment up to this point. For hauling a mile and stacking at the Stinson Place, however, two men would join me with the necessary wagon, equipped with a wide hay rack. Stacking loose hay is a science, in such manner as to shed rain and prevent spoilage. As usual, my job was tromping the loads and helping the stacker.

When the last cutting was in, Mother's two brothers, Lewis and John A. Hunt, would come and bale the entire crop with their horse-powered hay press. It was now ready for market. Quite remarkable was the fact that all the foregoing extra services were free of charge, "to help the missionaries." Friends and neighbors kept abreast of our needs, along with those of other missionary families, and took turns with their assistance. It was part and parcel of the church program, supervised by the bishop of each ward, and represented a community spirit rarely equalled in the annals of human affairs. Moreover, it was cheerfully done. Never was there a gripe or complaint. Even when buyers showed up, those with cash in hand were steered to our door. Mother had no difficulty disposing of the hay at going prices or better.

Home Horses

Probably the biggest blow to my pride at Dad's departure was the sale of our work team. Beet, a red roan, worked on the off (right) side, and Neil, brown and bald-faced, the near. Of medium weight, slightly under eleven hundred pounds each, they worked together in perfect unison, either for heavy hauling or buggy purposes. Each took a pride in not being outdone by the other, but instantly obeyed the various signals for their joint or divided action. Named for his reddish color, Beet was a Richards horse from Joseph City. Neil was a range colt carrying the F (Flake) brand and was named for "Bucky" O'Neil of Spanish War fame, always full of fire and horse dignity. "The Gang," my ten-to-fourteen-year-old sidekicks, and I often used Beet at the swimming hole and he enjoyed it as much as we. He was perfectly gentle and thought nothing of barging into water ten feet deep, carrying as many naked kids as could find room on his back. He swam lazily with only his head above water, groaning his pleasure as we used him for a diving board. Neil was too high-spirited and haughty for such monkey business. On rare occasions when Dad would let me take them both, I rode Neil alone. Always on the go, he swam with such vigor that his back remained above water.

As for horse character, Neil had it. Raised on the open range, his wild instinct was never totally subdued. Neither Dad nor I could walk up to him loose in a pasture, and occasionally he refused to be driven to the corral. With head and tail high he would scamper from one end of the enclosure to the other, enjoying himself thoroughly at our expense. Eventually, this would lead to one of the strangest phenomena within my experience. Having watched our unsuccessful attempts to capture this renegade, Mother (Annella) would don her sunbonnet, pick up a tie rope and walk out across the field directly up to Neil, who stood there and never moved until she tied the rope around his neck with which to lead him in. She did this several times, to the consternation of us all, including herself. How she could exert such an influence over a wild beast, by comparison with the fruitless efforts of Dad and myself, will have to remain a mystery. Some kind of horse psychology had to be involved. Did he reason and thus react that she had never given him a cross word or caused him any trouble, and therefore none was anticipated? Or did he, as I prefer to think, somehow join human counterparts in associating her with everything good and wholesome, rating her as an outstanding something to be revered and obeyed? Will we ever know?

But the real beauty of these two animals was the way they worked together. Dad was an expert at training horses, work teams in particular. One would hardly expect the best results from two horses of directly opposite dispositions, but the docility of one offset the fiery action of the other, and vice versa, thus striking a happy medium. We always kept them well fed, in good working condition, and to drive them was my pride and joy—analogous to present day thrills of youngsters with a new automobile. They could trot all day on a buggy, to my particular delight, or pull heavy loads in slow motion as occasion called for.

As for as the latter, one incident may be told as typical of their joint capabilities. After supper one evening in late 1899, our attention was drawn to a light six-horse freight outfit stuck in the heavy sand of Cottonwood Wash, which skirted our place a mile above its confluence with Silver Creek at the lower end of Snowflake Valley. Six scrawny gray ponies were hitched to two light wagons loaded with government stores for Fort Apache. They were getting nowhere in their half-hearted struggle to move the cargo. Shouted profanity of the Spanish variety and loud cracks of the whip permeated the atmosphere to no avail. Dad told me to harness the team and we would help the man out.

It was Juan Padilla of Holbrook who welcomed our arrival. Dad told him to remove all six of his horses, that he thought our two could handle the load as wheelers (next to the front wagon) and they pulled best with nothing in front of them. Padilla complied, very much in doubt that two horses could do what his six could not. All set, we shoveled sand from in front of the eight wheels for a slight aid in starting. Sensing the difficulty, Neil was chewing the bit and twitching his muscles, while Beet remained calmly alert for the go signal. Dad soothed them with his soft "St-e-a-d-y" command. As he clucked to proceed, their response was instantaneous and thrilling to witness. Each squatted for purchase in the soft sand, with perfect balance on the double-trees. Several seconds elapsed before the wagons began to budge. It was nip and tuck. But once started, there was no holding the victorious team until it reached hard ground thirty yards or so distant. Padilla was astounded. "Ah, que buenos caballos!" he shouted flamboyantly. He could hardly believe his own eyes. As he was to camp there for the night, after a pause for the horses to catch their wind, the wagons were pulled off the road to a suitable location. Then, drawing a buckskin sack from his pocket, he offered to pay, which of course was refused. He chattered over and over his appreciation in Spanish and broken

English—choice material for my natural tendency to mimic people for the fun of it.

Here was vivid proof of how horses will serve you to the limit of their capacities in response to ample feed, kindness, and sensible training, and of how man can become attached to them almost as members of the family. To part with Beet and Neil was one of the trials and sorrows of my young life and made me wonder at the time if Dad's mission was so important as to warrant their sale, perhaps into the comparative horse slavery of Juan Padilla's crow baits. Of all the teams furnished me to operate the alfalfa farm, although adequate, none compared with Beet and Neil in neat and efficient performance.

Old Gov as a Swimmer

Although wandering somewhat out of sequence, it seems appropriate to include here a swimming incident involving a horse we acquired a couple of years later, Old Gov. He was a long-legged, ten-year-old government horse, branded IC by the army at the time of sale, meaning "I Condemn," because his lazy temperament made him unfit for government service. Cottonwood Wash drains a wide watershed into Silver Creek just north of Snowflake. Both drainages are subject to occasional floods from heavy rains or spring snow melt. One such occurred in the Cottonwood about two months prior to our wild-horse chase, perhaps in March 1904. A good segment of townsfolk was out at "the Flume" viewing the torrent. A flume across the wash carried irrigation water to farmland on the west side. Trestle work at the east bank caused floodwater to make a diving swirl and a roaring sound, resembling rapids of larger streams. Watching along with the crowd, my thoughts turned back to the good old days when we swam horses for fun, either in clear, still water, or muddy-brown floods like this, which carried silt, litter, and debris. I could not resist the urge to reenact one of the old antics of our gang.

Of course, I knew what Beet or Neil would do, but they were gone, and none of Dad's present horses had been used within our knowledge in such a venture. Old Gov should be able to take care of himself, I thought. If we became separated, each could swim out alone, somewhere downstream. Or, if I could stay on him—some horses rear over backwards and paw around in deep water—no doubt he was equal to a quarter-mile swim with the current.

I slipped up home, several blocks southwest, and stripped, but for an old pair of Levi's, put a rope on Gov, with a nose-loop, and rode him bareback to the flume. Menfolk saw me and shouted, "Let's see you do it!" But the women and girls began to scream, "You stay out of there!" It tickled my vanity to be the center of attention, despite some misgivings as to what the outcome might be. In reality, there is far less danger in swimming a horse than would appear, especially with no saddle or other gear in which to become entangled if anything goes wrong.

Gov did not like the deal and took some prodding. At belly depth he lost his footing and we plunged out of sight into the swirling torrent near the east bank where the crowd stood. Holding my breath and tight grip, I thought he never would come up for air. He seemed to have had no idea what he was getting into, for it was not until he sucked water instead of air that he made any effort to swim. But that all changed, and fast. He scrambled straight up to the surface, about fifty feet downstream in swift current, stuck his nose out and blew water from his nostrils. Fighting for breath, his action was that of a fast-trotting horse, which in water makes him a vigorous, natural swimmer. But, strangely enough, he swam with hind parts two feet under water, and only withers, neck, and head showing in front. Once his nose and lungs cleared of muddy water, however, a better swimmer would be hard to find.

Down one block from the flume, Gov was unable to climb the perpendicular bank that had formed since the flood began, and we were forced on down—swimming with the current—several hundred yards to a landing he could make. He shook himself and puffed disgust at such goings-on. He resembled a huge drowned rat and I could boast no less. But we had made it and put on a show for the books. The crowd moved a block east to see what we looked like as we passed south toward home and a double washup with clean water.

Was this stunt smart, or merely a show-off? You guessed right. It was mostly the latter. Our only casualty was Florrie Allen, my own age, who fainted when we dove out of sight under the flume.

Chasing Wild Horses

By A.D. 1900, there were literally hundreds of thousands of wild horses ranging over plateau country in Arizona. Their jumbled ancestry includes some strains of Spanish invasions of the sixteenth and seventeenth centuries, to mix with those the Indians already had. Various crosses also occurred with horses brought in later by the big cow outfits from Texas, and farther north, including the better breeds introduced by Mormon and other early settlers. Horses are prolific breeders under range conditions at all favorable, and tend to go wild unless handled frequently by man. Given freedom in the wild, they develop uncanny protective instincts, the equal of any other wild animal, and become difficult to capture or control. This was the horse situation on ranges extending from the Mogollon Rim to the Little Colorado. Huge roundups were held each year by various owners to brand the colts and mavericks and to hold broke saddle horses and wild individuals of promise for that purpose.

When school was out in May 1901, William J. Flake, at my request, proposed to Mother that I go along on the annual community horse roundup as a day herder, saddle-horse wrangler, and general roustabout. I was so enthused with the idea that Mother gave her rather reluctant consent, fearing for my safety and general welfare. Arrangements were made to irrigate the alfalfa in my absence, and the west segment of the roundup would be over in time for the first cutting of hay, about July 1. Because I did the same thing in 1902, covering largely the same country, the two years have run together in my mind to the extent that few incidents can definitely be tagged to one or the other. It seems best, therefore, to treat these two horse works as one.

We outfitted at Snowflake, taking on chuck-wagon supplies at Flake Brother's Store, doctoring up saddles, cinches, and other equipment, assembling beds, tarpaulins, and appropriate personal effects. Large rolls of Manila rope were necessary for lariats, as were larger, looser twists for tie ropes and hobbles. Our first camp was at Twelve Mile on Cottonwood Wash, due west of Taylor. The boys on circle had already picked up several bunches of wild horses, mixed with semidomestic strays from the nearby towns.

In four weeks' time we worked the north slope of the Mogollon Rim, twenty miles wide by fifty long, to Chevalon [or Chevelon] Canyon. Every day brought new thrills in this wilderness area as bunch after bunch of unwilling wild horses were out-winded, out-smarted, and herded to the nearest stockade corral by experts in the business, riding saddle horses of tested stamina and endurance. These men not only knew the country, but they understood horse psychology and each day mapped out strategy much as a general in war combat. They had a pretty good idea of where the different bunches would be found and could describe or name the stallion in charge. Water and feed conditions entered into their calculations along with the more direct tracks and trails. Even so, they were often outdistanced on the first day's run and would go back on fresh mounts for a second and usually successful heat.

One of our main campsites was called Rice Seeps, six or eight miles east from Heber where there was a round stockade corral. It lay midway between Mogollon Rim to the south and open country around Dry Lake north toward the river (Little Colorado). Circle riders worked in all directions from this point over a radius of fifteen to twenty miles that took a week or more to cover. Hundreds of young colts were branded there, and males two to four years old were castrated and bobtailed for distant identification. Geldings from such previous operations were caught, hackamored, and tied overnight to trees. By morning they would be so exhausted and their necks so raw and sore from constant struggles to break away that they could be led anywhere or turned loose in the day herd for later handling.

Broke saddle horses were gathered along with their wild associates. Some had gotten away from their owners and gone back to their native habitat, while others had been turned out the fall before for lack of home feed or pasture through the winter. Often they were as wild and hard to run down as their unbroken counterparts and would buck their hearts out at the first saddling. A horse, like man, loves his freedom, and he is capable of surviving hard winters, drouth, and other adversities that spell doom to cattle or sheep. They tend to get smaller with each generation in so doing, but remain tough and persistent.

One day at Rice Seeps, the drive brought in a young iron-gray horse named Blue Dog. Uncle Bill Flake, Wm. J. as he was called locally, informed me he had a fresh mount, "just right for you!" Up to that time my mounts had been gentle at least, mostly lazy, second-rate nags, good for little more than day herding or wrangling. I said nothing at the time, but there ran through my mind two important facts: One was Uncle Bill's reputation of putting youngsters or greenhorns on any horse that came along, with little regard for what might happen, and the other that I knew this Blue Dog beauty better than he. John T. Flake, Uncle Bill's youngest son, and our mutual friend, Port Adair, a local half-Indian horseman of some reputation, had broken horses the previous summer at the old Flake ranch a mile south of Snowflake. I had spent considerable time with them, riding the non-buckers after a few saddlings and helping around the corral. It so happened that Blue Dog was one among the twenty to thirty head they were breaking, and, next to a "singer" called Squealer, was the wickedest bucking horse of the lot. So, as well might be surmised, I wanted no part of the handsome Blue Dog.

Foul Burk, mentioned above, was then a man about fifty, but still one of the best horsemen of his time. No roundup in that general area was complete without him. It will be recalled that Dad and I camped with him at Perkins Farm in 1894, before I was eight years old. It also comes to mind that I helped him trap wild horses at the mouth of the canyon north of Snowflake in the early spring of 1901, along with Orson Kay, a young fellow from Taylor. These genial contacts with Old Man Burk were to be of value to me in this situation, although in the goodness of his heart he might have done as much for any fifteen-year-old in similar difficulty. Uncle Bill Flake kept pressing the point that Blue Dog was just the thing for me, and I shivered in my boots. I could see even a good rider, such as Port Adair, having plenty of trouble staying aboard that blue devil, and there was no doubt in the world that he would bog his head with anyone attempting to ride him fresh from the range. It would be impossible for me to ride him, and he would probably get away with my saddle.

Trying not to lose face, I was stalling. Old Man Burk slipped up and said softly, "Do you think you can ride him?" My answer was a definite no. In a subdued voice then, Foul said, after I'd told him what I already knew about the horse, "Let me uncock him for you, then maybe you can get by with him." Coming from an old bunged-up man, old at least for that business, it didn't seem right to accept his offer. But the fact remained, I had no intention of trying to ride the Blue Dog.

At all events, we caught the horse and saddled him in the corral where he refused to buck without a rider. Some horses buck themselves out with the saddle and can then be held by a careful rider. Not so with this character. So Old Man Burk led Blue Dog outside the corral to be free from picket posts and the center snub and with help got on him and set. What an exhibition! No man alive could have kept Blue Dog from doing his utmost to throw him off, and that was plenty. At the same time, Burk rode him perfectly, as if glued to the saddle, a past master of the trade.

But Blue Dog was not to be outdone. When he realized this rider was too much for him in fair contest, after eight or ten terrific jumps, he deliberately keeled over on level ground, a thing no rider can cope with, other than to shake loose and try to avoid being crushed to death. The old veteran executed the latter as only the ex-

perienced can, rolling fast to one side like a barrel from the instant
he hit the ground. It was the only way out as there was no time to
get on his feet and run for it. The horse rolled toward him, but not
fast enough to do him harm. We grabbed the hackamore rope before
Blue Dog could get up and dash for freedom with the saddle while
the old man brushed pine needles and dirt from his clothing, glad to
be alive and unhurt.

Too much emphasis on this workaday incident in wild-horse circles may perhaps be pardoned in light of the strong impression it
left with me, if not with other participants and witnesses. Uncle Bill
took a ribbing from older hands for assigning such a horse to a mere
stripling, but countered that he assumed Blue Dog had been thoroughly gentled the summer before. As for Old Man Burk, no motive
could be finer, nor more genuine, than that which prompted his
protecting a kid in a tight spot, for each hand was expected to ride
whichever horse was assigned to him, regardless of age, or be accused of being a coward and having no nerve. Had I not known Blue
Dog, watching what he was like in the corral, I might have made the
grave mistake of trying him and getting myself badly hurt. My
gratitude was, and has remained, in like proportion to his kindness.
Rarely did we meet after the horse works of 1902, but in each case
the Blue Dog incident was relived, and once more my appreciation
expressed. Incidentally, no further attempt was made to ride the
Dog by anyone on that roundup. There was too much work ahead to
fool with him. He was merely placed in the day herd for later treatment by bronco twister, Port (Porter) Adair, who was not with us at
the time.

There are those who think that live horses did not exist on the
Western Hemisphere after their extermination in ancient times, until they were introduced into Mexico about 1519 by the Spaniards.
Spreading out to the north and south, it probably took another hundred years for escapees from domestication to establish themselves
in the wild and revert to basic instincts of the original wild animal.
These are most fascinating to observe. The average bunch of ten to
fifteen brood mares with their foals, colts, and fillies is always domi-

nated by a stallion who has maimed or killed all contestants for his harem. He remains alert at all times and maneuvers cunningly when danger approaches.

At sight of a range rider, for instance, in open country a mile away, he stands motionless for a full minute or so, trying to make out the object for certain. He issues a shrill blow, almost a whistle, as a warning to his charges, then runs at top speed directly toward the horseman for a better view. Stopping at a safe distance, with head and tail high, he presents a picture suitable for the best Hollywood movie. All members of the herd watch his movements intently until he is satisfied of the danger and whirls to run back. At that instant the mares start running back also, knowing the master will be along, and fast.

Just how he directs their course is often a puzzle, for he stays in the rear to be nearest the approaching enemy. To be sure, he swerves from side to side according to the direction he wants them to take, but how those in the lead a hundred yards away can instantly sense and obey these maneuvers is hard to believe. Invariably, he takes advantage of the terrain, heading for a hidden pass, rough country, or other point that means the greatest possible handicap to a pursuer. If a horseman can stay in their dust long enough, he may overtake mares with one- to five-day-old foals unable to keep the pace. True to nature, the mother stays with her offspring, despite rough pressure to stay in the running, for as long as the stallion dares delay.

But the foal has performed an incredible feat. Running abreast of, and leaning against, the dam's shoulder, it has covered at least five miles at herd speed. Is there another animal on earth whose day-old offspring can do such a thing? Veteran horse chasers were often heard to marvel at this quirk of nature as they related personal experiences in the game, and I was no exception when permitted to leave the day herd, or remuda, to join the chase. With a gestation period of eleven months, most range mares bore their young in the month of June when the larger roundups were going on and this phenomenon could be observed. Among the many thousands there was scarcely a mare three years old and up that failed to bear and raise a colt each year, thus accounting for the rapid increase in horse populations under natural conditions. Hardly ever were there sets of twins, but they did occur and, barring accidents, were usually raised well by a hardy dam.

Having any part in a horse roundup is a fascinating experience. Thus it was for me at ages fourteen and fifteen, respectively, with the works of Flake, Freeman, and Burk. We completed the rounds in each case and were back in Snowflake by the first of July where less exciting farm duties awaited my attention. But I had tasted of a lasting range lore that resulted in wrangling for the Long-H outfit five years later and in much more proficiency in cowboying, which was a great aid in the fieldwork on horseback with the U.S. Forest Service from 1913 to 1930.

Old Gov and the Point of the Mountain Bunch

Lessons learned at these roundups also had a large bearing on an incident that took place in May 1904. Grandfather John Hunt had a sorrel mare running on the range fifteen miles southeast of Snowflake near the head of the Millet Swale, which he was anxious to catch up to and use her. Likewise, Dad owned a gray stallion, the majordomo of what had come to be known as the Point of the Mountain Bunch, ranging in the same vicinity. So they conceived the idea of a joint effort to capture the two animals. Grandfather would take a team and wagon with food and supplies while his son, Taylor (sixteen, by a second marriage), Dad, and I, worked the country horseback. The idea sounded great to me, although it's a wonder I was around home long enough to be available. By a streak of luck we found the sorrel mare on the first day out. She was with semi-gentle horses that were easily corralled at our campsite.

When the wagon arrived, Grandfather was pleased. Our job was halfway done, but what of the other half? It was not to be as simple. Hay and grain were brought along for our horses, as was an ample supply of camp chuck for ourselves, and after a good night's rest we saddled up for whatever the day might bring. The year before, Dad had acquired two gray horses, among others, about as opposite as could be, except for color. The one, Old Gov, was so named for having been condemned as a cavalry horse at Fort Apache and sold at auction to Flake Brothers. Of Kentucky saddle-horse strain, he was sound as a dollar, but too lazy for cavalry maneuvers. The other, Poss (for Opossum), was a fiery Freeman horse, raised on the range west of Snowflake, never to become perfectly gentle. They were both fresh, having been led beside the team out to camp. Our strategy was first to locate the Point of the Mountain Bunch and give them at least a trial run. My close friend, Port Adair, had told me Old Gov was the longest winded mount he had ever ridden in pursuit of wild horses and we were counting on him for a final try, unless by some miracle we might be successful the first day out.

The way Poss acted up at saddling, I wondered if, after all, he were not the iron horse needed to subdue that wild bunch, which time after time had eluded such experts as Billy Gibson, riding Black Skylark, Flake Brothers' best in the business. For the first mile out it was all I could do to keep Poss from bucking. He snorted and twitched with energy that belied his limited endurance. We split four ways, traveling north toward the Point of the Mountain— named for the sharp, north terminus of the high black mesa between Snowflake and Concho. Grandfather still rode well at age seventy-one, but made no pretenses of riding long circle in that rough, heavily cedared area.

Dad, at forty years of age was essentially a farmer, an expert with workhorses, but had had little experience riding range. Taylor, my cousin, was an energetic lad, not too well mounted, but a good hand. The two older men kidded me about all that experience earlier on larger roundups and averred I should be able to outsmart even the Point of the Mountain Bunch, with anything like an even break. I demurred on grounds that the experience was mostly wrangling and day herding, and a kid of seventeen could hardly be classed as an old head in any line.

There were horse tracks everywhere and several small bunches were sighted, but none with our gray stallion in it. Riding alone, this went on until midafternoon, when all at once, through an opening in the thick cedars on the north rim of Millet Swale, the gray stud came into view a quarter mile away. He had been attracted by our noise or scent and, typical of his kind, was taking no chances on a surprise attack. Signaling his brood with a loud whistle-blow-snort, he whirled and ran obliquely to my right. Taking a short cut, I turned the skittish Poss horse on for the first time at full speed, and he could run. Escaping cedar limbs with only a few scratches, we ran smack-dab into the bunch at an opening about a half mile from where the stud was first seen. Knowing too well they could not be held up while fresh, I simply rode along with them south for a mile toward the head of the Swale, to an open flat. There was enough left in Poss to turn them at this point back to the north in more open country. My idea was to tire them down out where we might be seen by the other riders who would come to my assistance.

It worked for awhile, but the farther those horses ran, the faster their pace—or so it seemed by comparison with Poss who was beginning to fade. Another half mile and he was done for. Only those who have met with similar defeat can appreciate my disappointment at seeing the gray stallion, who ran always in the rear, pass out of sight in heavy woodland to the northwest. It was the end of the trail. Poss would do well to carry me the eight or ten miles back to camp in a slow walk.

Removing the saddle, I wondered if it were to be my bed. Poss was covered with sweaty lather. Rapid respiration and thumping heartbeats shook his frame, when only that morning he had bluffed the part of an invincible. He stood still for thirty minutes catching his wind, an object of pity. I removed the bridle bit and let him nibble sacaton grass. Nearby was a small pool of water from which he was allowed only a part of what he craved, lest the extra weight become a handicap.

The sun was low when we started for camp. To my satisfaction Poss showed signs of partial recuperation. After a slow start, he broke into a jog-trot that put us in camp by good dark. The other men had come in early and were eager to learn if my late arrival had any significance. Shocked at Poss's lowly appearance, Dad watered and fed him while I washed up and dove into a pot of beans, Dutch-

oven biscuits, and other substantial camp food. My story was fascinating to the three men, none of whom had sighted the P.M.
Bunch, nor cut sign of the chase. They did scout a lot of country and
corralled a few gentle horses. One was a bay saddle horse of Uncle
Bill Flake's, called Snip for the white spot on his nose, which Grandfather wanted to hold for his old friend. We sat around the campfire
and mapped a program for the following day. All agreed that Old
Gov was our only hope, providing his stamina was up to its reputation and we could again locate the wild bunch.

Breakfast was over by sunrise and the wagon loaded with beds
and equipment. Grandfather started for town with extra horses tied
on either side of the team and two at the rear. Seeing him safely on
his way, Dad, Taylor, and I rode north through the general area of
yesterday's encounter. Old Gov groaned, squirmed, and wrung his
tail with each touch of the spurs, a miserable mount to hack along
across country. Dad was on Snip, fresh from the range, as was
Taylor's mount, the sorrel mare. The two were being ridden mostly
in fear of their not leading well with the wagon, but they should be
good for a run of five miles or more, as well. They diddled and
pranced with vigor while Gov took goading to stay up with them.
We separated for a while, agreeing to meet at a certain spot near
the Point if the wild bunch was not sighted. We had scarcely reassembled when out of the thick cedars to the west came tearing the
gray stallion and his mates at full speed, no doubt boogered by some
other danger source than ourselves. They appeared to have been
running for miles already, which was all in our favor.

We took after them together under a plan merely to stay in sight
of them until they began to tire, before attempting control. Old Gov
came alive! It was as if all his laziness had been purposely designed
to store up energy for this very thing. His long legs took smooth
stride that belied his apparent lack of speed, his ears darted back
and forth with excitement as he kept an eye on the wild bunch and
picked his footing at the same time. Within a mile the fleeing horses
circled back west into the thick cedars. The three of us reached the
spot together, but the other two were soon to be outdistanced.

And what a ride! Gov was cold-jawed and hard to handle but

knew what he was doing. With little slackening of pace, he plowed through cedar branches, jumped gullies and boulders, never losing his feet nor the hot trail of horses we could barely glimpse now and then through the trees. My own task was not so much to guide our course—since Gov was seeing to that—as to prevent being brushed off or hurt by cedar boughs and snags. It took ducking and swerving from side to side while gloves, jumper, Levi's, legs, and arms took a terrible beating. Time after time we were trapped by bushy trees with intermingling branches, only to slash on through between main stems and trust to luck that Gov would not trip and fall.

At least five miles were covered before the trees thinned out at the south edge of Concho Flat. We were close on the heels of the gray stud, running as usual behind the rest. He snorted defiance and drove his herd at new speed. Gov felt strong as ever, but I was content just to follow. They ran south, through cedars again, clear to Millet Swale, beyond where I had first jumped them the day before. That could have been the upper limit of their range as they offered little resistance when turned for the first time—back the way we came. It was still touch-and-go back to Concho Flat where some fatigue began to show. My strategy now was to keep up the pressure, but confine them to the open flat if possible. The stud was now short of wind, the easier to be sighted by Dad or Taylor Hunt, and mad enough to eat Gov alive were it not for that uncertain quantity atop his back.

Acting as if to stop and blow, we crowded them on downcountry. They broke to the right, but Gov was master now and quite easily headed them off. They tried the left, but that failed, too, as did several other attempts back and forth to reach the woods. This went on for some time until finally we reached the box canyon of Silver Creek three miles north of Snowflake. They wanted to stop, but we turned them back toward the flat and continued the pressure. As we entered the lower end our stud headed for a water hole made by recent rains. This would clinch the deal. Checking rein on Gov, the whole bunch gathered around and drank to its full capacity, which meant twenty to thirty pounds added weight per horse. They were all so out of breath it must have taken thirty minutes to water between blows. The more they drank the shorter their breathing became.

As nearly as could be estimated, Gov had carried 160 pounds and a 35-pound saddle, running hard for a distance of fifteen miles without a single letup—a feat for any horse to match. Bloodlines will show when put to the test is my only explanation. When I dismounted and loosened the cinches, (those wild horses weren't going anywhere just now), he took several deep breaths, then settled down for more normal breathing than any in the lot. He and the others were covered with white lather. Streaks down their legs marked the flow of sweat from their steaming bodies.

Personal experience, and that imparted by veterans of this sort of thing, had taught me two major principles observed on that day's run. The first was always to wear a wild bunch down, regardless of direction taken, before attempting to drive it in. The second was what we were doing now. After a long run, where water is available, let the wild ones drink their fill, but not your mount. I led Gov to a smaller water hole fifty yards away, took the bit from his mouth, and allowed him eight or ten swallows as a fractional offset to his dehydration. He wanted all he could hold, of course, but had to be restrained. It was a dejected wild bunch that stood there, still panting for air after running little short of twenty miles to this our first stop. Their bellies bulged with the overdose of water. They eyed me in terror, but were too exhausted to move. Even the gray stallion was content to just rest. Gov nibbled sacaton grass.

It was late afternoon and the job remained to put these outlaws in a substantial corral before dark. Cinching the saddle again, I mounted and made a run at the horses to test their condition. They whirled and fled. But Gov's remaining strength and interest were both astounding after all he had been through. We crowded them hard up the center of the Concho Flat—even rump-whipped the stud with my double throw-rope. He squealed like a pig but was helpless to do anything about it. Another mile marked the end of the line. It was all the "invincibles" could muster. With mouths wide open and tongues hanging out, they gradually slowed to a walk despite shouts and whipping. Excess water gave the final touch. As I rode to one side, they stopped dead still. This was it.

I got off and led Gov around, lest he cool too fast, and scanned the landscape for any possible help on the drive into Snowflake. Fortunately, it was to be forthcoming. A horseman came into view from the east, a mile up the flat. It was Taylor and the sorrel mare. He had cut sign [followed the tracks] all this time, trying to ascertain which way we went after the mare failed to stay in our dust. Without a hat—it had been brushed off in the early rounds—I waved my arms and yelled, an unnecessary gesture, however, as Taylor saw the outfit at once and headed our way. He had not seen Dad or me since entering the first cedars and was completely surprised that any of the three would wind up with the "snakes" [the wild horses].

Our plan was laid to corral the wild bunch. I would lead, and Taylor keep up the rear, along a wood road that led into town. After some trouble getting started, the bunch followed Gov west through a wooded section, making only minor attempts to escape. Once out of the woods our troubles were about over. They balked at crossing the red wooden bridge over Silver Creek east of town, but Taylor managed to spook them through with Gov's leadership for assurance. Coming up the quarter-mile lane to Back Street (now known as Stinson Street), we turned south a block and a half to Flake Brother's "high, board corral." No one was in sight to open the gate, and in doing so myself, the horses broke by me, totally desperate and confused at finding themselves surrounded by the works of man. I leaped to the saddle, told Taylor to fasten the gate open and stay there to head the bunch into it from whichever way they came back around. Gov was still ample and eager, overtaking them in no time for a round of several blocks that sent women and children scurrying for cover. "Point of the Mountain Bunch on Main Street," I thought as we rounded the last corner toward the corral. Taylor was there for the shoo-in, and thus our mission was accomplished. So was the wildest ride in all my experience. As for Old Gov, no other horse ever carried me that far in the same length of time, or with such eagerness to subdue a wild bunch.

He was tied outside while we inspected the horses. Word flashed around that we had the P.M. Bunch. Marion Flake, another cousin, clerked in Flake's Store. Through the window he saw us pass by and went to the corral as the horses entered the gate. Back at the store, Billy Gibson refused to believe we had them, and came over to see for himself. He walked around Old Gov in amazement, fully realizing the master feat he had accomplished. He asked for details and followed my story with intense interest. About then Dad showed up on Snip. He had beaten us in and gone home for something to eat. He exuded great surprise at sight of the gray stud through the corral fence. Snip had also failed miserably on the first dash that morning, so he gave up the chase. Taylor and I left the crowd that had gathered and went to our homes for much-needed food for ourselves and mounts. The excitement over, and Gov changed from a walk to a slow trot, not without considerable urging. He was back to normal, lazy and listless as ever now, with real fatigue mixed in. With about half the water he wanted from the well trough, I fed him oats and alfalfa hay, while Mother prepared a big meal for me. When finished, Gov was allowed all the water he could drink and given a thorough rubdown with curry comb and brush, ridding him of all the dried sweat and grime. Actually, he looked little the worse for wear and I thought to myself, "What a horse!"

In the age-old horse versus dog debate, as to which is man's best friend, I choose the horse. As a retiree in urban surroundings, the things I miss most are a good horse, a well-fitted saddle, the soft jingle of spurs, the jog-trot cadence along a mountain trail, beyond the smell of monoxide gas, and a set of quick ears that twitch at each glimpse of natural hiding creatures.

CHAPTER TWO

Adolescence

Both Mother and Dad played the guitar and sang. Mother also was one of the Hunt sisters, who were locally famous for their beautiful singing. I was taught to sing and play guitar accompaniment at scarcely seven years of age. At twelve I began playing an undersized violin, a sweet-toned copy of Stradivarius. It had been a relic in Uncle John Addison Hunt's family for years, without strings or special care. But the inspiration I got from that fine little instrument kept me practicing incessantly as other tasks allowed, mostly by ear, but with some grounding in sheet music as well.

By age fourteen I was playing on church recreation programs and for kid's dances in the Flake brothers' hall atop their general store. Within a year I was playing with Claude T. Youngblood, seven years my senior and considered the best dance fiddler in the area. No opportunity to hear him play had been overlooked. A teenager learns fast that which he loves to do most. Hearing a tune once was ordinarily sufficient for me to memorize and play it on the little Strad. Before long we were playing together and very much alike. Many old favorite waltzes and two-steps were adaptable to harmonizing parts, on which I specialized, to produce in effect the double-stop or duet. This was new throughout our territory and gained such popularity as to place us in constant demand.

Another factor to our advantage was the appearance of Frank

Pruitt, a Texas cowboy fiddler with the touch of an artist on cattle-country hoedowns that were well suited for square dances, or quadrilles. Rarely did he play for dances himself for lack of volume or accompanists, but his rhythm and perfect coordination of finger and bow were extraordinary. Pruitt was a cowhand, and a good one, on the notorious Hash Knife outfit, but he kept his family in my home-town of Snowflake. As good a cowhand as he was, his true image was that of a fiddler, sitting on a wagon tongue at day's end, cheering the souls of music-hungry riders of the range. We followed him around to hear him play, Claude and I, and we learned his tunes and copied his style, thus adding materially to our repertoire of dance orchestra numbers.

Playing the same pieces, and very much alike, served Claude and me well in coping with the long, drawn-out square dances of the Texans, thus adding to our popularity for their Saturday night jubilees along the railroad, particularly Holbrook. It is too much for any fiddler to play a fast hoedown—"breakdown" as the Texans call it—for a full twenty minutes without stopping, then do it over and over again the whole night through. Instead of complaining, we told them to have at it as long as the caller had breath. After a few stanzas, either Youngblood or I would drop out for a rest, come back, pick up the continuity, and play while the other rested. Where we had two or more accompanists, they would do the same. Hence, with half time out, no caller or dancers could outwind us, and they liked it.

In 1902 Claude and I decided to go in for dance playing in a big way. The general situation was that although cash money was scarce, and day wages low, we were well paid for our music, and my own income from that source helped balance the family budget. This was not, however, without the disadvantage of being thrown into bad company at a tender age. In most places on our circuit the drinks flowed freely and were hard to resist, especially on arduous assignments like the all-night shindigs common to ranch country. Being able to handle one's liquor in copious amounts was looked upon as a feather in one's cap. Youngblood and I developed such capacities to our detriment, but never, as I recall, was either of us unable to continue playing a dance through. Much of this came later, however, as I was scarcely sixteen when Dad came home. Even so, a year's experience along these lines, coincident with a rapid transition toward manhood, created a rather cheap, reckless attitude on life in general. For some time I had ignored mother's exhortations to stay away from Holbrook, Winslow, Adamana, Navajo, Pinetop, and other dancing communities where liquor was available, this in spite of an unswerving adoration for her at all times.

Trouble with the Church

Meanwhile, all was not well in my relations with the [Mormon] church authorities, a source of worry to my parents. Because of the circumstances surrounding my activities as a dance fiddler, it is not surprising that Grandfather John Hunt as such, and as bishop of Snowflake Ward, was also deeply concerned. Backed by his counselors, William Jordan Flake (previously mentioned) and John Henry Willis, he ruled the town with a stern hand, a hangover from the strict discipline that had been indispensable to orderly colonization by the church. At sixteen I was physically grown up and right at that critical age when careful leadership is so important to a young man's future. Grandfather's blunt chastisement for the slightest infraction of church dictum became offensive to me and, not being able to hide my resentment, our troubles grew worse. He was known to deal more severely with his own posterity and told me several times I was the most "impudent" grandson he had. This only stirred the flame and drove me further into a don't-give-a-damn attitude. He was not used to back talk, especially from young people. When he spoke in that deep, gruff voice, which many of us inherited, it was law and Gospel, not open to challenge. Somehow, by nature, I could not resist talking back to him if I thought the point sufficient, only to be considered by him as impudence.

This state of affairs continued through 1902 and a showdown was inevitable. Harb Cooper, Sam Rogers, and I walked by the bishop's office one Sunday after church, having no idea we were involved in an official action by the bishopric. First Counselor Wm. J. Flake hailed us, saying, "You are just the boys we are looking for." Timidly, we entered the sanctum where the three men were in executive session. Grandfather John was spokesman. They had received a report that the three of us were guilty of disturbing the peace a few nights before, of such a serious nature as to warrant disciplinary action. Grandfather explained our right to a hearing in the matter and asked what we had to say. Harb and Sam were reluctant to say anything in an atmosphere of such high dignity. Consequently, the deliberations were carried on largely between Grandfather and myself.

What happened was that on the night in question Sam Rogers and I slept with Harbert Cooper in his father's cow shed in the extreme northwest corner of town. The nearest residence was a full block to the south, being that of the Joseph Cooper family in the same enclosure. It is quite the custom in rural areas for teenage boys to spend a night with their pals, especially in summer, out under the stars. Nor is anyone unfamiliar with the tendency of kids that age to indulge in boisterous scuffle and play, to which we were no exception. We denied the charge, however, that obscene or profane language was used on this occasion, or that we knowingly disturbed the peace of a living soul. I wanted to know where they got such information and Grandfather obliged.

Samuel D. Flake, our good friend, and about our age, son of James M. Flake and grandson of William J. Flake, was guarding a bumper crop of watermelons that night on the Cooper place. Harb's dad was noted for his fine melons, and that year's crop had been sold to James M. Flake in the patch. Some stealing of watermelons in season is always a possibility and Sam Flake's job was to prevent it here. We were totally ignorant of his presence, although he could have been stationed within a few yards of the shed. What he might have told his dad was never too clear, except that stealing melons was not among the things complained of. We suspected Sam dutifully reported the melons intact, but that Harb, Sam Rogers, and I made a lot of racket on the shed before settling down to sleep, and the grownups took it from there with strong suspicions we were up to no good.

At any rate, the bishopric was convinced an offense had been committed and imposition of an appropriate penalty was in order. The three men of that body were unimpressed with the point I tried to make that we could not disturb the peace when only one person was within hearing distance of our noise, secretly at that, since we were totally unaware of his presence. It was then a matter of imposing sentence.

Grandfather deliberately started, I think, with the other boys first in asking that we "show cause" why we shouldn't "ask Brother James Flake's forgiveness." Could I believe my ears? Ask Brother James Flake's forgiveness when he was not even present at the scene of the "crime!"—secretly, or otherwise?

"How about you, Brother Cooper?" Granddad was saying. "Are you willing," and so forth.

"Yes, Sir," was Harb's meek reply.

"Brother Rogers?" His response was the same. I was flabbergasted. Of course, we were taken by surprise, with no chance for a conference among ourselves.

"Brother Kenner?" Grandfather looked me straight through, a trait that cowed many a hardened criminal during his long years as a sheriff in Utah. I was scared, but I felt so strongly the verdict was unfair, and therefore I could not make myself agree to such unwarranted humiliation. I returned his gaze, determined not to be stared down. Tense moments passed as I thought out what to say. He sensed my opposition and turned red with anger. Finally, I repeated that no peace had been disturbed, in fact, and therefore I owed Brother James Flake no apology.

Obviously, the wrath of Bishop John Hunt came down upon me. His graying beard shook as he expressed it in no uncertain terms. Included was another reminder that I was the most impudent grandson he ever had. To me, this was uncalled for. It displayed one of his very few weaknesses of character. I was on trial in the Bishop's Court as a member of the Snowflake Ward, not as his grandson. And I told him so. Once in the fray I said other things, too, bluntly and ill-advised, of which I was later sorry. But the heated exchange ended with his barring me from the dances and other ward amusements, a penalty often imposed for infractions of church rules.

Lest an inference be drawn to the contrary, I always held Grandfather John Hunt in high esteem. He was a great man, an outstanding frontiersman who made history in the West, an impeccable character with natural leadership among men, and a tireless worker for the right as he saw it, with the courage of sound convictions. Our personalities clashed early, to be sure, but only because of his gruff mannerisms and implicit faith in the doctrine that church members must obey their authorities without question. I thought he was too strict, too exacting, prone to ignore the other side on occasion. One question has always intrigued me. What would he have done in my place at the bishop's trial? No one ever shoved him around and that is what I figured was happening to me.

My "sentence" was accepted with indifference since Claude Youngblood and I were playing steadily for dances at other places, once to several times a week, traveling on horseback carrying our violins, or by team and buggy. No effort was made to regain my standing for three months or more, until Dad, who had been ill with malaria contracted on his mission, recovered sufficiently. Fresh from his mission, he could not stand the thought of my being at outs with the church.

We had several meetings with Grandfather, who at first was belligerent and uncompromising. My defiance of a bishopric decision, in his view, was even more serious than the original charge of disturbing the peace, which I still denied. Neither had time altered my stand that Jim Flake's forgiveness would never be asked in these circumstances. It is doubtful, in fact, that Jim ever expected such a thing. But, Dad was so anxious to have the matter cleared up that I suggested going to Grandfather with this proposal: since Sam Flake was the only witness in the case, I would apologize—as opposed to asking forgiveness—to Sam, and no one else, providing he felt in any way offended by the incident. Dad thought that was fair, and we got another appointment. Grandfather was more friendly, but pondered the proposal for some time before making up his mind to accept it. I went from there to Sam Flake, who told me right off there was no offense as far as he was concerned, and I owed him nothing at all. Forthwith, our conversation was reported back to Grandfather, who, in a nice way, gave me some good advice with respect to living our religion, seeking good company, and avoiding pitfalls attendant upon playing for dances around the country. He removed the ban on attendance at ward dances and socials, which really meant little to me, but much to my good parents.

Tranquility reigned for a time, but the road ahead was not altogether smooth. Budding into physical manhood at sixteen, I reasoned, mistakenly, that I was very much a man in all other respects as well. Two years without paternal control at that critical age made it difficult for both Dad and myself to effect a proper adjustment. Establishing new friendships over wide expanses of Navajo and Apache counties as a popular dance musician, in an atmosphere of gaiety and celebration, brought about in me a radical change of viewpoint. No longer could I be satisfied with the modus vivendi of a single hamlet and its narrow concepts of the outside world.

Leaving Home

Growing differences resulted between Dad and me that could not be reconciled. Between dance engagements I helped him on the farm but came and went as I pleased, despite violent arguments and occasional whipping. The latter served only to embitter my soul and to strengthen a determination to get out from under Dad's jurisdiction. He was too much physical man for me to fight and when his temper got out of hand, probably his worst failing, he went entirely too far. Hence, there could only be a parting of the ways. Let it be said at this point, however, he was an honorable man, trying to handle as best he knew one of the most difficult problems in family life.

On the night of February 14, 1903, our stringed orchestra played for a St. Valentine's Day dance in the county courthouse at Holbrook. My close friend, George Elmer Richards, seventeen, of St. Joseph (later known as Joseph City) was there, and we enjoyed meeting again. Similar in disposition and at the age of irresponsibility, we made medicine that was to affect my course of action for the year ahead. We speculated the country around there was too small for "men" of our stature, and something should be done about it. We would go to Kingman, Arizona, and get a job. Sleeping on the matter intensified our determination to leave home, notwithstanding the likelihood that February was a poor time of year for such a venture.

It so happened that Dad was in Holbrook for freight or supplies and I was to ride back to Snowflake with him. He was disappointed when I told him the plan had been changed and I was going to visit with Elmer for a few days in St. Joseph. Never was it my inclination to tell a lie, "white" or genuine, but the circumstances seemed to justify at least the former in this instance. Neither did we make known our real plans to anyone. It would be fun to let our folks wonder what had become of us, we thought.

Accordingly, on February 15, 1903, Elmer Richards and I boarded a Santa Fe passenger train headed west for Saint Joseph, with two small suitcases and my violin. We counted our money and it wasn't much. It would break us if we bought fares clear to Kingman. So, when the conductor appeared, we purchased tickets only to Flagstaff, 165 miles less distant. Arriving there that midafternoon was something to remember. Six inches of snow blanketed the landscape, beautiful if forbidding. We were up in the tall pines at seven thousand feet elevation, on the south slope of the towering San Francisco Peaks, the highest points in the territory. We shivered across Front Street to Whiskey Row and entered the famous saloon of Sandy Donahue. The huge potbellied, coal-burning stove felt good. A dozen other saloons stood side by side on the row, but Sandy's Place was the most popular. Big John Customeyer from Missouri was tending bar on the day shift. Everybody knew him as "Mizzou." He called us over and "set 'em up" on the house, at the same time ascertaining who we were and where from. Jobs were scarce he told us, but if I could attract customers with my violin, no doubt Sandy would put me on steady. I went to work at 8 P.M., and played until midnight with a fair hobo pianist.

The crowds came to drink, gamble, and make merry. Cowpunchers patted their feet and whooped it up. Loggers were in from the camps, among them Archie Cody, who step-danced to "Miss McCleod's Reel" with a glass of whiskey on his head. Archie was a bachelor, big and handsome, brought in especially from the logging woods of Michigan by A. L. & T. (Arizona Lumber and Timber Co.) on his reputation as being the best canthook man for deck work in the business. This was one of his periodical time-outs for recreation, and between our music and his dancing the place was literally packed. Three bartenders were kept jumping, the gambling tables did a land-office business, and my own reputation was established for steady employment—of the kind.

Sandwiched between saloons, in about the center of the row was the old Commercial Hotel, also owned by Sandy Donahue. Elmer and I rented a cheap room there. We ate at the American Chop House, owned and operated by Chinaman Charlie. He served good meals for twenty-five cents. Other necessities were equally cheap, but so were wages; hence the economic balance was in approximate ratio with the present.

Elmer looked about town for a job, most anything, but without success. My four-dollar a night (one-dollar per hour) as a saloon fiddler was hardly adequate for our needs. Within a week he grew weary of the outlook and decided to return home. We pieced together enough fare money for him and said good-by at the little red-stone Santa Fe depot. The depot still stands, now relegated to secondary use, a symbol of the railroad's early 1880s. And so ended the air castle built by Elmer and me to accomplish great things together. As the train pulled out I could not suppress a feeling of nostalgia. My only close friend in a strange environment was heading home without me. I should have gone too. But it was too late now, and besides, that burning desire to leave home for an extended period was still dominant, and I determined to follow it through.

The shiftless life of a saloon fiddler kept things going for a few weeks, but it got increasingly boresome. Having been brought up in a better way of life, I could not escape a certain feeling of shame as well. It also became clear that no money could be saved. After a nine to ten o'clock breakfast, there was little to do but hang around the saloons, and by 8 P.M. shift time, wages from the night before were gone. As part of the crew, I was treated nice enough by bartenders and operators of the gambling tables. Sandy, an ex-logger and whale of a man, liked the hoedowns and often sent up drinks from the bar.

To mention a few others, Johnnie Donahue, a brother, was head bartender at night with extra help as needed; "Spot" Roberts ran the crap game; "Chris"? the roulette wheel. Al and Jeff Hudson, brothers, were in charge of poker, faro, and blackjack. Hugh Lane changed off, or ran the extra tables according to demand. They all wore fancy clothes and were accepted in the community as substantial citizens. At that time, gambling, like wrestling, was considered a legitimate business and strictly on the square, only to degenerate through the years. The breed of these men has largely vanished from the American scene.

Few people dropped in whom I had known before, but one night two old friends, George Rogers and Joseph A. Robinson, came to the music stand as we finished a number. George and his wife, Ida, had lived in Snowflake before moving to Flagstaff, where he had a contract to furnish sawed wood to A. L. & T. for their wood-burning locomotives. Joe, who worked for him, was a hometown boy, five years my senior, but an intimate friend. This was a pleasant surprise and lessened my feeling of isolation. George offered me a job sawing wood with Joe, which I was glad to accept. Since the management was entitled to a few days notice, I continued playing regular shift over the weekend but looked forward to the change with anticipation. It also provided the time needed to shop around for a camp bed and suitable gear for the job and the wintry weather, payment for which was guaranteed by George.

Lake Mary, south of Flagstaff, lies in what used to be called Clark Valley. Logging operations of A. L. & T. were centered in that vicinity, and furnished employment for large crews of crosscut sawyers, trimmers, teamsters, skidders, deck hands, loaders, rail-roaders, and railroad construction workers. Several trains a day brought ponderosa pine logs to the mill, west above town, and hauled back equipment and supplies for the camps. They also fur-nished transportation for the workers, job seekers, and freeloaders. Nondescript "passengers" dotted flatcars going out and loaded cars coming in. Hoboes shirked and ate a few days before moving on. Regular timber stiffs worked sometimes as long as three months be-fore drawing their pay and heading for a big time in town.

Archie Cody's type rented a room, bathed in a real bathtub, got barbered and fitted out in new clothing, all before touching a drop of anything intoxicating. But the end result was the same as for those who, with all good intentions, visited the bars first. In either case, it was only a question of how long it would take to drink and gamble away their last dollar. Never had I seen hard-earned wages thrown around with such disregard of their true value. Many slept on pool tables, or the piano stand, as they passed out or reached exhaustion, without even removing their hobnailed boots.

Saloon men accepted this as part of the business and watched over their customers to prevent theft of bank rolls or other foul play. Old Mose, the colored janitor at Sandy's, fired up the big stove as needed for their comfort, around the clock. Finally, with pockets clean and heads rumbling, they could mooch only enough drinks at the bar, or from friends, to settle their nerves, or even avoid delirium tremens. The time would come to think about clearing out. The A. L. & T. was experienced in the ways of the professional log-ger and had learned to fit his town phase into its own modus operandi. Watchers made daily rounds to check on whether any revelers were ready to call it quits. If so, a team and wagon came down from the mill to pick them up and see that they were safely aboard the next outgoing log train.

To say there were no exceptions would be quite inaccurate. Some of these men never drank to excess, if at all, had families in town whom they visited on Sundays, and rarely missed a shift in the woods. Why they represented a decided minority, however, is a question for the ethnologist.

George Rogers, Joe Robinson, and I hustled to catch the early log train that cold, windy morning in March 1903, with a week's food supply, personal effects, and equipment. George's wood camp was a whistle stop eight or ten miles out in Clark Valley. There was room for my bed, suitcase, and fiddle in one of the tents, and the three of us shared equally the cooking and cost of food. Our work was to cut dry pine wood to proper sizes and place it in ricks beside the track ready for use in those old-time steam locomotives that made history long before the Model T Ford. In proper lengths, the wood was our finished product. As it was loaded onto the tenders, the ricks were then replenished. We snaked or hauled medium-sized dead logs to the siding by team, there to be hand-sawn for length, split to maximum size, and ricked for handy loading.

Breaking in on a crosscut saw and then working ten hours a day is a tough experience. The first thing a rookie must learn is not to ride the saw. Its own weight is enough. Next he learns to pull only, never push. His partner on the other end of the saw, takes care of the return stroke and visa versa. It took several days of such training and sore muscles before I could be called a hand, but steady practice with plenty of food and sleep put me in good shape for the job. Joe and I did most of the sawing, George the splitting and ricking, although interchanging was common, and we became a smooth-working team.

Quite by coincidence, insofar as our planning was concerned, Joe played the guitar and had his instrument in camp. We played together at night, often at George's request, while he washed dishes or buried a pot of beans in the fire hole for all-night cooking. And what beans they were, cooked in this manner. George also loved to dance and conceived the idea of Saturday night parties in a new little schoolhouse at Flagstaff, for which Joe and I would furnish music. George and Ida had a nice group of young married friends who were just as enthusiastic for such diversion and leaped at the idea when notified on the next Saturday afternoon. As for Joe and me, it was an opportunity to meet and mingle with respectable people and add a few dollars to our weekly income.

That first party was a huge success. Square dances were still much in vogue and our hoedowns went over well. The most popular round dances were the waltz, two-step, polka, and schottische. Occasional novelty numbers were called for, like the Chicago glide, minuet, "Coming Through the Rye" (rye waltz), and varsovienne (or "Put Your Little Foot"). At midnight, closing time, Joe and I were showered with compliments on our music and engaged to play every Saturday night thereafter. We, too, had a good time even though some of those long quadrilles were tiring to play for. A guitar is harder on the fingers than a violin and Joe had several blisters that gradually disappeared as the usual callouses formed.

This setup was much more desirable than playing in a saloon. We went about our work with greater zest, looking forward to the weekend party and Sunday off. Acquaintances thus made were extremely nice. They invited us to dinner and took interest in our welfare. Too bad it could not continue the year through. My bills were all paid, with enough left over for dressups and other necessities. Joe was in better shape still, having been there longer and more inclined to spend wisely. George's wood contract expired in April and he chose not to renew it. He owned several teams of horses and wagons and figured there was more money to be made freighting. Accordingly, he moved to the Grand Canyon, from where we will hear from him later.

Work, Then Fiddle

Of course, Joe and I were out of a job. We did have free access to the Rogers' home, not yet disposed of, and batched there after a fashion. Sandy's place was short of musicians, so when we showed up they wanted me to resume night playing at once. Joe was introduced as my guitar accompanist in place of the hobo pianist who had blown to other parts.

Hardened in as we were on the wood saw, and being used to early rising, there was something distasteful about the occupation of saloon musician. Joe could not adjust himself to it and my own preference was something else. Saginaw and Manistee Lumber Company was another big outfit, whose mill was at Williams and main logging camp at Fort Balley to the northeast. There were no power saws as now for felling timber, and our experience on a crosscut should have brought steady woods employment had there been openings. At any rate, we would give it a try, and after a couple of weeks at Sandy's, we advised him of our leaving.

Good-byes were said to the Donahue staff as Joe and I boarded a Santa Fe local for Chalender Junction, about twenty miles west. Saginaw and Manistee's Railroad left the main line here, leading north to the Fort Valley logging area. We must have been conspicuous with our bulky luggage, camp beds, suitcases, guitar, and violin. Chalender's only habitation was the inevitable saloon. A kindly bartender, with no customers, gave us information on log-train schedules, conditions at Fort Valley, and the unlikely prospects of our getting work there.

Just the same we piled our stuff on a flatcar of the next log train and were at the main camp for evening mess. A genial bull cook beckoned us to seats at one of the long tables where we ate our fill of excellent food. He then showed us where to unroll our beds in vacant bunks for the night. It was standard policy of both A. L. & T. and Saginaw to feed and lodge men honestly looking for work—at least within reason.

At the field office we received little encouragement, but were invited to stay over a day in case something might turn up. The following forenoon was well spent looking over logging in action, from saw to railroad spur. As trees were felled, trimmed, and bucked into logs, the "wheels" snaked them to the nearest landing. A dozen or more carts with wheels at least eight feet in diameter were each drawn by two fat horses weighing fifteen- to eighteen-hundred pounds apiece. Logs were chained at the ends to a crosspiece between the wheels while the other ends dragged the ground. Those horses had done nothing else in their lives and what a delight it was to see them operate.

That afternoon I replaced a Swede sawyer with an upset stomach on a crosscut saw and bucked freshly felled trees into log lengths. My partner, "Ole," was an old head in the trade, muscled up and tough as nails. He noticed every little action on my part that did not come up to the man off sick. Yet I liked his accent and wisecracks, especially his consideration for my age and comparative in-experience. At quitting time he said, "Me boy, Oi cood make a sawyer outa ya!" Fresh green logs saw somewhat differently from the dead ones at George's wood camp, but with frequent applications of kerosene to clear soggy gum from the saw, it was actually easier.

Ole's partner soon recovered and took his regular place the next morning. Joe and I took stock. Saginaw was full-handed and no telling how long it would remain so. We both were fascinated with the layout, the tall timber and the hum and buzz of logging; the warning shout of "timber-r-r" echoing through the forest as trees cracked and swished to the ground on the exact angle planned by felling crews, and also with the jovial, accommodating attitude of the personnel. That the latter were largely Scandinavian can be traced to the fact that Fred Linstrom (Lindstrom?), a big Swede of long woods experience in Michigan was logging superintendent. When the company transferred him to Arizona, many of his better hands came with him. To say they knew their business is to put it mildly.

But Joe and I must work, or soon go hungry. We rolled our beds, arranged open-air passage by log train to Williams, and waved at the Chalender bartender as our train switched to the main line. Williams was a typical western railroad town, only more so in certain respects. There was the usual Whiskey Row across from the depot, interspersed with Chinese restaurants and hotels. By contrast with Flagstaff, women of ill repute infested the saloons, often with rooms in the back or overhead.

Named for Bill Williams Mountain looming to the south, the town is nestled in a beautiful valley fringed with ponderosa pine. It lies near the western edge of the largest belt of yellow-pine timber in the world, which extends east through New Mexico and on into west Texas. The Santa Fe's branch railroad to the Grand Canyon, sixty miles north, had been completed recently, thereby increasing tourist trade and also the population of the town by resident railroad personnel.

It was approximately May 10, 1903. Around the bars we learned about a city waterworks project south above town. Jake Kaufman was superintendent and George Winslow timekeeper. We hoofed it an upgrade mile to their camp and applied for jobs. Jake was snappy and to the point. If we could each handle a span of "hard tails" (mules) on a slip scraper ten hours a day for $1.25 and board, we were on. Assuring him of our qualifications, we were hired. He sent a hack to town with us for our beds and traps and assigned us a box tent. Breakfast would be called at six and we must have our mules harnessed and ready to go by seven. A pretty tough prospect, but at least a job.

By some hookup between the municipality and the Santa Fe Railroad, Williams was to have its first water system. It would also supply water tanks near the depot for the company's steam engines. Jake was building an earthfill dam to store drainage from the north slopes of Bill Williams Mountain, by horse-mule power and hand labor. Primitive, to be sure, by present standards, but Jake knew his business from long experience and pushed ahead to the limit of his men, materials, and equipment. Four-horse plow teams kept the scrapers in loose dirt nearest the dam, and two circles of slips kept moving from 7:00 o'clock to noon, and from 1:00 to 6:00 P.M., six days a week.

Some adjustment from horse to mule experience was necessary, but our first day on the job got us in good with Jake. He had many kinds of "teamsters" to deal with, some of whose qualifications were limited to the desire for a square meal. He could tell by the first round whether a new man was worth keeping, either from the standpoint of experience or an honest desire to learn. Those hard tails were ornery critters, but once in the harness they could stand the heavy grind and long hours far better than most drivers.

The corral boss, part mule himself, we jested, was on hand to help harness. His main job was getting blind bridles on the more cantankerous individuals, which were, or pretended to be, touchy about their long ears. In some instances it was necessary to wrap a tight wire around their upper lips and put on the pressure, at which feat our corral boss was a hardened expert. He knew the disposition of every mule and barked out instructions to new drivers accordingly. Hooking the tugs to double trees on the scrapers was also hazardous, lest either mule kick a teamster's head off.

There were humorous moments in a day's run. Joe was a natural comedian and saw the funny side of every happening. When he was right tickled his mouth flew open with loud guffaws of contagious laughter that frequently brightened our otherwise gloomy situations. One day he was next in line with a novice driver who urged his mules on with a constant "Chibby-Hut, Chibby-Hut" command, and to watch Joe get him off was a scream. Other ham-and-egg skinners could get themselves into more trouble with less reason than one would imagine. Something would go wrong when the slip was empty, the mules would get away and high-tail it for the corral, scraper and all. Or an outside tug would come unfastened and the hybrid on that side turn around facing the driver, flapping his ears forward and back and wringing his tail. Occasionally, a mule would get a hind foot over a chain tug, throwing him into a kicking rage. In nearly every case it was due to the driver's lack of know-how, or indifference, of which the half-ass, half-horse phenomenon was quick to take advantage.

It was soon apparent we must take better care of our feet if we were to stand up under long hours of walking in dirt and dust. Only by soaking them in hot water at night, applying synol soap [perhaps a medicated soap] to rash areas on calves and shins, and daily changes of heavy sox, could we stand the gaff. Even so it was a tough grind, and Joe especially was fed up with it by the second Saturday pay day. He and the corral boss were sort of crosswise, too, and he decided to quit. I wanted to stay another week or so, but Joe's mind was made up, and for me to work on seemed a bit disloyal to an old buddy. So, on drawing our meager pay, we both notified Jake of our leaving.

It seemed Jake was aware of Joe's trouble with the corral boss and expected him to quit, but supposed I would stay on and make him a regular hand. I appreciated his praise of my work, but disagreed when he said I could not afford to be tied to a fellow like Joe. Having struck up a sort of mutual admiration with Jake, I did hate to leave him. Back of his white eyes and leathery face there was character, as well as nerve and unbounded energy in his 150-pound frame. He was tough as a boot, yet kind and sympathetic as occasion prompted. Never having seen or heard of him since, I still wonder how he came out on the reservoir project and what happened to him thereafter.

Once again Joe Robinson and I were out of a job. We did the silliest thing—or was it so silly at that? After playing two or three nights with pianist Birdie Ray, common-law wife of Dick Hopkins, in the Palace Saloon owned by Hopkins and Alex Chisholm, the management decided there was not enough business to support the expense. Hence we started looking for something else, almost anything at all. As nothing turned up, we conceived the idea of making our beds down in an empty boxcar standing on a side track. Whither it went was immaterial, we agreed, and it might take us to a job somewhere to our liking.

A loud clang waked us about three o'clock next morning, signaling connection with a string of cars attached to a locomotive. There was some switching back and forth, but soon we were chugging along at good speed, as if headed for Los Angeles or San Francisco. We were on our way, but where? Our feeling of wild adventure and curious anticipation soon subsided when the switch engine brought the car back from the vicinity of Saginaw Mill and sidetracked it within a few yards of where it had stood the night before. No luck.

We went to breakfast at Gee Jim's restaurant on Front Street, between the Johnny Jones's and Mike Reneckie's (spelling not guaranteed) saloons, and held a "board meeting" on what to do next. At least we could go back to playing for Sandy Donahue at Flagstaff, and there appeared little likelihood of something better. Just why we expressed our beds and suitcases there and hoboed our own way there in an open coal car is not clear at this writing. It must have cost nearly as much as passenger fares, which would have permitted checking our baggage free of charge. But such was the kind of judgment we sometimes used. As we detrained at Flagstaff with Joe's guitar and my violin, you should have seen our sooty-black faces and clothing as a result of direct exposure to smoke from the coal-burning engine.

We left our instruments at Sandy's, causing some merriment over our disheveled appearance. We took a late breakfast at Chinaman Charlie's and proceeded to clean up. Only an itinerant of the open road can realize what a task it is to get thoroughly rid of coal smoke and cinders once he is fully saturated. Never again would we pull such a stunt, let alone select an empty coal car just a few cars back of the belching engine.

But they received us well at Donahue's and thought perhaps we could soon go back to work. However, business was slow and not expected to pick up before the next monthly payday of the A. L. & T., June 10. So we were asked to stick around a few days and they would see that we did not go hungry pending a better outlook. We did play a few pieces that night for practice, receiving tips of a dollar or so, but it was the wrong time of the month for much excitement at the bars or gambling tables.

Severe economics were necessary to cope with austere circumstances. Joe and I gave up our room, kept our instruments and suitcases behind the bar, pooled our bedding, and slept together on the ground at the east end of the Santa Fe freight platform. No one seemed to mind, and being so accustomed to railroad noise, we lost little sleep on that account. Chinaman Charlie provided a tin wash dish, hot water from the cookstove, towels, and a small mirror, where we washed up for a breakfast of "hot clakes," bacon and eggs, and coffee. Charlie was a typical Chinese restaurateur of the period, whom we learned to respect for his intelligence, honesty, and good-will—an excellent example for anyone to follow. We explained our circumstances and asked him for a few meals on credit until we could get straightened out. He sized us up, asked a question or two and said, "Allite, you eat, two bitty, get job soon." When Joe Robinson and I paid our bill he was pleased. He liked to help anyone who was trying honestly to help himself. Charlie's wife and two small children made their appearance occasionally, the first Chinese babies we had ever seen.

Meanwhile, we ran into Joe Tanner, an Indian trader from Tuba City, who spoke fluent Navajo, and just then was planning a trip to Grand Canyon with a load of Navajo blankets for the tourist trade. We had met him previously as a friend of George Rogers at the schoolhouse dances. He was of the opinion we could get work at the canyon and offered to take us along without charge. Our immediate worry was getting by for a week until Tanner was ready to start, but we thrilled at the chance of seeing the huge chasm and whatever else it might bring.

Although business was dull at Sandy's, there were occasional "live ones" who thirsted not only for intoxicants but for music as well. Joe and I picked up a few dollars from this source, especially playing old-time songs they loved to sing. We were hoarding every nickel now, and to help the cause, I took an afternoon shift in a little restaurant back of Jim Vail's saloon washing dishes, peeling potatoes, and waiting counter at a dollar a shift and board for the two of us. Our open-air sleeping quarters saved room rent, and thus we made out till payday when Sandy hired us again to play regular shift from eight to midnight. The place was packed for two or three nights as the time drew near for our trip to Grand Canyon.

One evening, when the merriment was well underway, I saw Dad enter the front door. Why he had come was quite obvious, and I bore down on the piece we were playing with nervous gusto. Elbowing his way through the crowd to the music stand, he exchanged a smiling nod with me and waited for us to finish the number. We shook hands cordially enough, and he had known Joe, of course, at Snowflake. We finished the shift while Dad viewed the revelry in obvious amazement. Some little conversation developed as our instruments were placed behind the bar, but mostly it was in the nature of bringing each other up-to-date on happenings during the four months I had been away. It was getting late, he said, and suggested we get some sleep, but he wanted to talk to me the next morning about going home with him.

When Joe and I laid out our camp bed under the stars, we knew there could be little sleep in light of this sudden development. We discussed my situation pro and con. Of course, Joe would go to

Grand Canyon in either case, but I wanted to go as strongly as he. The problem was how to get by Dad. After discussing the matter for several hours, I decided upon a course of action. My best diplomacy would be used in trying to convince him the canyon area offered good opportunities and that I should stay out long enough to come home with good clothes and a substantial bankroll. If this and all else failed, I would keep in touch with Joe and rejoin him on the first chance to break away.

The three of us met for breakfast at Billy's where I worked. (Billy is the only name we knew for the dark little mustached man who ran the place.) When it was over, Dad said he wished to talk with me in private and Joe left us alone. It was clear at once that Dad had made the trip determined I should go home with him and was in no mood to consider any entreaties to the contrary. In fact, he was quite arbitrary and blunt in telling me I must do as he said, which, of course, opened old sores and increased my determination to do otherwise. The conversation heated up and when he threatened to bring in the law, on grounds that I was a minor, I agreed he could probably do so, but told him if he did, I would leave him the next time for good, and guaranteed he might never see me again.

At this point it seemed to break through to Dad that I might do that very thing, for he changed his line of approach. Fully aware of my love and respect for Mother, he played up the anxiety and sorrow I was causing her, bringing forth tears I could not restrain. Yet to give in was still unthinkable under the circumstances. When he realized nothing short of the law could change my mind, he thought better of that course and asked that I come home as soon as my finances were sufficient to obviate an appearance of failure. My reply has always been a source of regret, although let it be said our differences were patched up in later years and no bitterness remains. I would come home when the time was right, I told him, but only to see Mother and the children, not him. And so we parted, each going his separate way.

Strained relations of this sort between father and son are indeed unfortunate. In the main, however, they served in my case as a blessing in disguise. Out on my own resources, the facts of life came thick and fast. I gained experience early that was to bolster self-reliance, independence of thought and action, and lay the groundwork for a broader, more comprehensive existence. My teenage gawkiness soon disappeared, as did the inclination to butt in where it was none of my business. To keep my mouth shut unless there was something worth saying and my eyes and ears open came as lessons indispensable to fixing one's proper place in the society around him.

Life, as I had come to know it here, was a far cry from the clannish atmosphere of a small town whose church membership was all of one faith, where everybody knew everyone else's business and talked about it freely, disparagingly or otherwise. My early training was to feel sorry for people not members of our church, whereas I found people of high education, honor, and integrity actually feeling sorry for me because I was a Mormon, so called. While this had never shaken my allegiance to the church of my parents, it did open wide a field for thought. It enabled me to respect the religion of any man, conscientiously pursued, and to appreciate more fully a nation founded in freedom, including that of religion.

CHAPTER THREE

On My Own

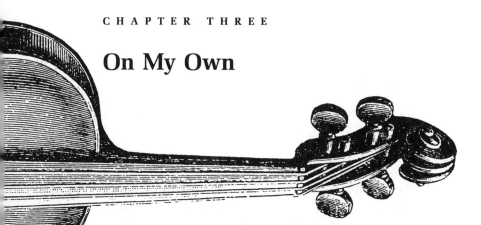

We stay together! Joe was waiting, his curiosity at fever pitch. He was pleased at the outcome but sorry it could not have been on friendlier terms. He wondered if Dad blamed him in any way, but I reassured him our differences were of long standing and that Dad gave me dubious credit for exercising my own volition in matters he frowned upon. Joe had a good code of morals and strove to be on good terms with all his acquaintances. We hunted up Joe Tanner to learn he would start for Grand Canyon the following day. Also that a husky young fellow, Neph (short for Nephi) Johnson of Kanab, Utah, was going with us. Neph was returning to a job at Grand View from a vacation with relatives in Snowflake. Tanner also had a seventeen-year-old Navajo chore boy by the name of Tsegini, which made us a party of five. He spoke no English, but was intelligent and a hustler at anything Tanner told him to do in his native language. It was my first experience around a white man who spoke fluent Navajo and quite a treat to observe their conversations and to watch the reactions of this young Indian to Tanner's strong sense of humor. His black eyes danced with joy at every witticism, and his hearty laugh spoke merriment itself. Joe Tanner was good to him and doubtless was giving him opportunities not to be had about the family hogan on the reservation.

A ton of Navajo blankets and five men with their beds, suitcases, instruments, and traps made quite a load for our wagon as we left Flagstaff that morning in mid-June 1903. But Tanner's heavy span of well-fed horses was equal to it and traveled right along. Our road-bed led northwest through Fort Valley and skirted the west slopes of San Francisco Peaks through Hart Prairie about thirty miles to Cedar Ranch where we camped for the night. Our cooking was catch-as-catch-can, each man doing some part, except Tsegini, who cared for the horses, greased the wagon axles, and did other chores directed by Tanner.

As we sat around the campfire that night at Cedar Ranch, Neph Johnson unfolded his story, helped here and there by leading questions from the two Joes and myself. Christened Nephi, he was a twenty-two-year-old, six-foot, 190-pounder who had been on the dodge for some three years. Unlike some fugitives from the law, he told his story freely in a most interesting way. A handsome blonde, straight as an arrow, beaming with virility, and with a striking personality, he could not help being attractive to the opposite sex, an item that started the trouble. He was blamed for an illegitimate pregnancy in his hometown of Kanab, Utah, for which he was quite sure he was not responsible, but had no way to prove it. Rather than marry the girl under those circumstances, or face a court trial, he left home in the night. Heading west, he hired on as a cowhand for an outfit in Nevada, where he rode for possibly a year before Charlie Button of Kanab got wind of his whereabouts and sent a deputy after him. The other cowboys knew of Johnson's plight and what to do in case of emergency. When the deputy made known his mission at headquarters, he was told that Neph was out on the works, but would be in sometime that evening. They made him welcome and took care of his horses.

In the meantime, one of the boys rode out in a hurry to tell Neph what had happened and keep him out there, while another saddled his private cowhorse, packed another with his bed and personals, and rode away as if on some company mission entirely foreign to the issue at hand. With his own fresh mount and packhorse, Johnson made cross-country haste a hundred miles or more to another cattle outfit. Button's deputy was thus eluded slick and clean, in keeping with the standard code of the range. Returning to Kanab empty, he was well aware of the conspiracy that foiled his plans. But making a cowboy talk when a buddy was involved just did not happen, and that included the range foreman. He could be so dumb the wonder was he held a job. And being the only source of information, its paucity was too great a handicap for the law to cope with.

It could be Neph was taking advantage of a statute of limitation in talking so freely, even among friends. He related at least one other incident wherein he successfully eluded Button's men through similar cooperation of his cowboy friends and traced his movements on into Arizona. Visiting relatives at Snowflake under his true name would indicate he anticipated no further trouble, despite the likelihood of telling correspondence between kinsmen at Snowflake and Kanab. While the Johnson name was nonexistent among Snowflake residents, "Aunt" Janette Johnson Smith was his father's sister, making her eleven daughters and one son his own cousins.

Rays of the morning sun streaked through notches of lofty San Francisco Peaks as we broke camp at their northwest base and departed from Cedar Ranch on our second day's journey. This had been a halfway campsite for heavy tourist travel between Flagstaff and Grand Canyon for many years prior to the automobile, and up to the completion of the Santa Fe spur line railroad from Williams to Bright Angel (now Grand Canyon Village) only three years before, in 1900. A long thirty-five miles of rock and dust lay ahead from Cedar Ranch to our canyon destination. Summer rains were yet to come in quantity, and the country was hot and dry. Our bumpy wagon road meandered northwesterly downward and across the broad open plain that separates the peaks from timbered country along the canyon rim. A ten-gallon barrel of water lashed to the wagon took care of our needs at the noon stop, since we would not reach Hull Tank before midafternoon, the first open water to be had. Barely using enough to make coffee for ourselves, we let the horses drink the rest, and they wanted more. They were fed hay and grain and in an hour's time were fit for the final lap of our journey.

Joe Tanner was an interesting host. His background among the

Navajo Indians was ample basis for many a story that staved off monotony, which otherwise would have attended such a trip. Tsegini drove the team while the two Joes, Neph, and I made ourselves comfortable by freight-wagon standards. Wherever possible, the team was pressed into a trot and we arrived at Grand View on the South Canyon rim before sundown, fourteen miles east of the railroad terminus at Bright Angel.

At the Grand Canyon

To describe one's feelings at first sight of the incomparable Grand Canyon of Arizona, something more than words are necessary. Being raised in hilly to mountainous country with all its crags and box canyons was no preparation at all for Joe Robinson and me to view for the first time that granddaddy of all chasms throughout the world. The other three had been there before, but still marveled at its vastness and scenic splendor. Nowhere else on the earth's surface has erosive water and wind, freezing and thawing, gouged out such tremendous quantities of original formations and borne them down to the sea. Capped by a heavy layer of Kaibab limestone, formed under our ocean, the area has gradually risen over countless millions of years to its present elevation above sea level of seven thousand feet, while the turbulent, silt-laden Colorado River sawed its way incessantly to maintain a waterline grade. The average distance from rim to rim is thirteen miles, with thousands of "temples" and other weird rock formations, labyrinths, and side canyons in between. From rim level to stream bed is a vertical mile, yet the shortest trail to the river is about seven miles, along sheer canyon walls and precipitous switchbacks.

Grand View boasted a two-story hotel operated by Smith and Page, and a smaller hostelry and saloon combined, owned by Pete Berry. Neph Johnson was returning to his job at Pete's as driver of a four-horse stagecoach, transporting tourists from Bright Angel to Grand View and to various scenic points along the rim. Pete needed another man for odd jobs around the place and hired Joe Robinson at once. In addition to their larger tourist business, Smith and Page were contractors to deliver copper ore by mule and burro pack train from the Last Chance Mine, located in the bottom of the canyon, to Grand View Point three miles to the north of us. They were short a packer and gave me the job.

And so, our Grand Canyon idea was panning out as we had hoped. I moved three miles north by wagon road to Grand View Point, and took up batching with George Noakes, from Neph Johnson's hometown of Kanab, Utah, and a mysterious old bearded man we knew only as "Dad." He lived on a pension and came in handy by doing most of the cooking, even though paying his third of the grub bill that averaged around twelve dollars a month per man. Noakes was in charge of fifteen pack mules and I was given twenty-two burros. Hosteen John, an old Navajo Indian, night-herded all the animals on good grass nearby, and a younger husky "Navvy," known only as Juan, was our helper on the trail. We three whites bunked and cooked in a small two-room log cabin that has been preserved to this day by the addition of a galvanized tin roof, while Hosteen John and Navajo Juan had an outdoor camp nearby and lived mostly on beans and meat.

My first pack trip with Noakes and Indian Juan was an interesting experience. By daylight that morning our three saddle horses, fifteen mules, and twenty-two burros were brought to the wire corral by night-herder Hosteen John. Each animal had his special grain box which we filled with oats to the level of his tested capacity—a gallon can full to the horses, two-to-three-quart cans to the mules, and two quarts or less to the burros. Horses and mules were partitioned off from the burros, partially to prevent fighting. Every pack animal had his own marked saddle and blanket and was trained for the job at hand. We finished our breakfast about the same time the animals did their oats, and saddling began for the day's run.

We packed several mules with groceries and equipment for the mine and started down the trail. George Noakes took the lead with his mules, while Juan and I followed with the burros. My brown saddle horse was a good one, called Biscuit. Noakes rode a more showy black, and Juan a tough, but lazy Indian pony. In each train the better travelers were placed in order, front to back, with each succeeding mule or burro tied by halter rope to the pack saddle rear of the one ahead. This method had been adopted by trial and error after several animals had been crowded off the trail, sometimes falling five hundred to one thousand feet straight down to the nearest shelf below. Of course they were killed instantly on first impact and it was not feasible to recover any part of the pack or gear, nor was any attempt made.

All this was routine for the experienced man or beast, but to me the thrill of a lifetime. Looking down over my outside stirrup in the more precipitous sections of the built trail was actually frightening and dangerous at first, with nothing below but an abyss of death for the unfortunate who made a misstep. That, and gazing across side canyons at sheer rock walls a thousand feet high, made me dizzy. In order to keep my composure it was necessary to look only at the pack train ahead and reason it out that if the others could take it in stride, I could force myself to do likewise.

Reaching "the Switchbacks" a mile down, I noticed the ease with which each animal made the turns, taking particular care not to step close to the trail's edge. This was over a quarter-mile, ninety-degree slope of ledges and shale that took three times the distance to negotiate by trail. The bottom leg bore to the east across Red Canyon Saddle and north another mile on the west face of a high, narrow ridge, deep red in color, almost maroon. From there to the mine was more open terrain with here and there a reverse grade as minor depressions were crossed. A trail crew was kept busy on repairs to washouts and cave-ins, some of the latter being caused by falling boulders from strata overhead, which, of course, is part and parcel of the perpetual erosion in the canyon area. They had cautioned me in advance to take the best cover available upon hearing the thunderous boom of a falling ledge segment, unless we could be certain its path was well away from our immediate location. In the higher elevations, winter freezing and spring thawing loosen vast quantities of exposed rock, which sooner or later tumble to the bottom of the nearest canyon. During the following three months we heard hundreds and saw a few of these phenomena, but I never knew of any loss of life they might have caused.

It was hot at the Last Chance Copper Mine when we arrived there before noon, in keeping with the reduced elevation by some three thousand feet in three miles travel. Superintendent Johnny Kearns was there to greet us and take charge of the camp supplies in our packs. He was about forty-five, tall, ruddy-complexioned, with a shiny bald head, and a bearing that bespoke his prowess as a hard-rock miner. A pot of coffee from the cook shack touched off sandwiches brought from the Point, which we ate in cool shade at the mouth of the mine tunnel. Also refreshing was a large, burlap-covered jug of cold water for miners and visitors alike, kept there at all times.

In the mining operation high-grade ore was brought to the surface by means of a hand car, pushed horizontally over tiny steel rails a distance of several hundred feet. Kearns sorted out the least profitable material and dumped it over a hundred-foot, perpendicular cliff a few feet away. The rest was placed in heavy burlap sacks of sixty, seventy-five, or one hundred pounds, respective capacities.

With cinches tightened and blankets set straight, the loading began. The ricked sacks of ore had been placed in two parallel rows, with room between for the pack animals and a man on each side. In this way both sacks for a given animal went on simultaneously, thus disturbing its balance hardly at all. Rope loops of proper length hanging on either side were brought up around the sack and hooked over the saddle, a simple operation which, with experienced hands, took less time than to tell about it. At least ten of Noakes's heavier mules carried two hundred-pound sacks apiece, the other five taking two seventy-five-pounders. "Old Sandy," my largest burro, could tread up under two hundred-pounders along with the best of them. Three or four other burros carried seventy-five-pound sacks, while the balance were loaded with sixties. At this rate, our total load approximated fifty-six hundred pounds, four hundred short of three tons, almost evenly divided between mules and burros.

All set for the long, hard climb, Noakes led the mules, I led the burros, and Navajo Juan brought up the rear. You can expect some life and spirit from mules, but never before had I seen the lowly burro exhibit such ambition as a beast of burden. They seemed as anxious as the mules, or we, to get the job over with. Rather than having to punch them along, our main difficulty was keeping them back in their places, to prevent crowding, a critical factor in dangerous sections of the trail. Old Sandy, as leader, knew where he was going and rarely tightened the lead rope. Unlike a horse, when something goes wrong with the pack on a mule or burro, he will make it known by twisting and squirming. Perhaps a gouging cinch ring, a twig under the saddle, a wrinkled saddle blanket, a broken breast strap or breeching would be the cause. Whatever it might be, the entire forty animals, including our mounts, had to be stopped and kept quiet while the trouble was eliminated. Rest stops were also made on the steeper grades, particularly through the switchbacks.

Noakes's habitual shout of "Hike away!" echoed from cliff to cliff. Nearing the top, each animal exhibited an urge to get there first, to be relieved of his burden, grained, and set free. We topped out around four o'clock. A mile an hour, loaded, was good time. My cliff dizziness had gradually disappeared. As time wore on, in fact, I went to the other extreme of exploring crevices, crawling around under ledges as a curious youngster might be expected, the thoughts of which now bring a shudder!

Unpacking was systematically routine inside the large wire corral. Noakes and I worked on opposite sides of each animal as Juan led it into place. The sacks of ore were placed in three separate piles according to weight. Handling the one-hundreds first made the seventy-fives and especially the sixties seem like child's play to husky young men. Halters were removed and pack saddles hung in place. The animals rolled in the dust and nickered for their oats. The day's work was done. Night-herder Hosteen John was on hand to drive the herd out to grass.

In the cabin George Noakes and I washed up and doctored our copper-infested scratches, a daily must to keep down open sores on our hands and arms. "Dad" was ready with a pot of Irish stew, vegetables, and fruits fit for a king, and ample to surfeit our greedy appetites. After supper chores were the usual bachelor type—sewing on a button, washing socks, an occasional bath in a washtub, shaving, and even cutting each other's hair as needed. At least half the mules and burros had feet rough enough to work without shoes. The other half and our horses must be kept shod to withstand the wear and tear of stony ground. Where necessary, the herd was held up from going out to graze while missing shoes were replaced, thereby avoiding delay the next morning.

Shoeing horses on a farm and ranch had been routine, but here was my first experience with mules and burros. Some of the mules were so cantankerous we had to tie up each foot, or even throw them down. Burros were more docile but required careful handling to avoid being kicked by a hind foot. Special shoes were made for them by some manufacturers, resembling those for mules, but smaller. We still had to cut front shoes shorter at times so the hind feet would not catch on the protruding ends. Our equipment included an anvil, cold chisels, nippers, rasps, horseshoe hammers, shoes and nails of various sizes, furnished freely by the company on order. Along with the rest, this phase of the operation was good experience for me that came in handy over the years.

My amazement at the performance of those burros never ceased. Well fed, shod when necessary, and taken care of, they were the equal of their larger contemporary beasts of burden and offered no apologies for their output. Emaciated specimens of the Old Countries, India and Mexico, might as well be a different breed entirely. It was a lesson indeed on the response of lower animals to the needs of man when properly treated. Imagine this lowly creature bucking in play and braying his pleasure on being turned out for the night after a hard day's work, a common occurrence on Grand View Point.

That first trip was typical of the daily runs, six days a week, except that one cargo, usually on Saturday, was of a different kind and even more valuable. A vein of some of the finest asbestos in the world, glistening white and three to five inches thick, was located three miles beyond the Last Chance near the river. It was sacked in about the same weights as for copper ore and enough accumulated during the week to make a load for our outfit. Seven or eight packs operated daily between the asbestos diggings and Kearn's camp, but we handled both outputs from there to Grand View Point, as also incoming supplies for them. We preferred the asbestos for handling, since it was noninfectious and cleaner than copper.

Our delivery of copper and asbestos ore to the point was only the first step in its transportation. Both materials were hauled from there by wagon some twenty miles to Anita Junction on the Santa Fe's Grand Canyon railroad, and then taken away in ore cars to its final destination. This is where George Rogers comes back on the scene. It will be remembered he had moved that spring from Flagstaff to the canyon with his family and four-horse freight outfit. He established headquarters at Pete Berry's and took the freight contract between the point and Anita Junction, hauling equipment and supplies on return trips. Dynamite for mine blasting was among the supplies. He told us of a narrow escape for himself and the whole outfit when a case of the dynamite exploded in his rear wagon from a severe jar over rocky road. The incident caused us all to handle the stuff with extreme care.

Some of the stuff we packed down to the mine was near the impossible. Tools, groceries, clothing, pots and pans, and all other items of reasonable dimensions were, of course, ordinary routine. But when it came to cook stoves, lumber, large trunks, and other big articles that could not be knocked down, our work was cut out for us. Extra lash ropes were used for such packs with wooden kayaks on either side to form a platform. It was there I learned to throw several versions of the diamond hitch, box hitch, squaw hitch, and others best suited to the immediate pack problem. Our gentlest and most tractable animals took the brunt of these bulky loads. A bright yellow mare mule called Poppy was the most reliable of all. Placed out in lead, she would stop and start as told, carry a stove or other huge article with an even pace that caused a minimum of side sway, and make switchback turns with utmost care. A misstep at certain points would have hurled her overboard to sudden death below.

Once a load of lumber came in by freight wagon, part of which was not to be cut shorter than ten feet—another job for Poppy. We fashioned a pack that gave her little headroom between boards, but she was quick to adjust herself. With head low and neck straight, she maneuvered cautiously down the trail, stopping instantly at the whoa command when something went wrong. Board ends, front or back, would catch on rock side walls, making it necessary for a man on foot to lift them out of the way. Switchback turns were not engineered for such cargo and we encountered plenty of grief getting through them. At one turn we had to unpack and carry the lumber around by hand. We arrived an hour late at the cook shack, where Johnny Kearns and his crew were at lunch, and they marveled at our ungainly pack. Poppy had done enough for one day, except to return up the hill empty.

For the next two months our daily trail routine was about as above set forth. We had Sundays off, and for recreation, George and Ida Rogers talked Pete Berry into having Saturday night dances at his one-room bar. Joe Robinson and I furnished the music. The dancers included Pete and George and their wives, Neph Johnson, George Noakes, and several couples from Smith and Page hotel— even tourists on occasion. Married men brought their families. Women and children in a bar room, where "drinks flowed free," looked a bit out of character at first, but such was the carefree atmosphere in these wide-open spaces.

From Buglan Ranch to Bright Angel

To stay in one place for long was not in keeping with the impulse that prompted my leaving home to start with. Down the trail and back, day after day, developed into a monotony that called for a change. There were certain personality clashes with Noakes that made matters worse, and I decided to quit. Martin Buglan had a ranch east of Grand View with which he had merged a small tourist business. People who wished to visit Moran's Point and other scenic areas, either on foot or horseback, were brought in by regular stage from Bright Angel,there being no roads at that time. Buglan needed a guide for those using horses and I took the job.

It was quite a change from the daily packing routine, which I found both interesting and educational. Li, the Chinese cook, was really the only other regular employee. On advance notice he could feed a dozen people, but rarely were there more than four or five extras. He griped at my excessive use of canned milk in coffee, or to moisten a dry piece of pie, to which Civil War veteran Jim Brashear, a boarder, took exception. He told him, "No Mongolian is going to tell the kid how much milk he can have!" which seemed to settle the matter. Jim had a contract to fence the Buglan homestead and his board was part of the deal. One other steady boarder was Harry Schlee, a retired railroader from Williams, out there trying (?) to overcome an advanced case of alcoholism.

The job itself kept me tied up seven days a week, but very little work was involved. Tourists trickled in, two or three at a time, only part of whom wanted horses while hikers were on their own. Half a dozen gentle saddle horses were never all needed at one time. Just the same, there were occasional problems. Some of those tourists came from far-flung points of the earth, spoke no English, and had never been on a horse. One such character from India was placed on Bay Billy, the best trained and most docile mount of the lot, but slightly tender mouthed. It was my first encounter with a grown man who had no more idea how to get on a horse than the man in the moon, much less which side to mount from, or how to handle the reins. After lifting him bodily to the saddle, I saw him begin yanking back on the reins, nearly pulling the horse over backward before I could stop him. It was necessary for his own safety to do away with the bridle and lead Bay Billy with a tie rope.

By and large, our customers were men of means—professors, geologists, engineers—and in most cases they spoke good to broken English. Their many discussions, scientific and otherwise, were of value to me as we made the rounds, and at headquarters as well. But there was one drawback that served to shorten my stay with Mr. Buglan. Some days we had no visitors, while others brought only hikers, and it left too much time to be spent at the ranch. Frankly, I could not work up a liking for Schlee, nor Li, and they left no doubt that the feeling was mutual. An older man perhaps could have resolved the difficulty, but my untrained diplomacy was hardly equal to it. Jim wanted me to stay on, but I had had enough friction for one job. When thirty days were up and the paycheck came, I said good-by to my close friend Jim Brashear and went by stage to Grand View.

I spent two or three days around Pete Berry's, visiting with the Rogers family and Neph Johnson in his off hours. Joe Robinson came in to help play for what was to be our last Saturday night dance at Pete's bar. Everyone was in a gay mood, including Joe and myself, who had been out of communication for over a month. Drinks from the handy bar came thick and fast to our makeshift music stand, to "wet the strings," as the dancers put it. Thus fired up, we were in shape to play all night, especially after a midnight lunch brought in by the ladies. Pete thought better of that, however, and closed around 2 A.M.

Sharing my bed with Joe, we talked over our experiences and speculated on the future. Unless I could land another job in the vicinity there was no telling when we might meet again. A good breakfast made up for loss of sleep, and Joe headed north via Grand View Point to the Last Chance. It was our last meeting for a year, until he drifted back home in the fall of 1904. We had been close pals in forbidding circumstances, through which a lifelong friendship was formed. His older head was a stabilizer to me as well, at a time when reckless youth and vigor crowded out common sense or serious planning for the future.

Pete Berry's four-horse stagecoach left early that Monday morning for Bright Angel, fourteen miles west, to pick up any interested tourists coming in by train. I was aboard with violin, bed and bags, along with the regular driver, Neph Johnson. He introduced the first man we met, who was none other than the famous tourist amuser, John Hance, likewise on his way to meet the train, representing Fred Harvey's eating house and mule-back trips to the river. They met almost daily in this business, and Neph had already described Hance to the letter. He recommended me for a job and the old man said he would ascertain what might be available. Meanwhile, I could cache my baggage in the bunkhouse and sleep there without charge.

Neph booked several passengers and was soon on his way. John Hance steered others to the Harvey House, stuffing them with wit and tall tales en route. When the flurry was over, we sat down to talk, and a more interesting, unique individual could never be found. His three-score and some years were evidenced by gray hair and a long white beard that waved in the canyon breeze and which vibrated accompaniment to his constant chatter. Now and then an unruly denture shook loose from excessive enunciation, only to be mashed back in place while he caught his breath for the next sentence. Loose in his pants pocket was a hundred-dollar gold note for frequent, "accidental" exhibition as he fumbled for a match, pocketknife, or small change. John Hance had a quick wit and was full of tall tales, which tourists repeated around the world and which brought many a chuckle. It's no wonder Fred Harvey paid him well just to lie.

We walked over to the corral where Harvey's saddle mules were kept. One I had often heard mentioned in canyon conversation, called Snyder, was pointed out, a drab-colored veteran of medium size and gentle disposition. Tourists who knew about him wired ahead for Snyder reservations, so wide was his reputation as a reliable mount on Bright Angel Trail. This seemed quite unnecessary, however, after learning how long and thoroughly all mules were trained before trusting them in regular service. There were experts who did nothing the year-round but train Missouri mules for the business. Their finished product knew every inch of the trail, was conscious of his own safety and that of panicky riders. Only a small percentage of the animals tested ever made the grade, and be it said for the thoroughness of Fred Harvey that very few serious accidents occurred over the years, despite the thousands of inexperienced riders making the trip.

The man in charge took my application for a job, wishing I had come along sooner as the active season was about over. But he suggested I stick around a day or two and it was apparent John Hance's recommendation bore a lot of weight, evidencing the respect in which he was held. Yet the last of September was rather late to expect steady employment. Two or three days went by without sign of a job. They were hardly wasted, however, what with tourists coming and going, the changing hues of the canyon, depending upon the time of day, the worthwhile conversations with people from afar, and the antics of John Hance. And speaking of his antics, a New York dame of no little self-importance hurried up to John one day and said, "Where is the Grand Canyon? I don't see any canyon." John's very dignified reply, standing there in full view of the great chasm, is one of the classics. "Lady," he said solemnly, "there *is* no Grand Canyon. It's all a myth!" It can be said of John Hance that he went down in southwestern history as the greatest and most pleasing liar of his time.

It is a matter of regret that I did not ride a mule down Bright Angel Trail to the river though I was invited to do so by the foreman. Whatever the reasoning, it would have been time well spent. Instead, I boarded a train for Williams. This was within a day or two of October 1, 1903. On my arrival, Dick Hopkins at the Palace Saloon seemed pleased to see me, shoved out a drink on the house, and inquired about Joe. Dick was a good-hearted Texan, blonde and blue-eyed, once a slender cowhand, but now growing obese from too many years around a bar. He took me to a vacant room at the rear, which I could occupy for the time being in return for a little music during periods when it might stimulate trade at the bar. He and his partner, Alex Chisholm, had installed a music stand and piano since we left there in May, and his wife, Birdie Ray, soon learned to harmonize with my fiddle tunes. We became quite an attraction, in fact, for such business as there was.

The best tailor in town was a beer-guzzling Dutchman known only as "Dutch." He took my measurements for a fine suit of clothes for which he was paid in advance—a good thing, too, considering that my $150 bankroll was dwindling fast. The plan had been to dress up good and go home with a showing of prosperity. But I made a bad mistake in not purchasing a ready-made outfit, thereby eliminating three or four weeks of waiting for Dutch to finish the suit by hand. He had other orders to fill with no extra help, and "rushing the can" took part of his time.

With time on my hands, in a saloon environment, there could be but one result, regretting which, I think of the great Barrymore and his comment, "A man realizes failure when his memories turn to regrets." The world looked easy. Everywhere I went people were cordial, more especially saloon keepers and gamblers, ever alert for a "live one." I played poker, roulette, and shot craps, all on a moderate scale, but nonetheless ruinous in end result. Some days I won, largely at draw poker, the most fascinating game of all, and at that time considered straight. There is a certain thrill to outwitting an opponent through studying his facial expressions and maneuvers, the number of cards he draws, if any, the amount wagered in proportion to the size of the pot, whether it be on a good hand or bluff, and all the psychological fine points that veterans use. Watching professionals in action, like the previously mentioned Hudson brothers and Hugh Lane at Flagstaff, was an inspiration, and I toyed with the idea of being somewhere in their class.

But there are too many things the amateur does not learn at once, for instance, when to quit. It can be mighty disheartening to win a hundred dollars in a five-dollar change-in only to wind up loser by playing on and on. Gamblers are experienced in such matters and do everything nice to keep one in the game. Too many free drinks tend to lower one's guard and make him feel invincible. He starts plunging when he should fold up, the very thing they want him to do, and I was no exception to such manipulation.

Whatever may be wrong with gambling, and although it hastened my going broke in this instance, I still enjoy a quiet game of poker among friends, on a moderate scale where no one is unduly hurt. It separates good sports from soreheads—the latter being few—sharpens the wits, and broadens one's understanding of human psychology. Even if a "fool and his money" were parted in a week's

time at Williams, there were certain educational values that served
not only to even the score in time, but to accelerate a teenager's at-
tainment of maturity in the highly competitive game of life.

The Perrin Ranch

A mile west of town, north of the railroad, was the headquarters ranch of a Dr. Perrin and his wife, Lila, consisting of a
modern, two-story residence, barns, corrals, fences, some farmland, and a thousand-acre pasture. They ran both cattle and sheep
on surrounding forest range. One day Dick Hopkins, knowing my
circumstances, told me the Perrins were in need of a ranch hand and
my name had been given their representative as a qualified prospect. With funds running low, and tiring of daily saloon life, I called
at the ranch for an interview. Robert Perrin, an elderly bachelor
brother having some unknown interest in the operation, was there
to do the questioning. In oral form he took my history from birth to
date and the deal was made. My pay would be eight dollars a week,
including board and room with Sundays off. There was nothing
about the job I had not done before, the better for all concerned. It
consisted of milking a Jersey cow night and morning, making sure
all was clean and sanitary, chopping and carrying in wood for the
kitchen range and various heaters about the house, caring for the
work-and-buggy team, taking the family out for a drive as often as
they wished in a rather pretentious surrey, hauling in wood by team
and wagon, cleaning stables and corrals of fertilizer and spreading
the same on garden plots or land used for growing oats and barley,
fence repairs, and miscellaneous other odd chores that go into ranch
maintenance.

Tom Brown, a typical Texan from San Angelo, was foreman over
the cattle spread, and Steve Brown (no relation) was in charge of
the several sheep herds. They both were interested in my limited
career and in turn told me about their field operations. Tom loved
hoedown fiddle music—a Texas weakness—and had me playing for

him every trip in. He went with me several Saturday nights to the
Palace Saloon where I played with Birdie Ray Hopkins on a regular
schedule. Although he never drank to excess, he would buy several
rounds at the bar and thoroughly enjoy the evening. We had to walk
through a railroad underpass going home, and on each occasion Tom
would draw his trusty .45, just in case.

One of the duties I liked most was taking the family out for a
buggy ride two or three times a week. The old work-team trotted
well in the harness, considering the two had been selected specially
for their gentle laziness so that the son, Lilo, and his mother could
handle them when necessary. Kept always fat and sleek, their extra
grooming for these jaunts made them look the part—in keeping with
a late model surrey and a flashy set of harness. Mrs. Perrin and
Robert thought I was the best teamster they ever had (thanks to
early training on the farm, perhaps), which might explain their
planning trips more often than before. We visited their cattle and
sheep camps, picnicked on Bill Williams Mountain, shopped in town,
or just breezed around for the ride.

Weeks rolled by in routine fashion. Hauling wood was completed
for the winter. Saturday was payday and I never missed spending
the evening in town. Besides playing the violin at the Palace, I sat in
several games of draw poker and just about won back the money I
had lost earlier. There was plenty of time at the ranch to ponder errors and factors that had cost me a fair bankroll. I was determined
not to repeat them. Losing on one's better judgment cannot be
helped, but falling into an obvious trap through sense-dulling liquor,
or being too modest to quit when ahead, is inexcusable. It was often
amazing how Saturday night revelers threw their money away by
violating these two simple rules, and now I was profiting by having
learned the rules the hard way.

Other errors are frequently committed by youngsters that turn
into regrets. I got word that the postmaster wished to see me at his
office in town. Accordingly, I saddled one of the Perrin's pet black
horses and rode in to see what was up. As might have been expected, Mother had written the postmaster to ascertain my
whereabouts, and he remembered my calling for mail. He was a

kindly man (the name escapes me) and gave me a good talking to about the debt we owe our devoted mothers. I hadn't written home in several months, and it's no wonder Mother was worried. The lump in my throat prevented free conversation for a moment, but I thanked him for his interest, apologized for causing the inquiry, and wound up using his desk to write Mother there and then.

Many a young fellow away from home is remiss in this regard, not from any lack of love and respect for his mother, nor real aversion for writing, but the shabby habit of putting off, of not fully sensing the anguish she is apt to suffer through his negligence. In this instance Mother replied by return mail and was so happy to hear from me that I resolved never to go that long again without writing.

One incident at Perrin's is unforgettable. The townsfolk and ranchers had been advised that President Theodore Roosevelt was due on a certain train from Grand Canyon and would make a speech at the rear platform. People came from far and near to honor the popular Teddy, who was the first president many of us had ever seen in person. Everyone was thrilled with his snappy talk, spectacles and bared teeth as shown in numerous portraits, and his dynamic personality. As the train pulled out to the west, some fifty mounted cowboys from outlying ranches whooped it up with hats held high and a loud "Hurrah for Teddy!"

Christmas was approaching and for Williams it was always white. Merchants and saloon men looked forward to a busy season. Windows were gaily decorated and mahogany-framed, back-bar mirrors glittered with appropriate paintings by soap artists of the period. Anticipating a business upsurge at the Palace, Dick Hopkins offered me a steady job playing violin at better pay than at Perrin's. It was a hard decision to make, however, for the Perrins had been good to me. Besides, I liked the ranch job, and with Saturday night fiddle earnings, plus winnings at poker, I was doing all right. Perhaps an influencing factor was having a woman boss. Mrs. Perrin was a fine person, but boring at times with her constant shifting of assignments around the place, each before the other could be completed. Notifying her a week in advance of my leaving was an embarrassing task. She knew of my playing in a saloon and spoke kindly against it. In fact, I almost backed out when the time came, they appeared so disappointed—as if I were more a member of the family than a come-and-go ranch hand. But the die was cast. Dick was bent on having music seven nights a week during the holiday season, and if he hired other players, my Saturday nights would be cut off in the bargain. We shook hands all around, the Perrins and Chinese cook wished me luck, and I thanked them for their many kindnesses.

For the next month and a half, it was daily routine around the saloons, including a nightly four-hour shift playing the violin at the Palace with Mrs. Hopkins, pianist. Steady practice greatly improved our harmony to the extent that we drew cowboy-logger elements, which comprised a good majority of the spenders. Occasionally, Johnny Jones and Ben Sweetwood dropped in to see how we did it. They operated separately the two most attractive bars on Front Row, located at opposite corners on the main street leading south from the depot. A classical violinist worked for Sweetwood and attracted music lovers to a degree, but as Tom Brown would say, "It's no good. You can't even pat your foot to it!" Jones had an accomplished lady pianist and singer who was a bit too highfalutin for the common guy seeking amusement.

Home Again

It happened before, and now again. I was getting tired of saloon life as a steady diet. By hard knocks I had learned a few lessons in frugality and thrift, and by mid-February 1904 was doing quite well in the pocket. Room rent was cheap, three dollars per week, meals, twenty-five to fifty cents each, and there was no sense in repeating earlier purse-flattening procedures. My system for draw poker worked out well on a moderate scale, namely never to lose more than ten dollars at a sitting, or try to win in excess of fifty dollars, except as it might accrue in the last pot. Checking-out winner took some chiding from losers, but real gamblers respect the right of any player to cash in at will. Although learning to cope with

these surroundings on a mature basis was not without some satisfaction, there was still something lacking in that general type of
living which impelled another change.

Coincident with my decision to get out of Williams while the going
was good came another surprise. Unlike the one at Flagstaff in June
1903, this was to fit beautifully into my own plans. On shift at the
Palace, Mrs. Hopkins and I were playing away one evening when I
noticed Dad entering the front door. This time I was really glad he
came and told him right off I was ready to go back with him.
Homesickness per se has never plagued me greatly, but frequent
letters from home since the fall before had kindled a yearning to see
the folks, Mother in particular, and whether Dad had come or not, I
was ready to pay them a visit. Dad explained that he had not come
after me but was in Holbrook and decided to drop out and see how I
was getting along. His attitude had changed completely in respect
to forcing me home and all was pleasant, as such a reunion should
be. Saloon owners, bartenders, and gambler friends were delighted
to meet "the Kid's Dad," and spoke words of praise that made him
feel good, despite his unalterable disagreement with their mode of
life and the part I was playing in it.

There was some delay for such as laundry, dry cleaning, and odd
chores, but when we were ready to go, a group of the above associates accompanied us to the train. They were inquisitive about Snowflake and surrounding Mormon towns, an opportunity for Dad not
only to describe them, but to expound their religion as well. We
bade good-byes and boarded old Santa Fe No. 10 for Holbrook, a
year almost to the day since Elmer Richards and I left home February 15, 1903, "to see the world." At Flagstaff, Whiskey Row was a
familiar sight that brought back memories. I recognized friends
among the crowd gathered at the depot during a brief stop—a pecu-
liar town custom that remains to this day. Arriving in Holbrook late
that night, we carried my luggage, fiddle, and so forth, to the Co-op
corral where Dad had left his team and wagon in care of other
freighters. His camp bed was ample for both of us, but little did I
sleep in anticipation of going home next day.

We arose early, fed the horses, and walked to Sam Chinaman's for breakfast. En route we met Joe Knight opening up the Pioneer Saloon. He proposed and "eye opener," which I accepted amid questions and discussion concerning my absence. Joe was a good friend of whom more will be written. In two or three hours we were loaded with freight and on our way to Snowflake. Trudging along with a freight outfit was a far cry from old No. 10, and I thought we would never get there. However, the familiar scenes and landmarks lent spice to the slow, twenty-eight-mile pull that took about ten hours, by contrast with the thirty-minute drive nowadays over the same route by car or truck.

That "blood is thicker than water" was never more evident. Nor had I ever realized fully the depth of family ties until that evening when we entered the old home. They are wonderful and should never be allowed to disintegrate. Greetings were accompanied by tears of joy. At supper, Mother and the four kids kept me busy answering questions about the year's experiences. Some were soft-pedaled to suit the occasion, for saloon life, of all things, was farthest from family tradition and teachings. I was intrigued by changes in my brother and three sisters, how much they had grown in one short year, and how they could play guitars and sing together under Mother's tutelage. In like manner they marveled at my appearance of maturity and embarrassed me with veneration for their big brother. They were eager to hear the old fiddle again, especially the many new tunes I had learned, and thus we celebrated a happy reunion. Jenny was fifteen, Thalia twelve, Lafayette (Lafe) ten, and Leone eight. I was justly proud of them all, clean and sweet youngsters in mind and body only a wonderful mother could produce.

Thus came a happy ending to a formative year away from home entirely on my own, whether for good or bad being difficult to evaluate. It certainly taught me self-reliance and removed a natural reluctance to approach and mingle with strangers. It broadened my concept of the human race, its virtues and vices, put me squarely on my two feet to cope with the pitfalls of youth. Perhaps above all, it proved that the world owes one a living only as he is willing to work for it. On the debit side lies the fact that most if not all these attainments would have come about coincidentally with a college education, toward which a full year had been wasted and the desire to achieve it lessened. Despite gratifying recognition of hard work and commensurate advancement over thirty-five years of my professional life, all too often the lack of a college degree spelled handicap and sore regret. Wishing it were possible to live over one's youth is pure idleness, but it should serve as a warning to following generations who are prone to make the same mistakes.

CHAPTER FOUR

Country Fiddler
Dancing and Other Sports

For a week or more I was content to visit at home and around town. Old friendships were renewed and family gatherings were enjoyed on both sides of the house, as was customary in frontier communities. The first Friday night dance at Flake Brothers hall was delightful indeed. Girls I had hectored at school seemed so grown-up, pretty, and attractive it was hard to believe. Claude Youngblood and I took turns playing violin and dancing. My new tunes went over good and in a short time we were playing them together, as well as other pieces he had picked up in the same period. Such wholesome recreation and town spirit had never before so impressed me. Those people really made the most of their entertainment opportunities. They worked hard and they played hard—two fundamentals in the building of character and economic security. So much for a homecoming, the thoughts of which have been pleasant ever since.

There was little to do at Snowflake in 1904 but farm. Money was scarce and the only available jobs paid low wages—mostly in credit at a local store. These were drawbacks that made young men look to wider fields of endeavor. Having attained some popularity at dances in 1902 with our two-violin combination, Youngblood and I took up where we left off, specializing on hoedowns played in unison or relays for square dances and two-part harmony pieces for "round dances." The dual (two parts) feature was unique for that period and received wide acclaim in dancing circles throughout northeastern Arizona. "Youngblood and Kartchner" became a symbol of sociability and dancing fun to the extent that we were hard put to meet the demand for our services, especially on Friday and Saturday nights. There was little difficulty in booking other weekday nights if they were well advertised in advance.

Transportation was a problem at times. On the railroad we traveled east or west by train, but in all directions from Snowflake we had to go horseback—carrying our instruments under an arm— or by rented team and buggy. To offset these difficulties we jointly purchased a light hack or buckboard, with suitable harness, and converted our saddle horses into an excellent driving team. Wherever we went their proper care took top priority and, I must say in passing, no other outfit was ever allowed to pass us on the road. Thus by midsummer of 1904 we had a well-equipped business of sorts and we plied our trade at all major towns in Navajo and Apache counties.

Good accompanists were scarce for the most part. However, we had contacts with local guitar or banjo players of varying proficiency on whom we could depend without the necessity of hauling them from place to place. Notable among these was Antolino Tafoya of Saint Johns. Totally blind from smallpox suffered in early childhood, his other senses were remarkably keen. Aside from being the best guitar player we ever had, it was amazing how fast he could replace a broken string with a new one of proper size, all by the sense of feel. His rhythm and harmony were perfect, including appropriate modulations and minor sevenths befitting a master of musical science. He loved playing with us and was always on hand when notified by mail that we would be in Saint Johns or Concho on a certain date. For Concho engagements he either came the fifteen miles by mail stage or with friends. It was there, in fact, where most of our playing with Antolino took place. As an orchestra musician, I daresay his guitar would be as popular today as then. The poor fellow was one of the first to die when influenza ravaged the country in 1918–19.

Old Concho

Our association with the little Mexican-American town of Concho, starting in 1902, was unique. Among its three or four hundred inhabitants were well-to-do sheep and cattlemen, such as Juan and Rosalie Candelaria, David and Tom Ortega, Lorenzo Martinez, Lorenzo Baca, and others, all with medium to large families. It boasted two saloons, a bank, several small stores, a school, a dance hall, and the old coffin-shaped Catholic church north of town. The laboring class sometimes found jobs as sheepherders or cowboys, or else along the railroad. For those times it was a prosperous village, comprised of descendants of original Mexican settlers who had moved along the Rio Grande up through New Mexico to southern Colorado. This dated back to around 1700 A.D. after Diego de Vargas reconquered the area in 1692. Concho was one of the many outlying hamlets where these people came to settle. It came into existence in about 1869 when Juan Candelaria settled there with his sheep. Other founders were largely pastoral, branching westward from Albuquerque and vicinity in search of new grazing lands for their flocks.

Sometime in 1902, Concho leaders sent young Teodoro Lopez on horseback the thirty-five miles to Snowflake for the purpose of engaging the Youngblood and Kartchner dance orchestra for a three-day fiesta celebration. This was something new and we wondered about adjusting our music to their type and tempo of dances. We accepted the offer of extra pay plus board and room for ourselves and keep for two horses, providing they would hire Antolino Tafoya to come over and play with us. Teodoro readily agreed and the deal was made. He was the flashy twenty-year-old son of Benigno Lopez who ran a saloon and general store on a rise at the south end of the main street. Aside from Antolino's ability as a guitarist, his knowledge of the Mexican people, their language, their dances, customs, and temperament were invaluable to us in the new venture.

On the date set, Claude and I saddled early and rode east past the

Point of the Mountain to Rock Well twenty miles out where we had lunch and watered the horses. Carrying a violin on horseback is tiresome, but we were somewhat used to it and didn't mind too much. Topping the hill west of town we rode into Concho that afternoon amid cheers from the populace. People shouted "Los Musicos Mormitos" (the Mormon Musicians) in obvious anticipation of events to come. Antolino was there and we felt reassured. Our horses were taken care of and a nice clean room at the home of Federico Sandoval, a block west of the business center, was assigned us. Spanish courtesy was everywhere, exceeding our own in gusto. We were thrilled by it.

Not anticipated, however, was their standard custom of going around with the *gallo* (rooster). Barely allowing us time to wash up, a team and wagon with Antolino aboard called for us to make music through the streets, thus to advertise the *baile* (dance) that evening, to put dancers in the mood, and to leave no doubt the music would be on hand. For some reason they associate this with the crow of a rooster. We had serenaded in wagons at Snowflake in the wee hours on holidays, but here was our first late evening gallo. Our original embarrassment soon gave way to the thrill of enthusiastic approval on all sides. People cheered in front of their homes as we passed by and a large crowd assembled downtown at the finish. Any such introduction to a new and unique clientele in our business could not fail to sink deep in our memories.

Antolino spoke English, if somewhat broken, and knew all the angles. When asked why the dance was scheduled so early (7 P.M.), as compared with 8:30 to 9:00 opening time for the Anglos he said, "Well yoost the same like gallo, eet ees a custom of the Mexican people."

Sure enough, by seven o'clock the little dance hall next door to the second main saloon run by Old Man (Viejo) Gallegos and his two sons, Juan and Carlos, was filled to overflowing. They came in family groups, each strictly ruled over by its head of the house. Their young people danced at will but the slightest infraction of proper dignity was corrected at once. Each father or guardian carried a coal-oil lantern to light the way for those who walked, while others at greater distances came in wagons or on horseback, little folks and all.

We musicians sat on an improvised platform at the back of the hall, conspicuous for all to see. Wide-eyed youngsters stared at Claude and me as if we might have come from Mars. Older people were curious. Floor manager Federico Sandoval called for "un valse," which we played in duet form faster than ordinary, as coached by Antolino in preliminary rehearsal. The two-violin combination was a hit here no less than elsewhere, especially with Antolino's expert accompaniment. Next was a Spanish polka also in faster tempo. Dancers and wallflowers alike seemed delighted and encored vigorously. Then came a cotillion, a term I never understood, pronounced "koteelio." This was a Spanish quadrille similar to a square dance but without a caller. Our stepped-up hoedowns proved ideal for time, and we marveled at the grace and perfect rhythm with which the dance was executed. Beginners were few and rarely was there an error on the part of individual dancers. These three numbers are mentioned, in particular, since they occupied most of the agenda. Less frequent were dances of the Anglos—schottische, two-step, even Comin' Through the Rye (rye waltz). Their manner of closing was another new feature to us. At about 11 P.M. the different family heads rounded up their broods, lit the lanterns, and simply left for home. There was no announcement or request for the "Home Waltz," to which we were accustomed. They just quietly cleared the hall and the baile was over until the following evening.

Twice more we went around with the gallo to proclaim the second and third bailes respectively. Strangely enough, the third fell on a Sunday night but, as we learned, this was not unusual. Most of the residents attended mass at 6 A.M., perhaps other religious rites during the day as well, and danced that night as though it were a part of their Domingo (Sunday) observances.

Our three-day contract fulfilled, the dance committee paid us off in full, not counting a few dollars in tips. It was a little embarrassing to accept a tip at first, not being used to it. But it was their way of showing appreciation for certain pieces they especially liked. Antolino explained it as a common custom; to refuse was considered an offense to the giver. We said adios to our new-found friends, all of whom appeared to have enjoyed the music and had a good time. They said "Venir otra vez," or, "Come another time." We did go on many occasions afterwards, perhaps an average of four to six times a year, at holidays or weddings.

Mexican weddings were always interesting. We must have played for a dozen in a six-year period, mostly at Concho, but at least one each in Holbrook and Rio [de] la Plata (Silver Creek above Shumway). The latter was little more than a group of sheep ranches near the head of Silver Creek. The day began at sunrise with a grand march from the bride's home to the church, headed in our case by two violins and a guitar playing slow march music to accommodate the pace of old and young. Pictures of such a procession would be priceless now. Unfortunately, I cannot recall that any were taken. Claude and I sat in church with the paraders during rituals performed by the priest, following suit as the audience knelt several times in prayer. To the best of my knowledge, Father De Richmont of Saint Johns conducted the marriage ceremonies in each case, the one in Holbrook being a possible exception. He was cordial the few times we met personally. Once he commented about our joint responsibility for a successful occasion.

At the conclusion of church rituals our parade re-formed for its march back to the home of the bride's parents or, where necessary, to larger quarters especially prepared for the day's festivities. A long table was set with every manner of food and drink open to all throughout the day. Our contract called for continuous music for an hour or so and to stand by for requested numbers the whole day long. Seemingly, no expense was spared to honor and joyfully celebrate these occasions. Friends and neighbors dropped in with gifts to congratulate, eat, drink, and visit. Rapid but softly spoken Spanish flowed like music. The bride and groom always dressed beautifully and acted their part with decorum and appropriate dignity. Crowning the day's events was the wedding dance beginning around 7 P.M. and closing at 11:00 to 11:30. They were little different from other dances except for the grand march to start them off and a few extra hall decorations.

Never have I regretted this closer association with Mexican customs and traditions. Not only was it educational, but it served to create many friendships that were renewed on occasion in later years. As a case in point, upon entering the Forest Service in January 1913, I was assigned the park ranger district of the Sitgreaves National Forest on which several sheep outfits held grazing permits during the summer months. It was my job to count each herd to make sure permitted numbers were not exceeded and to work with the owner or "caporal" in effecting even distribution over the range. In addition, for three consecutive seasons I had to count some sixty-five thousand other sheep coming up each spring from the Salt River Valley over the Heber-Reno driveway that crossed my district. Practically all the herders were Mexican acquaintances who at some time or other had danced to our music, a circumstance that was to facilitate my official work as a counter. Riding horseback from herd to herd on the trail, I was often greeted with "Hello Cannery," and in every such case given full cooperation toward an accurate count.

Of course, the moniker "Cannery" was an attempt at pronouncing my name Kenner. It was used rather widely by Mexicans I knew, having started around 1900 when Lorenzo Baca moved his large family from Concho to Snowflake for a term of school. Near my age were Hilario, Mona, and Benito with whom I became well acquainted. They were smart in school, but their English was decidedly broken. Benito's was noticeably improved when I ran into him in the early 1920s working in a store at Gallup, New Mexico.

Over and above these advantages, I gained a fair working knowledge of "sheepherder Spanish" that came in handy, especially among those who spoke no English. There were many such people in mountain villages in the Manzano National Forest in New Mexico with whom it was necessary to confer on their use of the forest for grazing and taking out of cordwood. Spanish was also much in use around Reserve, New Mexico, on the Apache Forest to which I was transferred in September 1925. It is amazing how much faster one adds new words and phrases to his vocabulary in a foreign language where those with whom he must converse can talk nothing else. Conversely, in my case, a few years of total nonuse causes one to forget much of what he has learned. With each generation there has also developed a wider knowledge of English among the Mexican Americans such that it is rarely necessary to speak Spanish anymore.

Early opening and closing of Mexican dances of that period had another angle. Not often, but occasionally, a fight would start on the dance floor. Invariably that meant the baile was over. Family heads hurriedly gathered their broods and left for home in a matter of minutes. We were always paid in full, although a dance might have lasted but an hour or two. Offenders were usually high in their cups and thoroughly resentful of being chastised by the management for boisterous conduct. Other incidents might involve jealousies between two rivals for the same señorita's attentions. We witnessed a number of fistfights that got pretty well along before they could be quelled and by that time no girls were left to dance with.

Foot and Horse Racing

Major sporting events in the early 1900s invariably were tied to a big dance for which we frequently furnished the music. For this reason Claude Youngblood and I attended holiday celebrations, matched horse and foot races, baseball games and similar events more widely than average sportsmen in the area. A few such occasions come to mind.

Sometime around 1907–08 Jesse H. Pearce, a professional foot racer himself, and Ez Walker brought an undersized thoroughbred racehorse named "Silver Kid" over from Farmington, New Mexico. They went from place to place matching races of either variety and usually won. Ignacio Bazan, a reputable and well-known stockman of Rio [de] la Plata (Silver Creek, some fifteen miles south of Snowflake), had a store and saloon there and occasionally put on a small rodeo and dance. In his employ was a Mexican caballero (his name escapes me) of mysterious origin and questionable character, who owned a blue-roan horse he imagined could outrun anything extant that might walk on four legs. Pearce and Walker bantered him for a race between Silver Kid and his blue-roan, which he accepted at once with a show of some self-importance. Forfeit money was posted and a date set for the race to be run at Rio [de] la Plata. If Ignacio Bazan was involved in the betting, he kept it undercover and took no part in the row that followed the race. But he recognized the crowd-gathering potential of such an event and decided to stage a dance that evening. He contacted Youngblood and me for music and spread the word throughout the neighborhood. Had it not been for this added feature, our presence at the matched race would have been unlikely. As it was, Youngblood, who had had some experience and whose light-weight was in keeping with the trade, agreed to jockey for Pearce and Walker on Silver Kid.

Accordingly, on the morning of the race Pearce, Walker, Youngblood, and I went from Snowflake to Rio [de] la Plata, fifteen miles by team and buggy, leading Silver Kid at the side. He was a pretty thing, in fine condition with bloodlines flowing throughout his makeup. His small size was attributed to having been stunted as a young colt for some cause or other. However, this hampered his speed but little, if at all, for short distances of three hundred yards to a quarter of a mile. Trotting him fifteen miles before a race on the same evening would ordinarily have been poor judgment on the part of his owner-trainers, but they correctly judged the blue-roan's inability to run anywhere close to the little thoroughbred in three hundred yards, even though the latter might have traveled twice the distance to be on hand.

As expected, a good crowd gathered to see the race in late afternoon. We met Arch Ruth, a husky young cowboy much interested in the matter and having a stake in it. He had ridden across from his Forest Service fireguard station near Linden as previously planned. It was he, in fact, who promoted the race. He was one of four or five tall brothers raised in the ranching business and known for their fine horses. Moreover, he knew and understood the flashy Mexican cowboy who imagined his common blue-roan cow pony was no less than another Man of War on the track. Little attention was given the .45 Arch carried at his belt, since it was still a partial custom thereabouts.

Final wagers were made (some three or four hundred dollars in all) while Walker groomed and Youngblood warmed up Silver Kid. The best three-hundred-yard track available was a smoothed roadway through rocky ground and not entirely straight. But they agreed this was as fair for one side as the other. The prancing blue-roan appeared, ridden by his owner who was dressed in gaudy colors with a dazzling silk bandana around his neck. His confidence was complete as was that of his half-dozen backers and numerous fans. Wagons full of women and children lined both sides of the outcome, along with equestrians and people on foot. Judges officiated at both ends of the track. The air grew tense with excitement as each jockey maneuvered for position.

"Aye corriente!" someone shouted and the race was on. As much as to say "There they go," at tracks where English is used. Here came Silver Kid with his ears laid back and bit in teeth expressing disgust, as it were, for being placed in the same class with any such nondescript opponent. True to his pedigree, he ran the three hundred yards at such terrific speed as to make a farce of the whole affair. He beat the touted blue-roan "as far as you could throw a rock," to use the expression. Subdued groans came from partisan onlookers, especially the losers who could hardly believe their eyes. We ourselves had not expected such a rout but were nonetheless jubilant over the outcome.

To suppose the matter ended there and that wager money was paid over willingly is not to understand the temperament of unscrupulous individuals of hot-blooded Latin-Indian origin. Nor was Arch Ruth oblivious to what might happen in wearing his gun. For our flashy braggadocio and his backers the shock was too great. They were so sure of themselves, so bent upon teaching the gringos a lesson, plus collecting the spoils, that they simply could not accept what they had just witnessed as anything but some sort of crooked mystery. The Flash, we shall call the owner and rider of the blue-roan, rushed back to the outcome and jumped off his horse fighting mad. Approaching our group of gringos, he shouted a diatribe in Spanish too fast for us to get it all, but leaving no doubt he was spitting defiance and telling us he refused to pay the bet.

With odds of five to a hundred or so, the present situation was grave indeed. We had no way of knowing, in addition to the bettors, who or how many bystanders might join them in case of a fight. As it turned out, however, the bulk of local citizens were as disgusted as we with Flash and his cohorts, reducing the enemy to about three combatants to our one. Realizing our disadvantage in numbers, Arch Ruth pulled his gun and said, "We run you a fair race and we want our money!"

I was standing at his left. A chunky Mexican national made a run at Arch's back, presumably after his gun, but called it quits when I knocked him down. Another of Flash's comrades rushed Arch from the right side but was thoroughly subdued by an unusual defense tactic. Out of the corner of his eye Arch watched the maneuver, gun in hand. Just as the assailant was about to make contact, he threw his whole two-hundred-pound weight into him with a terrific chug of the right elbow that knocked all the breath out of him and sent him sprawling over and over through the malpais rocks. It was two down but how many to go? And where was the Flash? He was conspicuous by his absence. Had his flamboyant bravado taken a sudden nosedive? So it had.

By now I was looking for Arch to kill one or more of them any second. He twirled the revolver on his finger and shouted, "The next son of a bitch that makes a crooked move, I'll kill him!" The expression on his face left no doubt that he meant every word. Normally rosy-cheeked, he turned pale as a ghost, particularly around the mouth, spelling readiness for the worst. No law officer was present, or if so, none put in an appearance. Again Arch demanded the money and wanted it *now*. I have never experienced a tenser moment. But if any of the Mexicans had a gun they were content not to make it known, a factor that may have had some bearing on the bloodless outcome. Naturally, we were alert for any move toward what might be a secret weapon.

Finally, the sheepish Flash, scared stiff and thoroughly convinced his bluff was doomed, came from nowhere with hands raised saying in broken English, "Don't shoot! Don't shoot! We pay! We pay!" Stake-holders gave me the money while Arch held his gun at a safe distance for possible action. He was taking no chances lest this be a ruse or there be an attempt at foul play. It all happened so quickly and I was so preoccupied on rear-guard duty to protect Arch from behind that I failed to notice how the other three boys were faring. But we wound up together and counted out each man's share of the bets. In fact, we remained together in case Flash might seek some underhanded revenge.

The dance was staged in the loft of a large red barn, much as if nothing had happened. A stairway had been fashioned for ingress and egress. We had played in worse halls, at that, and those people really enjoyed themselves. There was no trace of friction, and we suspected Arch Ruth had something to do with it as he sat beside us the whole evening still wearing his gun. None of the Flash gang was there and the only thing we noticed—somewhat amusing, but indicative of tension—was the extra room given Arch by the dancers. Several moved quickly away upon finding themselves too near him. No doubt community leader Ignacio Bazan was a factor as well. He expressed to us his regrets for the fracas and counseled his people against further trouble.

Joe Wood had a fast cow pony that he and Dick Greer backed against Silver Kid, the race to be run on July 4, 1908 (I believe), in connection with other holiday sports at Holbrook. How well I remember the loss of three ten-dollar gold pieces to Joe Wood personally on what I thought would be a cinch and the jovial kidding he gave me for showing such poor judgment—actually against his own advice. Joe was a great guy, a good citizen, likable, and later a topnotch sheriff of Navajo County.

We who bet on the Kid that day—the few of us left—still believe he was the faster horse by a substantial margin. But contrary to his behavior at Rio [de] la Plata, he balked at the starting line. Hi Richards, the rider, had difficulty staying aboard as he reared, pitched, ran backwards and sidewise for a matter of thirty minutes. Whether the belated start was at all fair has remained controversial ever since. But the gun was fired. Instead of running straight, Silver Kid veered wide of the track through rabbit brush and weeds for perhaps seventy-five yards before taking a sudden notion to get back on the track and really run. By that time, it was too late. Joe Woods rode his horse across the finish line barely in front as the Kid came near to closing a gap of eight or ten lengths. Had the race been 350 yards rather than 300 we still would have won going away. But a race is a race. Despite our protests it was ruled that since both horses left the score on signal, the race was official and they were on their own. "Oh well, you can't win 'em all," I thought, even with the fastest horse. My loss approximated Rio [de] la Plata winnings.

It was a serious blow, however, to Pearce and Walker, who had lost about everything they owned except a balky racehorse. Walker confided, incidentally, that they were able to purchase Silver Kid only because he had been track spoiled. If in the mood, he was tractable and ran a superb race. If not, he threw a fit and very likely the race, as demonstrated at Holbrook. Pearce and Walker were desperate. They hadn't enough money left to pay livery and other expenses. Jesse Pearce was in training and could run a hundred yards in ten seconds flat, perhaps less if crowded. He proposed a match with our old Concho friend Tom Ortega, then living in Holbrook. Tom had a reputation as a sprinter, especially among the Mexicans, and had been known to win substantial sums in various matches. They found Tom and made a deal to run a hundred yards late that evening on a cinder path along the Santa Fe Railroad tracks in front of the depot.

Just who put up how much is lost to memory. One-armed saloon man Jose Nuanez seemed to be calling all bets backing Ortega. Pearce mortgaged his brother's freight outfit—possibly with Silver Kid thrown in—to a Holbrook merchant for a sum thought to be around five hundred dollars cash, which he bet on himself. Harry Scorse's offer to bet one hundred dollars "on the gringo," I believe, was also covered by Nuanez and Ortega. Tom was a prosperous sheepman and no doubt went fifty-fifty with Nuanez. (The latter's son, Louis, was one of our guitar accompanists and played with us for the dance that evening—not in Antolino's class but a pretty fair ear musician.) Miscellaneous small bets probably ran the total wager up to a tidy seven hundred dollars.

Stripped down for a race, Jesse Pearce had all the points of an outstanding athlete. Also, he knew how to train and kept himself in top physical condition between matches. He was normally calm going into a race, but the terrific pressure in this instance showed plainly in his maneuvers at the starting line. He must have been called back a dozen times for jumping the gun. But he had to win this one. "Not an inch of advantage must be lost," he thought. We had to reassure him, off to one side, before he would give Ortega an even break. Once they started, however, it was about as one-sided as the horse race at Rio la Plata. If you ever saw a human "claw gravel," it must have been Jesse. This was no time to take chances on his usual policy of just winning by a hair in order not to divulge his best time for the hundred. But Tom was a pretty fair runner and did his best even though beaten by upwards of fifteen feet. The day was saved for Pearce and Walker. Reliving its events ran high at the Pioneer Saloon and on into the dance that followed.

Jesse Pearce, about sixth in a large family of boys and several girls, was the son of James Pearce, an early pioneer, who had moved from Shumway to Snowflake in the mid-1890s. Both Jesse and I were about ten years old at the time, he being slightly the younger. At that early age he demonstrated superior speed at games of run-sheep-run, hide-and-seek, and so forth. One evening in particular I was surprised at not being able to catch him in a race for the goal, an incident often recalled in connection with his later career as a professional sprinter.

The fact was that Jesse was proud of his ability to outrun all comers in his age class. Doing it so often, as he grew up, had a lot to do with his development, by age twenty, into one of the top sprinters of his time. He excelled in track through grade and high schools but his reputation was not firmly established until about 1906 when he trained under a high-school coach by the name of Pointer for a matched race at Farmington, New Mexico, against a member of the sporty Hatch family.

Joe Lee, who for many years ran the Gap Trading Post north of

Cameron, Arizona, was a runner himself and had been beaten by both Pearce and Hatch. Since Pearce "took him" by a wider margin than Hatch had done, Joe told Hatch that he knew a young sprout from Snowflake he would back against him in three weeks time for double the amount he had lost on himself—probably two to three hundred dollars. When Hatch called the bet, Joe immediately placed Pearce in the hands of athletic coach Pointer for some serious training, Jesse's first on a scientific basis. Pointer taught him the fine points of starting from an all-fours position, smoothed up his nine-foot stride, and allowed him to run the full distance only once in three or four days rather than every day as had been his custom. He directed more time be spent on calisthenics, rubdowns, and such, and set up regular hours and a proper diet. It was exactly what Jesse needed to realize his full potential. By race time Pointer was proud of his product. Cooperative throughout, Jesse had advanced from raw material to a scientific running machine. Hatch was no match for him. Joe Lee got double his money back and shared his winnings with Jesse for expenses.

Ez Walker and the Silver Kid passed out of the picture in time, but Pearce remained "open for engagements" for a number of years as a professional sprinter. Matched races were more infrequent. However, a few came along at moderate wagers, which helped that much with ranch expenses. Jesse Pearce was never beaten where worthwhile money was at stake.

Baseball: The Brilliant Boner

Baseball in Navajo and Apache counties from early frontier days would make an interesting book by itself. Unfortunately, it's too late for comprehensive coverage prior to 1900 for lack of participants to interview, and from that time on there is probably no one available to write it up. For purposes of these memoirs, only a few highlights associated with my own experiences are included— experiences that produced an avid television viewer of major-league

Kartchner's parents, Orin Kartchner and Annella Hunt.
Wedding picture in 1883. Photograph by J. Fennemore & Co.

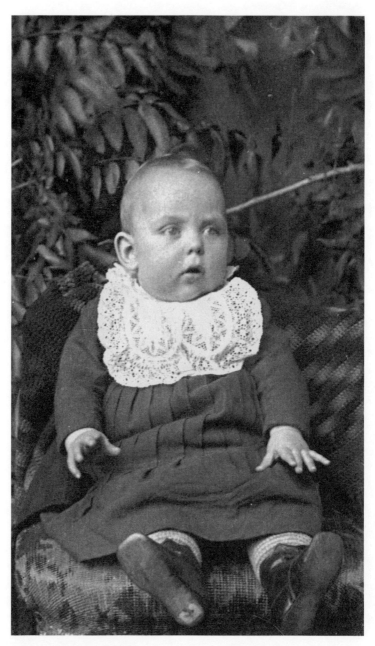

Kenner Casteel Kartchner at age three months

Kartchner, first row, second from the right, *with first-grade class, Snowflake School, 1892*

Kartchner, center, *shearing sheep about 1911*

Kartchner, right, *with sheepshearing friends Pete Greenhalgh and* *Bill Jenkins,* seated, *about 1912, in Montana*

Kartchner, left, *Al Frost, and Elmer Richards, fall 1907, in Globe, Arizona*

Kenner C. Kartchner and Adlee Lindsey Kartchner, March 1908

Kartchner, 1909, working in Joe West's store in Salt Lake City, Utah

Kartchner with wife Adlee, right, *and children,* left to right, *Stanley, Merle, Kenner, Jr., and Afton, on a field trip to Canyon Lobo near Mt. Thomas, northeast of Grants, N.M., in June 1922*

Kartchner, standing far right, *on a deer count on North Kaibab,
March 19–30, 1942*

Kartchner, right, *with F. Lee Kerby, forest supervisor, and O. C.
Williams, Arizona state land commissioner, on range inspection trip
through central Arizona, near Pine, October 1942*

Kartchner, second from the left, *at a Federal Fish and Wildlife Meeting, about 1954*

Kartchner, with Ralph Schmidt, Albuquerque, 1955, when he was assistant regional director, Fish and Wildlife, Department of Interior, over eight western states

*Claude Youngblood, Kartchner's fiddling companion, Nellie Merrill,
and Kartchner rehearsing at Nell's home, January 1959*

*Ike Isaacson, "Little Ike," and Kartchner at Kartchner's home in
Phoenix, January 1959*

Kartchner with sisters Thalia on guitar and Leone at the piano. Top, at the golden wedding anniversary of their cousin, Marion L. Flake, October 1963. Left, in Snowflake, June 1962. Note Kartchner's fiddling style.

ball as played today, who wishes he could turn back the pages of time or at least have made the big leagues. Of course, there are a few million elderly Americans in the same boat.

Coincident with my first recorded memories in the early nineties, there was much enthusiasm for the "Great American Game," as we have today. Dad was a pitcher for the Snowflake team. Despite meager equipment and slow transportation, there were occasional intercity and county contests that stirred up interest to no end. We country kids grew up playing town ball and cricket, later to take our places as grown-ups on contemporary baseball teams of the different towns. In baseball's Hall of Fame at Cooperstown, New York, are statues of big-league greats who were probably no better players than some of those country boys of Navajo and Apache counties might have become given the same opportunities. Schoolteacher –attorney and sportsman Marion V. Gibbons of St. Johns was one such individual.

In midsummer 1904, the Snowflake Wild Cats were practicing for a game at St. Johns. Their regular first baseman failed to show up. Captain Len Jensen said to me, "Kid, take that glove (lying nearby) and get on first base." Our pitcher was half-Indian Tom Adair, who threw a ball like a bullet. With a runner on first he would often attempt a pick-off and some of his sizzling pegs were low into the dirt. Luckily, I was able to come up with them including a few hot grounders and pegs from the infield without an error. At the finish, Jenson came to me and said, "How would you like to go with us to St. Johns?" Surprised, I asked, "What about your regular first baseman?" and mentioned the fact that my hitting was poor. He told me not to mind about either. He would take care of the personnel angle, and my glovework overshadowed any weakness at bat. Time was too short to recover from extreme soreness of arm and muscles under heavy training so the only out was to go easy on throwing and running but concentrate on catching and batting.

At seventeen past I was elated to get on the main team as its youngest member. St. Johns, however, could go us one better. Their nimble second baseman was none other than Marion V. Gibbons, a few months younger still. In 1904 their ballpark was on flat unfenced ground across the Little Colorado east of town. We took a brief workout, and everything looked well for the afternoon game. Rivalry ran high as might be expected, yet many lifelong friendships were formed through this wholesome competition. We were raised alike and had many things in common.

A large crowd of St. Johns rooters was on hand at game time and they gave us the works. It was my first good lesson in "holding your head" under terrific ribbing by the fans. All went well in the early innings with scores about even. At about midway a most unusual thing occurred, probably with few parallels in baseball history.

Marion Gibbons, first man up for St. Johns in that inning, got a single. Next batter got on and Marion took second with nobody out. Time was called over some difficulty during which Gibbons and our second baseman, Chase Rogers, engaged in conversation probably not along baseball lines. The plate umpire yelled, "Play ball!" whereupon the third man up hit a hot liner straight at Gibbons. Being right at home on the second-base spot, he caught the ball instinctively bare-handed and whipped a perfect peg to me at first before realizing his action had retired his side. The umpire could only call him out for being "hit" by a batted ball, the batter out on a caught liner, and the runner on first caught off-base after the catch. Some claimed the catch was illegal, being executed by a member of their own team. Even so, Gibbons was out either way; the ball remained in play and was in my possession on first ahead of the batter for two outs, leaving only a trapped runner between first and second almost certain to be run down.

The first decision stood. To say that general confusion ensued would be putting it mildly. Players closed in on Gibbons as if to scalp him on the spot. Spectators flocked over the playing field shouting indignation. The poor kid had made the most beautifully executed play of the game only to bring remorse to himself and the wrath of his townsmen down upon him.

Our group gathered to one side chuckling over our good fortune and the double-compound error that brought it about. Fully half an hour elapsed before play could be resumed. The final score is unimportant except that such a blow is enough to throw any team off stride just as it had that day at St. Johns.

Probably no other incident in local baseball history has been so frequently discussed and rehashed over the years. In 1960, some fifty-six years later, it was my pleasure to meet Marion Gibbons again in downtown St. Johns. Our reminiscences could not end without bringing up and having a good time over his famous bonehead of 1904. Up to that time only rumor offered any hint that perhaps his reflexes were a mite below par and for a specific reason. But Marion spelled it out in person. En route to the ballpark he met some friends, near Jake Armijo's saloon, who insisted he have a couple of drinks with them. For lack of mature judgment in such matters he could see no harm in that. It might even sharpen him up for the game. Out on the diamond his head sort of buzzed with exhilaration, but he thought nothing of it. In fact, he played errorless ball up to the instant that line drive stared him in the face. Reflex impairment was just enough to cover the split second it took to make the play, during which the physical took over by instinct. In many a ballgame thereafter, with Gibbons and against him, his play was consistently above average. Telling about his "brilliant boner" in later years "M.V." enjoyed the laugh on himself as much as anyone. He said, "My brother Andy would have killed me—if he could have caught me!"

We played against Holbrook quite often in those days and when Gibbons was available for the keystone sack it took a good bush-league outfit to cope with us. I recall one such game wherein their manager, Charlie Osborne, gave his base runners orders to steal second at every opportunity, a costly mistake, he decided, after seven would-be stealers had been tagged out by Gibbons. Our catcher, my brother Lafe, took pride in pegging to second within a foot of a certain spot, it being understood Gibbons would be there when the ball arrived. Our double-play combination was working well at that time also. Hugh Willis was one of our better shortstops, despite being the smallest player on the team. With a runner on first, any fieldable grounder to right or left bid fair to start a double play—Willis to Gibbons (or Gibbons to Willis) to Kartchner. The fact that "M.V." and I were still playing the same positions twelve to fifteen years after that game in 1904 when we first met on opposite sides is of some significance to us if not our various managers.

The last team I played on was the best. Several of our top players had returned from World War I in the spring of 1919, a short time before my transfer out of the area by the Forest Service. Another contest was in the making between the Snowflake and St. Johns stakes as part of a two-stake athletic meet sponsored by the Mutual Improvement Association (MIA). Special attention was given to baseball by our stake-wide committee, of which the late James J. Shumway of Taylor was chairman. Systematically, the committee set out to screen an all-star team from the various towns in the stake, roughly coinciding with Navajo County, by means of tryouts advertised in advance. When selections were complete, those from out of town came to Snowflake for a series of workouts, some at considerable sacrifice. Enthusiasm ran high and each man felt honored at having been chosen to play his favorite spot, including yours truly at first base. Here is the list of All-Stars chosen by the committee:

Catchers: Lafe Kartchner and Charlie Ballard
Pitchers: Big Southpaw fireballer George Smith and Curve-ball
    artist Gene Gardner
Infielders: Lester Shumway, third base, Hugh Willis at Short,
    Marion Gibbons, second base, Kenner Kartchner (myself) at
    first
Outfielders: Dow Shumway in left, Taylor Hunt, center, and Ham
    Fish in right

Old Pioneer family names will be recognized throughout the roster, and what a team it was. Of course, we speak here in terms of bush-leaguers, but had it been possible for this group to stay together and do nothing but play baseball as professionals do, there's no telling how far up the scale it might have gone.

After all the preparation and training on our part, the game itself was a miserable disappointment. St. Johns had concentrated on other features of the overall contest at the expense of baseball. Ironically, their main pitcher was none other than Ernest Shumway, brother of the two on our team, who taught school in St. Johns at the time. He could have been tough, with time to get in shape, but his lack of toughness was soon apparent. After about five innings of play, with a score of seventeen to one, Levi S. Udall, later to become chief justice of the state supreme court, announced they were conceding the game, that it appeared futile to "continue the farce." Their team could do nothing right, ours could do nothing wrong. All of our men got hits, from singles to home runs, and played errorless defense, another illustration of what training means to athletes.

Lest there be erroneous inferences, the two games described here are fifteen years apart and by no means represent the relative baseball standings between the two stakes overall. If the truth were known, they would likely be about even in the games' won-and-lost columns, notwithstanding Bill Freeman's wisecrack that the only way St. Johns could cope with us would be for their boys to marry our girls and get the stock started over there.

Fiddling and Our First Playback

Just prior to the November general elections of 1904, a group of Democratic candidates for office clubbed together for a tour of Navajo County precincts. As an added appeal to voters they hired the Youngblood-Kartchner orchestra to accompany them and play for the dance that followed each rally. Advance agents made hotel and livery reservations for the cavalcade traveling south of the railroad by horse-drawn buggies. A more congenial group would be hard to find. Campaign speeches were usually concluded by 10 P.M. in each little town, leaving a couple of hours for tripping the light fantastic, which goodly crowds seemed to enjoy. Candidates kissed babies and met the voters as they could get around to them.

Whatever credit might be given the dances in voter appeal, a great majority of office seekers in the party was elected. We musicians were treated on the same level as politicians and had a wonderful time throughout the trip, especially since we had no wor-

ries about the uncertainties of an election. When it was over we had
played for thirteen dances in fourteen nights. To make that possible
we filled an interim Sunday night engagement at Concho in Apache
County, rejoining our party the following evening. Twenty to fifty
miles a day for our jointly owned team and light hack were ordinary
routine in which we got no little satisfaction. Moreover, a fact not
fully realized at the time was the broadening influence of wide
circulation and acquaintances through the occupation of dance
musician.

Youngblood and I had promised to play for an all-night dance—old
year out and New Year in—at Holbrook, December 31, 1905. Word
was out to all the towns and ranches and a large attendance was assured. Knowing there would be great disappointment if we failed
them, we struck out from Snowflake facing a blinding snowstorm
that lasted through the twenty-eight-mile journey. Our saddle-
horse buggy team was grain fat and raring to go, but evinced dis-
pleasure similar to our own at facing the storm head on. Changing
off drivers, we kept them in a fast trot wherever the road was visible or they could stay in it by feel. The top was up on our light hack,
and we wrapped ourselves in a heavy blanket, except for the
driver's arms, hands, and face, which, in a short time, got so numb
the other would take over. Despite our heavy overcoats, overshoes,
gloves, and "long handles" [long johns], each conjectured to himself
on whether we could make it through.

At the well-known Wash Board, a rough-bottomed cross drainage
eleven miles out of Holbrook, we met Bill Lewis of Taylor driving
the mail stage. With their backs to the storm, he and his horses
fared much better than we who were going directly into it. He
looked us over skeptically, but grinned broadly at the shivered
query as to whether he might have aboard something stronger to
drink than ice water. He broke the seal on a full quart of Keystone
Monogram and said if we had the nerve to face that blizzard we
were entitled to any part or all of it. In our condition it actually
tasted good and went down as smoothly as spring water. Returning
the half-empty bottle, we hailed the date of his birth and told Bill he
had just saved the lives of two good men.

Scientific experiments in the far north have long since proven that men stand extreme cold much better with no liquor in their diets, but here was a temporary situation that defied tests. The snow fell increasingly, but the north wind that whipped in our faces for the hour it took to cover the remaining eleven miles seemed to lose its bite. Some expectant dancers spotted us as we trotted east on old Main Street and gave a war whoop to hail our arrival. At Smith & Smith Livery Stable, we ordered rubdowns and blankets for the horses in addition to plenty of hay and oat grain. It was our habit to take care of them first before looking to our own comfort. In turn they were always ready for service at our command. They did a magnificent job facing that storm in a fast, three-hour trot with no sign of tiring, although they resembled a couple of oversized drowned rats at the finish.

Not until we had cached our violins behind the bar and snuggled close to the potbellied heating stove in Joe Wood's Pioneer Saloon did either of us feel the slightest intoxication from the heavy jolts of Bill Lewis's whiskey. But in thawing out it was necessary to shed our overcoats and back away from the heat to avoid a threatened loss of equilibrium, and to refuse for a time repeated invitations for a nip at the bar.

We ordered thick beefsteaks, for which Sam Chinaman was famous, and were soon little the worse for wear. Youngblood asked me what my reaction would have been to a suggestion that we turn back prior to meeting the mail stage, at which we agreed either would have consented, but neither was willing to make the suggestion.

The dance was well attended despite the storm, many out-of-towners having come in ahead of it for holiday festivities. The people in charge doubled our pay in appreciation of our battling such odds to get there. They had really given us up until we came splashing down the street to end the bitterest three-hour drive in all our experience. Facing such a storm nowadays, comfortably, in a modern, glassed-in and heated automobile, I never fail to think back on the horse-and-buggy days and, more particularly, the battle of the blizzard on December 31, 1905.

Navajo, little more than a trading post on the railroad some fifty miles northeast of Holbrook, was the scene of many a cowboy dance in our general circuit. People came by train from east and west along the line and from ranches in all directions. In the fall of 1907 (sometime between a hitch with the Long-H outfit and a trip to Globe with a bunch of horses), Charlie and Sam Day, Indian trader brothers, gave such an all-night dance in the schoolhouse there, and we were on hand with the music.

Having time on our hands before the dance, Charlie took us to his living quarters and played some cylinder records on a brand new Edison phonograph. He also showed us a recording attachment that came with it and asked that we tune up and make some records. We complied, hardly able to imagine such a thing. Our first piece was the song made famous by Ada Jones's records across the country, "Alexander Tell Me Don't You Love Yo Baby No Mo'," a popular two-step, whose lead and tenor parts harmonized well throughout. A sheep inspector for the state territory sanitary board, whose name I have forgotten, quite ably announced the title when signaled by Day, adding, "as played on the violins by Claude Youngblood and Kenner Kartchner, ex-Long-H cowboys." The late Ed Gardner of Snowflake accompanied on the guitar.

When we finished, Charlie Day changed over and played the record back to us. It actually sounded better *to us* than the real thing, to say nothing of the awesome feeling that crept over us upon experiencing the seemingly supernatural reproduction of our own product. We wanted to take it home with us, to which Charlie replied he would not part with it for fifty dollars, but there were other blank cylinders and we were at liberty to make another for ourselves. We recorded that tune again and two or three additional numbers, with Charlie taking one set of cylinders and we the other. For lack of precedent, those records were quite a novelty. Patrons of the dance crowded around the phonograph to hear them over and over until dance time. During the dance, frequent requests came for the same numbers firsthand.

To fully appreciate the significance of the event it must be real-

ized that those were days before the radio or jukebox, let alone television, and even the phonograph was a primitive novelty to be
counted on one hand in all of Navajo County. The natural craving
for music and singing to be found in all people could be satisfied only
through "live" rendition. Thus, less is the wonder they made arduous journeys to listen, if not dance, to music they seldom heard.
But a new era was dawning—"canned music"—to be followed by
radio and the rest. Today, the remotest rancher sees and hears musical artists of world renown in his own living room or, perhaps
more to his liking, hoedown fiddlers with their harmony and pat-
your-foot rhythm of the cow country.

No. 7, Santa Fe's westbound reliable train for many years, was on
time at daylight for our return trip. Many were the dances that ran
all night in Navajo, with a big feed at midnight, and which closed
just in time for residents or people living out of Adamana, Holbrook, Joseph City, or Winslow to catch No. 7. On this occasion, after arriving by train in Holbrook and before hitching up our team at
Smith & Smith Livery Stable for the buckboard trek to Snowflake,
we played the prized records in Judd Lathrop's Bucket of Blood
Saloon. His was the only other Edison phonograph in town besides
the first one brought in by Frank Wattron for his nearby drugstore.

In playing the first record, Youngblood left off the sheep inspector's announcement of who was playing, just to see what the
reaction might be among a group of local friends. Sure enough, at
the finish, H. B. Smith, partner in the livery stable, remarked in
rough, facetious sarcasm that had we learned to play like that we
might have amounted to something. Without a word, Claude
replayed the record in full, whereupon H.B., his face red, told us
not only how many kinds of so-and-sos we were but that we could go
squarely to that place reserved for fiddlers and horse thieves, and
we knew where! It cost him a round of drinks and frequent ribbings,
but H.B. enjoyed a prank even at his own expense.

Now that we are "old and gray," fifty-four years later, in fact,
with Youngblood eighty-two and me at seventy-five, we would give
the world to dig up and play those old records. We were too

thoughtless then to realize their historical and antique value a half century hence. For lack of an Edison machine of our own, the records were left in Frank Wattron's drugstore among numerous others. No doubt they were eventually lost or destroyed, as perhaps was the set kept by Charlie Day.

CHAPTER FIVE

Work Away from the Farm

We now go back to the fall of 1904. On October 19 I became engaged to Electa Adlee Lindsey, and it was necessary to grub for a wedding stake. B. B. Crosby of Eagar, Arizona, was a sizable contractor, making railroad grade for the Santa Fe. Claude Youngblood was timekeeper on the project just west of the Colorado River opposite Topock. He wrote me by request of grade foreman Frank Campbell of Snowflake that a teamster job would be held open until I could get there, if I was interested. Crosby had found that local farmboys were better skinners by far than the average "itinerant of the open road" and showed his preference accordingly.

I could use the steady job and so proceeded forthwith by passenger train to Needles, California, thence back to Crosby's camp by local freight. Space was allocated for my bedroll, suitcase, and violin in one of the freight cars that stood on a siding for the contractor's use. I was pleased to find among the crew so many acquaintances from Apache and Navajo counties. After supper, Youngblood and I entertained in the mess car with a few fiddle tunes, not too satisfactory for lack of good accompaniment.

Next morning we were on the job bright and early. My outfit consisted of four horses driven abreast on a Fresno scraper, better known as a four-up, and we worked in a circle with a dozen such units. It was an improvement over Jake Kaufman's two-mile slip-scraper operation at Williams the year before, but still by present standards a primitive way to move dirt. Also there were loaders and dumpers so that all a skinner had to do was drive his team. Mine was among the better ones, but I got satisfaction out of correcting such defects as uneven pulling and handling between the four animals.

About the third evening, Frank Campbell told me I was to change over to a job as a finisher. That meant we were up to grade level as staked by the engineers and my four-up would be used for the finishing touches, leveling and widening as need be, while the circle moved to the next grade segment. My off (right) animal was a fiery gray mare of a fractious disposition. Called Belle, she was well trained and good to pull, but she required careful handling. Her instant observance of commands to start, stop, and steady down became the cue for the other three to act in almost perfect unison, no doubt a factor in the selection for grade finishing. One other finisher was Shorty Carlton, an Iowa farmboy. The two of us were thus occupied from then on, except for intervals when our work caught up with the circle.

One evening at quitting time, the high-spirited Belle mare was credited with saving the lives of herself and mates, not to mention a thoughtless skinner. In regular routine I unhitched from the Fresno, leaving harnesses intact. It being some distance to camp, I mounted the near horse to save walking. No trains were in sight, so I took a shortcut that put us on the main line. There was good vision ahead, but behind us the tracks disappeared around a point at no more than 150 yards distant. All at once and without warning a westbound passenger train rounded the bend at high speed with the engine's throttle wide open. If ever fast action was called for to avert disaster in the life of a teamster it was at that moment. Perhaps as much by instinct as deliberate thinking I yelled at Belle, cracked the end of a leather line over her rump, and yanked back on the left line attached to all four bridle bits. Never before had I barked at Her Majesty in such voice—out of deference to her nervous temperament—or applied the whip. Sensing terror in both, she lunged forward with the force of a racehorse out of a starting gate, to effect a complete left turn, she on the outside, the horse I was on forming an inside pivot. When the train swooshed by with its deafening noise, we were barely out of its way, but that we were, thanks to a high-strung mare who never could know what a heroine she had been. Her excitement spread to the other horses, and it took some doing to avert a runaway toward the camp. The corral boss was curious about their being unusually nervous. Feigning nonchalance, I let the matter pass, muttering something about train fright. Deep within, however, I was vowing that never again would I take such a chance. A lazy off-side horse at that moment would have meant bits of harness, horsehair, flesh, and bones (if not human as well) strung along the track for half a mile—a horrible carnage to contemplate.

Topock Marsh

During two months in camp alongside the Colorado River, we saw millions of ducks and geese on their wintering grounds north of the railroad. A few shotgunners took their toll unrestricted but with little effect on overall numbers. At age eighteen, the area had no significance to me, but quite the reverse would be true thirty-five to fifty years later. This broad expanse of swampland, over a mile wide and several miles long, came to be known as Topock Marsh in wildlife management circles. It has always been, and I trust always will be, an important winter feeding ground for many millions of waterfowl that migrate annually north and south along the Colorado Basin sector of the Pacific Flyway.

Market hunting steadily increased across the continent. Sport hunters killed birds without limit, foreboding a time when duck hunting would pass from the American scene. No one state or country could stop the wanton slaughter that continued year-round from Canada and Alaska in summer, to Mexico in winter, and twice across the United States in between. The situation became so serious that a treaty was negotiated with Canada for joint administration of migratory species, according to seasonal location. Congress confirmed the same by enactment of the Migratory Bird Treaty Act in 1916 and placed jurisdiction in the federal government, in cooperation with the forty-eight states. A similar treaty with Mexico was delayed until 1936, but in the meantime, U.S. and Canadian regulations had done wonders in saving ducks and geese, at least, from extinction.

Completion of Hoover Dam in 1936 and the apportionment of Colorado River water between the several states and Mexico created a conflict of interest between two government bureaus. Whereas the Fish and Wildlife Service, with backing from state game departments, was committed to a policy of providing maximum habitat for waterfowl, the Bureau of Reclamation was bent upon draining swamp areas, including Topock Marsh, and clearing out other obstructions to save every drop of river flow for "higher" uses. By 1940 a huge, specially designed dredge with which to channel the river and thus drain the marsh as dry as possible was in the planning stage.

Harking back to November–December 1904 and the memory formed of Topock Marsh as it existed then, it would have been unthinkable that some day I would participate in a struggle to save it from destruction. However, it came to pass, for while director of the Arizona Game and Fish Department from 1939 to 1943 I worked closely with California and Nevada against the proposed drainage, thus backing the stand taken by the Fish and Wildlife Service. A significant feature of the long, drawn-out controversy was a false claim by the BR that Topock Marsh had been created through its own flood-control program, made possible by completion of Hoover Dam in 1936, the premise being that it should have the right to remove a river impediment of its own making. It was here that my memory of actual conditions there in December 1904 came into focus. Representing the Fish and Wildlife Service at a number of conferences and hearings, I could assert from personal knowledge that, while Hoover Dam did stop the floods and yearly channel changes, it merely stabilized a valuable duck marsh existent through the ages—certainly not just since 1936. And thus, some importance was attached to my driving a four-up Fresno scraper on the banks of Topock Marsh so long ago, far beyond the meager wage of three dollars per day and board. In February 1947, it was my pleasure to traverse the marsh by motorboat, as assistant director of Region 2, Fish and Wildlife Service, in company with refuge supervisor George Barclay and Havasu refuge manager, Gale Monson. Our old railroad campsite of 1904 was pointed out, with attendant discussion of marsh conditions forty-two years before.

We Meet Commodore Owens

On completion of the grading at Topock, we loaded everything on the work train and headed east in early January 1905. Not being able to finish by Christmas as planned, most of the crew stayed on the job except for the extra day off. Youngblood and I found a guitarist and played in a saloon at Needles on the nights of December 24 and 25. It was my first Christmas at the low altitude of seven hundred feet and how delightful the climate by contrast with Williams in 1903, and all others at not less than a mile high.

On the Santa Fe's single-track main line, our work train endured the lowest priority schedule, hardly missing a stop at every side track for a passenger, regular, or local freight train. Resultant delays made it necessary to unload the livestock at Seligman, Arizona, for feed and water, although our covered distance was less than two hundred miles. Each teamster looked after his own four horses in the large stockyard corral where a mass consumption of water, grain, and a half ton of hay by some fifty head of good-sized workhorses took place.

Having several hours of leisure time on our hands, we were asked by Foreman Frank Campbell how many would like to meet Commodore Owens. The very name excited our curiosity, especially those of us who were raised in Navajo or Apache counties. Accordingly, eight or ten of us followed Frank north two blocks from the railroad to a frame, one-story building, where the famous ex-sheriff had settled down to a small mercantile and saloon business in 1900.

My first impression of Commodore Perry Owens stands out to

this day. As we entered the building, Campbell in the lead, Owens was standing behind a waist-high counter, or bar, looking us over intently. His quick glances from one to the other and the suspicious expression on his face were those of a man who had lived by his guns. At age fifty-one, he was much heavier than previously described. His traditional brown hair that had hung loose to the waist, was now cropped off at shoulder length, and seemed darker, almost black, though there was little trace of gray as yet. We (the youngsters at least) looked at the man in awe—possibly adding to his suspicion—having in mind his colorful background as the gunfighting sheriff of Apache County from 1887 to 1890. (Navajo County was combined with Apache County until 1895.) In a fight scarcely equalled in gun-battle history anywhere in the Old Southwest, history records an incident at Holbrook in which Sheriff Owens killed three gunmen by himself and wounded the fourth while trying to serve an arrest warrant. The lone survivor was Johnny Blevins. He was a fiddler of some note, and we became friends several years later. Earle R. Forrest in *Arizona's Dark and Bloody Ground* relates that Johnny was repairing his violin at [Sam] Brown and Kinder's Livery Stable on that fateful day when Sheriff Commodore Perry Owens rode in to put up his horse. Johnny immediately ran home to warn his older brother, Andy "Cooper," wanted by the law, that the sheriff was in town.

When Owens went to the [Cooper] home and tried to serve a warrant for the arrest of Andy Cooper (Blevins), the fight was on. As the smoke cleared away, Owens had all but wiped out the remaining male members of the Blevins family, single-handed. He fatally wounded Andy when he resisted arrest. A lightning-fast second shot from his famous Winchester—he aimed from the hip— shattered Johnny's right arm, Commodore having been barely missed himself by a shot from each of the brothers' guns. Reportedly, Johnny's shot killed Andy's horse, which was tied out front for a quick getaway. Mose Roberts, a brother-in-law, was next and received a mortal wound as he emerged from a window, gun in hand.

At this point the teenaged brother, Sam Houston Blevins, was the only "man" left, who was able to fight. Some said he was sixteen, others fourteen. Either way, he is said to have won a scuffle with his mother for Cooper's gun and tried to draw a bead on the intrepid sheriff. The latter, aiming carefully to miss the mother, waited to make sure of the boy's intent before dropping him in the front door with a bullet through his heart.

"I shot him," became historic words as used by Owens before a coroner's jury and in his official report to the Apache County Superior Court. Each encounter was described in brief detail, ending with the three short words, "I shot him." His report is still on file at the Apache County Courthouse, brought out now and then for inspection by officials, writers, and the curious. Long will it remain a symbol of a bloody era, which has seemed unavoidable in bringing civilization to our raw frontier. This incident was a major step in ridding the county of organized horse thieves and similar outlaws.

Of course, Frank Campbell was quick to introduce himself and state our reasons for dropping in, at which Commodore was affable enough and talked freely. He remembered Frank and one or two Crosbys and Maxwells from the Springerville-Eagar area, who were grown men when he was in office. Not so with the youngsters but he did recognize family names as we were introduced.

One item of the conversation especially comes to mind. Campbell asked Owens how he would feel about living over again those perilous times that carved him out as one of the most famous lawmen of his time. The answer was significant and unequivocal, that he would have no part of it. He said the record would show that he had never killed a man without good cause, but even so, each case had left unpleasant memories, to say nothing of the nerve-strain involved from round-the-clock vigilance lest he be ambushed or otherwise taken by surprise. There are always friends or relatives of a departed outlaw, he said, who are looking for the slightest opportunity to avenge his "murder," regardless of circumstances. Such were the considerations that impelled him to refuse re-election after serving three years as sheriff.

He expressed satisfaction with his present surroundings and spoke highly of his wife, the former Elizabeth Barrett of Seligman, to whom he was married April 30, 1902, his first and only marital venture. He wanted nothing more than to live in peace the rest of his days, a wish, incidentally, that came true. On May 10, 1919, he died at Seligman of natural causes in his sixty-seventh year. Just why he was buried at Flagstaff is not clear.

An excellent photograph of Commodore is found in *Arizona's Dark and Bloody Ground*. It was taken at Albuquerque in the early 1880s. Here are portrayed the marvelous physique, the long-flowing hair, heavy leather chaps, cartridge belts and guns. Any hint of vanity or sham at being pictured in such gunman attire is dispelled by the many deeds of valor, the unhesitating performance of duty under fire, backed by superb marksmanship and the nerve of cold steel. Having heard stories about him from childhood, it is little wonder that as we walked back to the work train, we rated this a memorable occasion, a day to be remembered.

Reloading the horses and chugging on east to Gallup, New Mexico, were matters of routine and without incident, but snow covered the ground, and men and horses suffered with the cold at this sixty-five-hundred-foot elevation. The Santa Fe was not ready for an operation of B. B. Crosby's capacity. Unhappy with the outlook, a number of us drew our pay and called it quits. The experience as a four-up Fresno skinner is not all bad to look back upon.

Shearing Sheep

Money was scarce and paying jobs few. We were inclined to grab at anything that came along to replenish the pocketbook. Shearing sheep was no exception, albeit the labor was as hard as any ever done by man, white or black. At one time or another between 1904 and 1908, before shearing machines came into general use, Dad and I were among crews that sheared for local sheepmen in a thirty-mile radius: Ignacio Bazan at Ortega Lake, southwest of St. Johns; Porter Brothers and Will Amos near Pinetop; William Morgan northwest of Lakeside; and several to the west of Snowflake at Chevalon Canyon and Lost Tank. These outfits depended on local shearers each year, most of whom were second-generation

Mormon settlers of Show Low and Silver Creek valleys. Dad was among the better shearers, having paid his taxes, or met other cash obligations, from this source over a period of years.

My "career" in shearing began with the spring of 1904 at temporary sheds set up at Five Mile Wash, northwest of Snowflake. We were in the third year of a severe drouth over the Southwest that featured high winds and blowing sand. Sheep were poor and dirty, spelling plague to experienced shearers and worse to beginners. We set up tents for sleeping quarters and purchased new shears, on account, at the commissary. Dad helped me fit out two pairs with buck straps and sole-leather bumpers, the former to prevent the hand from slipping forward, the latter to take up the jar of raw steel when the blades closed together. Old-fashioned hand-operated grindstones were provided to keep shears at the right thinness. Men worked them in pairs, alternating between grinding and turning the crank—an overtime job averaging an hour a day. Fine-grained oil stones finished off sharp, smooth edges. Honing of shears was necessary at least once for each sheep shorn and more often in dirty wool.

Little did I realize what an ordeal this was to be. The eight shearing pens, accommodating sixteen men, were full of sheep by seven o'clock starting time that first morning in April 1904, and the "plant" swung into action. Groans of agony and disgust could be heard from old shearers as they opened up necks and started down the left sides of their individual first sheep. They found a solid mat of sand and debris along sides and backs, not only difficult to cut through, but dulling to their tools in a matter of minutes. Two or three other neophytes and I held a psychological advantage in not knowing the shearing difference between clean and dirty wool.

It's a good thing our board was included in the five cents per head, for that first day netted me exactly seventy-five cents. Worse still were inside blisters on the right hand, and cuts and bruises from kicking sheep. Not a muscle in my anatomy escaped fatigue and soreness. The only consolation was the fact that others were in similar condition. By early bedtime, my right wrist had swollen twice its normal size and throbbed with pain. Intermittent sleep was made possible only by exhaustion. Getting-up time came all too soon. Every bone in my body ached. Every muscle, cut, and scratch hurt to the limit of endurance. Should I make the effort, ran my mind, or call the whole thing off?

Like soldiers in combat who perform heroic deeds lest they be open to ridicule by their buddies, I mustered the courage to get up and going. Moreover, once the decision was made, I thought I might as well bluff it through that I was little the worse for wear and in fact quite ready for the arduous task ahead. Strangely enough, playing the part served to convert pretense into reality. Such is the result of determination, supported by the almost limitless recuperative powers of youth. In two weeks time the whole crew had hardened down to a steady work basis. Most remarkable, however, was the speedy recovery from pain and fatigue made by the few of us youngsters who kept plugging away. Blisters hardened into callouses, abrasions healed quickly, and spent muscles bounced back twofold.

Aside from shearers, there were "wool stompers" (sackers), corral boys, cooks, and flunkies, mostly composed of local men. Sheep owner Clarence Morrow was corral boss—and a good one. Fast-moving, with tireless energy, he and his crew never failed to have fresh sheep ready as each pen of six or eight was shorn. Neither were there delays on account of rain. (Wool must be dry when sacked to avoid spoilage.)

Unabated, the southwest wind blew more sand into fleeces on the hoof. Veteran hands, used to scores of 125 or more sheep per ten-hour day when broken in, were shearing less by 30 percent and wearing out shears in half the normal time. Despite the dirty wool, however, beginners were learning fast. By the end of the job, which lasted about thirty days, we were shearing within ten sheep per day of the veteran average. No other shearing was available locally in 1904, and we went our several ways along other lines.

The spring of 1905 found the same crew—a few men more or less—again at the Five Mile location, under conditions exactly opposite to the dry, howling winds and dirty sheep of the previous season. Three years of drouth, the most devastating in the history of

Arizona's livestock industry, had come to an end with a vengeance, and early feed was everywhere in abundance. We sophomores made steady progress and soon were shearing a hundred or more sheep per day, along with the veterans. Even so, only by actual experience can one appreciate the physical shock that attends breaking in, the getting used to stooping over kicking sheep ten long hours a day, and developing a shearing hand that will stand the constant clipping.

Finishing the Five Mile hitch in mid-May, part of the crew moved to Santy Jaques' ranch northeast of Lakeside for a two weeks' run. The sheep were fat and clean, a pleasure to the lowly shearers, who by now were used to the daily grind. Santy was perhaps the youngest sheep owner in the district.

In 1906, having gained some experience, I branched out and went with Dad to the valley to shear where sheds had been set up on the desert east of Mesa. About half the crew of some twenty shearers were buddies from northern Arizona. The other half were "road-stiff" professionals—a breed apart, as I learned to know them—who did little else. They followed the season from early March in sunny Arizona to July and August in northern Montana. With few exceptions they were bachelors, ages twenty-five to fifty, hard workers and amiable, but with no particular aim in life other than to shear all the sheep possible on each run, wind it up with a binge in the nearest town, and walk away broke, in search of free transportation to the next job.

Sheep that wintered on the desert were fat and clean, except for the cholla cactus spines in wool that pricked our legs and had to be extracted. Antiseptic soap was used to keep down infection. Otherwise, this was the easiest cutting wool we had yet encountered, and the daily scores soon jumped to 125 or more. It was here I reached the veteran stage and Dad remarked that he must have taught me well. Of course, it takes more than muscle alone in any craft where tools are used. Keeping shears in top condition became a science by trial and error.

The desert run was over about the last of March when daily temperatures already topped ninety degrees. We proceeded by rail through Prescott and Ash Fork to Winslow, thence by wagon twenty miles southeast to a shearing plant on Chevalon Canyon. Nights were chilly and day temperatures some twenty degrees below those in the valley, punctuated by ever-present spring winds of the Little Colorado Basin. Wool cut harder for lack of heat to melt its gummy grease and daily scores fell off about 20 percent. Again the crew was divided between local shearers and road stiffs, the latter working their way north.

Finishing at Chevalon around the first of May, the crew scattered hither and yon. Cashing our paychecks at a bank in Winslow was something to remember, since only coins were used. Twenties, tens, and five-dollar gold pieces made up the tender, supplemented by silver to make exact change. Although folding money had come into general use, gold coins were available on demand up to 1934, when Congress passed the Gold Reserve Act under which they ceased to exist in international transactions. To some of us the handling of money since has never been quite the same. We local shearers proceeded to various small jobs between Holbrook and Pinetop, winding up the 1906 season about mid-June.

Having shorn through three consecutive spring periods, the Freshies of 1904 were accomplished seniors, equipped to hold their own in any company, and when February 1907 rolled around the feet started itching to get on our way. Dad was occupied on other business and passed up Valley shearing that year. E. P. Grover, erstwhile partner in the sheep firm of Grover and Nelson, set up a plant near the Arizona Canal on what is now North Central Avenue in the Sunnyslope sector of Phoenix. Six of us from Navajo County came down by rail to shear there, namely by pairs: Len Jenson and Lon Standifird; Charlie Shumway and Newt Knight (younger half-brother of Hyrum Knight of the Long H cattle outfit; Al Frost and myself. We were ten miles due north of Phoenix, which at that time had a population of only fifteen thousand. For some reason no sheep arrived for shearing during the two weeks we stayed there on free board, just biding our time. We pilfered delicious oranges, mostly picked off the ground, from extensive irrigated groves south of the canal. But then, citrus fruit was so cheap the owners paid little attention to such hand-to-mouth thievery, and how we mountain boys did enjoy them!

At last, word came that the plant would be moved to Queen Creek southeast of Mesa and that shearing would be postponed until after lambing. That, of course, meant we were out of a job with no free beanery to sustain life. They told us George Scott, George Wilbur, and John Nelson of Mesa each had need of two lambing hands and the six of us were hired for the purpose.

Jensen and Standifird wanted to work for George Scott, so when we arrived at Mesa, they hurried straight to his office and were hired. Knight and Shumway preferred George Wilbur, leaving John Nelson for Frost and me. As it turned out, however, ours was by far the best set-up of the three. John paid us two dollars per day and board on condition that we stay with him to the finish, which we did. His charming wife, Mollie—one of the Baca girls from Concho—worked closely with him in the sheep business, office and field. She drove a fleet span of horses on a light spring wagon, by which means we were transported ten miles to the lambing ground east of town. Her daily trips kept us in fresh vegetables, even beef steaks—as a change from mutton—pastries, and other items that made for high living in a sheep camp. No one willing to do his job well ever worked for nicer people than John and Mollie Baca Nelson.

As Frost and I were green hands in the lambing business, we did everything the hard way for a few days. But once we got the hang of it, backed by husky physiques, the daily routine went off like clock-work and brought praise from the boss. Besides Nelson and the two of us, there were five Mexican employees, including the caporal, Juan Torres of Holbrook, his handyman brother named Fermin, two herders, and the cook. Starting with two thousand, the number of ewes in the "dropping band" got smaller each day as lambs were born. Palo-verde brush corrals that each held about one hundred ewes and lambs were conveniently located around the main camp.

Most of the lambs were born at night, and their mothers remained with them on the bed-ground after the main herd moved out to feed at the peak of day. One man took charge of the sixty to one hundred head involved, seeing to it that the newly born got to their feet and took nourishment, twins and all. By late evening they were strong enough to move with their mothers to the nearest brush corral for the night as protection against predatory coyotes and bobcats. Each day the *tajo* (or cut—meaning a small bunch cut off from the main herd) moved on to the next corral in the chain, thus making room for those to follow and allowing mother ewes to graze as much as possible. Within five or six days the lambs were fat and frisky, ready for the tajo to merge with the new herd of ewes and lambs that was building up at the far end of the line.

Feed was everywhere luxuriant on the desert that spring, much to the delight of sheepmen wintering on public domain. Alfilaria grew like alfalfa, and its high moisture content, including the morning dew, made it unnecessary to water sheep at all. Nelson told us later that at marking time his lamb count was 2,200, or a lambing success of 110 percent, including twins and occasional triplets. Such biological mass reproduction was marvelous to me; likewise was the rapid development from first-breath to week-old creatures that ran and played like so many well-fed kittens. Mollie Nelson thought of everything, and her husband went along in reason with her numerous ideas. Twice during lambing she made the extra trip to camp after dark to take Frost and me to Mesa for a hot bath and change of clothes. Moreover, at the finish she hauled us to the Queen Creek shearing pens (on the railroad twenty-five miles southeast of Mesa), along with equipment they would need while their sheep were being shorn. They were an ideal couple as one learned to know them, happily working together to make a go of the sheep business. John's naturally stern expression belied a big heart and golden-rule disposition. Mollie's scintillating personality, quick wit, and fluent speech—Spanish or English—kept everyone around her in a jolly mood. Such pleasant surroundings impelled us to do our very best, and the lambing experience brought satisfaction in a job well done.

Al Frost and I had selected a shearing pen, set up whet rocks, and ground and fitted shears before the boys arrived from the other lambing camps. Len Jensen and Lon Standifird came in afoot, punching a burro packed with their bedrolls and effects, as ragged and dirty as they were disgusted with the whole deal. Spying Frost and me, Jensen yelled, "Now don't say a word," as much in earnest as in jest. Rumors had reached them of our rate of pay and of our being hauled around in the Nelson buggy, by comparison to their own miserable set-up with George Scott. And recalling they had literally run from the train to Scott's office in Mesa to avoid competition added significance of his demand that we not remind them.

Their story unfolded gradually. The same burro was given them for the twenty-mile hike from Mesa east to Scott's lambing ground. They received $1.25 per day and mediocre board like the other common hands, and they hadn't been to town or had a decent bath in three weeks. They despised the Mexican *patrón* [boss, foreman], and to add insult to injury, they found themselves saturated with body lice brought in by the herders. It was hard for us not to pour it on with joking reminders, perhaps the most pointed of which was the suggestion that a little consideration of others might have been in order, such as drawing straws to see who worked for whom, since the sheepmen had stated no preference.

How Shumway and Knight got to Queen Creek is forgotten, but they, too, were given a burro and hiked from Mesa ten miles to George Wilbur's camp, not far from Nelson's. After all, this was standard custom for ordinary sheepherders and had nothing to do with personal inconsideration. Frost and I were just lucky in having no preference, and yet stumbling into top pay and "cushions" for transportation. Wilbur paid $1.50 per day and treated the boys well, but none of us could understand the three different pay scales— $1.25, $1.50, and $2.00—between outfits so closely associated, but for one thing, they were not organized then as all industrial groups are today.

On completion at Queen Creek, our sextet pulled stakes and headed by rail for Winslow for a two-week run at Jack's Canyon, about twenty miles to the southwest. Joining us there were Dad and Claude Youngblood. Two highlights of that project were the fine step dancing of sheep owner Nate Bly's younger brother Fletch, and the fluffy sourdough biscuits of our Mexican cook, Dutch-oven style. The Blys were good sheepmen and well liked. After cashing our checks at Winslow, we locals went by train to Holbrook. At Joe

Wood's Pioneer Saloon we met Hyrum (Noche) Knight, foreman of the Long H cattle outfit, looking for cowboys to fill out his crew for the spring works. Whatever came over us, other than pure adventure, Youngblood, Frost, and I agreed to report for "duty" following certain arrangements to be made at Snowflake.

In the spring of 1908, I passed up shearing on the desert, but joined the crew again at Jack's Canyon and then went from there to local runs in the Show Low–Lakeside area, winding up sometime in June. I was married in the meantime [March 25, 1908] and in October of that year we made a trip to Salt Lake City to go to the Salt Lake Temple. An uncle by marriage, Joseph A. West, persuaded me to stay in Salt Lake and work in his gent's furnishing store and mail-order house, a valuable experience in salesmanship, bookkeeping, buying (for the shoe department), banking, and meeting the general public in the largest city we had ever been in—population at that time, ninety thousand.

But the salary was too low for decent living, and by the spring of 1909 I was on the lookout for a new position, or other means of increasing our income. It so happened that one of our store customers, Pete Greenhalgh of that city, was a sheepshearer. He brought up the subject [of sheepshearing] one day, and to the surprise of us both, our experiences had been much the same. He suggested I write Billy DeWolfe at Milford, Utah, if interested in a thirty-day run coming up there soon. Pete and his traveling partner, Bill Jenkins of Oakley, Idaho, were booked there as a starting point on their annual migration north with the shearing season. Upon receipt of a favorable reply from DeWolfe, I applied for a thirty-day leave of absence from the store. Joe West was sympathetically amused when I told him that the eight to ten dollars per day to be made shearing was necessary in order to "finance" the store job, and he granted the leave.

Shearing that spring term in Milford marked the beginning of a four-year association with Pete and Bill. We roomed and boarded together and became great friends. At the conclusion of the Milford run they would follow the circuit north and I would return to the store. Without exception Bill made the highest shearing score of all at every plant where we worked together—both with the blades and later on machines.

On Sundays or rainy days the little town of Milford hummed with business, especially the saloons. Another of Bill's talents was barbershop singing. At one of the bars he and I made the mistake of singing some old favorites in duet form, such as "Down by the Old Mill Stream," "Down Where the Cotton Blossoms Grow," "Silver Threads Among the Gold," "Sweet Adeline," and others. A large crowd gathered and business picked up to the extent that the management was after us to sing at every opportunity. On another day off, a young hobo, with an exceptionally fine tenor voice, came in and joined us. I switched to baritone or bass (Bill always led), and the resulting trio was all the more entertaining.

In 1911, for the third year, we three sheared at Milford for Billy DeWolfe in the same general pattern. From there, however, I made an important change in the plan that took me with them on their northern tour. Our first run, of short duration, was on the Crabtree Ranch in southern Idaho, my last time to use the blades. Power machines had come into general use at the larger plants throughout the north, and our next run was at Forsythe, Montana, where Pete and Bill had learned to use the machines the year before. There I joined the Sheepshearers Union of North America. Pete vouched for my ability to "beat" him with the blades at a meeting with the camp delegate, who then issued the card on the accepted premise that a blade man soon adjusts himself to a machine. I bought a new machine, along with a dozen combs and twice as many cutters. My single pen lay between Pete and Bill, who had filled the machine with oil and properly tensioned it. A shearing machine may be described as a king-sized version of powered barber clippers, with a tail that plugs into a flexible drop at each pen from an overhead power shaft. Cutters dull faster than combs, and both are replaced as needed. Used ones are turned in each evening to a man who does nothing but grind tools on emery paper glued to power discs. What a relief from the old-fashioned grindstone and the nightly do-it-yourself chore on the blades.

Knowledge of machine shearing came fast. Within a week my

daily score was higher than ever attained by hand—crowding 175 in a ten-hour shift. In the remaining three weeks several two-hundreds were recorded, despite the larger, heavier fleeced sheep of the north. When finished, Dave Rea of Rea Brothers (Jim and Dave) handed me a better than average check for around four hundred dollars.

We were next booked at a ten-man machine plant in the Little Belt Mountains of central Montana. With their pine and spruce forests, exhilarating mountain air, and cold-running trout streams, the Little Belts in summer present a refreshing change from the thousands of square miles of low, treeless prairie to the east. Big Baldy, their highest point, towers above nine thousand feet and is visible on a clear day for hundreds of miles. In these surroundings we pitched our tent, set up the usual crude shower bath, and prepared for duty.

These were the most nearly uniform sheep yet encountered, large and fully fleeced with excellent wool up to five inches long, yet without neck wrinkles or dirt to retard their shearing. The rainy season was underway, but no time was lost on that account. It seemed odd to be shearing away while the rain came down in torrents. To make this possible, huge "sweat sheds" had been provided that held more sheep than a day's run. Wool thus steam-dried during the night cut like butter next day, enabling one to shove his machine at full swathe as fast as he wished. With clocklike consistency my score ran 200 sheep per day, while the "Bull of the Woods," as Bill Jenkins was called, sheared 220 to 225. Pete Greenhalgh was satisfied with a more leisurely pace, at something like 175. That Jenkins would draw the big check was taken for granted, but for me to place second was a surprise, even in that small crew of professionals.

Failing in our attempts to locate additional shearing, we called it quits and headed south. Reuniting with the wife and two-year-old daughter, Merle, was such a thrill I all but vowed there would be no more road-stiff shearing with its long absences from the family hearth. Let it be said, however, that many a similar pledge is made by married men, only to be broken when the next season rolls around.

Instead of returning to the position at West's store, we moved back to Arizona by mid-July, having in mind the forest ranger examination, which I would take at Snowflake that fall. After the exam, however, having received no word from the Civil Service Commission by March 1912, I made preparations for yet another round of shearing similar to 1911. Accordingly, toward the last of the month I left Holbrook by Santa Fe train, transferred at Daggett, California, to what was then the Oregon Short Line, which took me to Milford.

Pete Greenhalgh and Bill Jenkins greeted me at the depot. They had already rented living quarters for three and arranged for meals at a new boarding house catering to transient shearers. The enterprising Billy DeWolfe had spent a lot of money converting his massive hand plant into a forty-unit machine operation, making possible larger scores than we had made there in previous seasons. As usual, stores and bars vied for the enhanced business, and the town had its wild moments on weekends and rainy days. Jenkins continued as King of the Hill in terms of sheep shorn, per day and in the aggregate. We kept hearing about two or three who allegedly could beat him, but if there were such men I never had the opportunity of seeing them prove it.

Transportation for the road-stiff sheepshearer up to 1912 had to be by rail, because cars were few and highways nonexistent for their use. Only side trips by wagon to plants off the railroad were the exception, furnished free by sheep owners. To beat railroad fares was common practice from hoboes to half-fare artists. Our best method was to learn from a local contact—usually a barkeep or saloon owner—what conductor going our way would cooperate in a half-fare deal. When his train pulled in we would board the smoker, luggage and all, no matter how crowded it might be, each having a piece of blank paper for a ticket. One of our group sat at the front end of the car where the conductor began collecting tickets. He would show his union card and pay cash for the number involved on a half-fare basis.

The front vestibule came in handy for such a transaction, as a means of avoiding suspicion by other passengers. "Tickets please," the conductor would bawl, assuming the stony dignity of a supreme court, while he punched the blanks and tickets alike. A dubious procedure, to be sure. We rode the cushions for half price on a par with the clergy; the conductor got it all, less a certain kickback to his contact. The average laboring man's conscience can easily succumb to a shady practice against a large corporation, saving face in the thought that, "The Company will never miss the loss." Much the same attitude existed when a farmer's cow was killed by a train on an unfenced right-of-way. She quickened from a nondescript of low value into a purebred of fabulous worth! But we probably saved fifty dollars each per season through the half-fare racket, which meant the shearing of five hundred sheep.

Our next run was with the Rea brothers in eastern Montana in a vast sheep empire. In general, those northern sheep were more easily shorn and our daily output rose by 10 to 15 percent. People from nearby towns along the Yellowstone River came out to see the plant in action, and by human instinct gathered around the shearer understood to be the best. Bill enjoyed the notoriety but remained nonchalant, ripping off fleece after fleece without looking up. To cap things off, we saw one of the professionals, reputedly faster than Bill, in action. Pearl Jenkins (no relation to Bill Jenkins) took a pen several days late, thrilling everyone with the prospect of a sensational contest between the Jenkinses. But there could be no contest as Bill outdid Pearl by a good margin, day after day for a week, until the latter flew the coop—together with his effeminate first name and pseudoreputation.

We kept hoping Bill Boreland would come along. According to statistics of the Union, he held the world record of 365 in ten hours flat. We understood the record was made in Australia, however, in small, "bare-belly" thin-wooled sheep, by no means comparable to the sturdy breeds of the northwestern United States. At any rate, we and Boreland were never booked at the same plant, and who was the better man remains as intriguing as a Jack Dempsey–Joe Louis prize fight, each in his prime. And so much for the sporting angle of sheepshearing.

We gave up trying for additional shearing and headed south for the last time. Parting for good with these warm friends marked the conclusion of a close, three-way association. We had shorn sheep and traveled together four consecutive seasons without friction of any kind, but rather with a growing mutual respect for each other's honesty, sense of humor, and hard work. It causes wonderment, if after all, we may not meet again sometime in another realm of existence.

As a footnote to my shearing career, in 1935, after twenty-three years without shearing a sheep—when times were hard and with nothing better in sight—I tried a comeback. Joining up with A. F. (Quill) Standifird, his late brother Lon, and Loren Merrill, we traveled in two cars from the Snowflake area to a job run by big Charlie Larson southeast of Kingman. No elaboration is necessary to imagine the handicap of flabby muscles and increased age and its reduced power of recuperation. Although the price per head had increased 50 percent, so had everything else. The eight-hour day seemed longer than had the ten-hour version of yore, and my daily output was to remain well under two hundred.

Four days of hard driving took the four of us through four states, to Buffalo in northern Wyoming where Bill Standifird took over supervision of a plant he had operated several seasons previously for a group of Basques. These people are noted for their skill as sheep raisers in the open-range country of the western United States, and many have become prominent citizens in their respective communities.

We were close to a month completing the Buffalo job. I had proven that a strong physique will do wonders, even at past middle years, when put to a severe test. No longer were my scores near the top as in times past, but about average, which was not bad considering the elapsed period of inactivity. On the last day we worked late to finish up, making possible my lone two hundred score and bringing to a close a career of ten seasons during which I had shorn all told an estimated forty thousand sheep. In labor circles one often hears the remark that "hard work never hurt nobody," with the true meaning of which we learn to agree.

The crew laid over a day for the annual beer bust, feed, and dance—put on by those Basque sheepmen at ranch headquarters out of Buffalo—to celebrate the conclusion of another shearing season. A special orchestra came out from town, as did a group of dance partners to augment ranch wives and older daughters we knew through their operation of the dining room and kitchen. Everything was free and no effort or cost was spared to see that all had a good time. The Basque people were loudly cheered when they performed a dance native to their French-Spanish Pyrenees homeland. A delightful occasion we all agreed and a pleasure to mingle with sturdy characters of foreign descent, well on their way to Americanization through a melting pot of races that has produced the greatest nation on earth.

Taking leave of our hosts near Buffalo, on the Clear Creek branch of the famous Powder River—the scene some sixty years before of hostile Indians wreaking havoc upon the white man's westward march—our four-man contingent in two Chevys began a circuitous trip homeward. We bought food and supplies at Sheridan and were equipped to camp out at leisure. Crossing over into Montana, our road led down the Little Bighorn to Custer Battle Field National Monument, where on June 26, 1876, General George Armstrong Custer and 260 of his soldiers were killed to a man by an intertribal force of five thousand Indians, well coordinated under such notorious chiefs as Sitting Bull, Crazy Horse, and Rain-in-the-Face.

Neatly installed where each man fell was a stone monument with his name and rank inscribed. Although this horrible massacre has been attributed by some historians to Custer's foolhardy charge into a well-planned trap—not in keeping with his reputation as a military strategist—our feelings were stirred nonetheless by the scene around us. We stood near the general's grave, and that of his lesser-ranked brother, and sang the chorus of "The Valley of Custer," in quartet form.

> 'Tis the Valley of Custer, the park with its cluster
> Of little log cabins spread out on the green,
> 'Tis the Valley of Custer, where oft we did muster,
> And drank to the brave from a soldier's canteen.

Except for the three weeks of struggle at Kingman to get back in even mediocre condition for such arduous labor, the 1935 venture was more a pleasure tour of the West than gainful employment. Suffice it to say, shearing sheep has had its place in the variety of occupations I have pursued. On the whole, it formed part of a groundwork for increased and more permanent responsibilities. In executive positions for the state and federal governments, knowledge of physical labor, use of tools, cowpunching, and the worker's language have all been proven assets—not to omit pat-your-foot fiddle music.

CHAPTER SIX

Punching Cows for the Long H Ranch

"**E**verybody ride your colts first and then often enough to stay even with them." Such was the order, that June morning in 1907, of Hyrum Jerome Knight, better known as Noche, field foreman and part owner of the Long H Land and Cattle Company. A hundred head of broke to half-broke saddle horses milled around in the circular stockade corral. We were starting the summer cow works from Stinking Springs horse pasture on the east edge of Greer Valley, between the Zuni and Little Colorado rivers in central Apache County, Arizona. Company cattle grazed a million acres of unfenced rangeland extending roughly from the Puerco River on the north, to Mesa Redondo on the south; from the New Mexico line on the east, to about Show Low, Snowflake, and Holbrook on the west. Noche (Spanish for "night") had cut our "strings," numbering six to eight horses per man. We were now on our own, expected to cope with any untoward incidents that might occur in transforming those heterogeneous specimens of horse flesh over from a life of ease to one of subjugation and hard work.

The fifteen-man crew, including Noche, his year-long straw boss, George Jenson, and newly married ranch hand, C. R. "Rue" Jarvis, anticipated the day's events and those to follow with a mixture of enthusiasm and nervous anxiety. Charlie Gillespie, Norman Bennett, Jim Sorenson, Joe Thomas, and others were seasonal hands of local origin, while Claude Youngblood, Al Frost, and I came in from Snowflake, unfamiliar not only with the Long H but also their tougher brand of cowpunching. Big Don Nichols belied his tender age of sixteen and asked no favors. "Little Ike" Isaacson of St. Johns would join us later.

Joe Knight, an older brother of Noche and probably the most experienced cowhand of the lot, reluctantly accepted the job of wagon boss and cook. Time was when he would have been satisfied with nothing less than a top string and commensurate responsibilities. But he had passed his peak and for some time had tended bar for Joe Woods at Pioneer Saloon in Holbrook. As it turned out, he was an excellent cook, an able supervisor of camp operations, and a good adviser to us younger men. He knew the country, the water holes, and how best to locate camps for the most convenient range coverage.

Starting out on beans and bacon, we soon found choice heifer beef on which we were never short thereafter. Joe's Dutch-oven steaks and sourdough biscuits were something to remember. No one could believe, until he saw, how many of each we young men could put away, day after day, indefinitely, along with dried fruit dessert and plenty of Arbuckle's coffee. We were in the saddle from daylight till dark, plus regular turns at night guard, and there never were hungrier men at mealtime.

The rule was two meals a day, breakfast by firelight and supper the same. We missed no opportunity, however, to poach "mountain oysters" on the range when there were bull calves to castrate, earmark, and brand. A man assigned to the fire not only kept the irons hot, but roasted oysters (fresh calf testes, no less) on the sharp sticks as they came from the "factory." Salt carried for the purpose just touched them off, and to say they were not relished by all would be a gross misstatement of truth. As beef eaters, in fact, cowpokes of the period could well have been classified among the leading carnivores of the animal kingdom, odd parts and all.

Obeying Noche's command that morning at Stinking Springs, each cowboy proceeded to rope out and saddle the horse from his particular string that seemed to him the most ferocious or most apt to buck. My six horses were Sampson, Crook, Little Z, Skunk, Croppy, and Grulla (Gruya). The latter two were "colts," ridden just enough the fall and winter before to fit them for the night horses or day herding at roundup time. After months of large-pasture freedom, however, there was no telling what capers they might cut, and this included some of the older cow ponies as well. To become beasts of burden was in direct conflict with their instinctive ideals and not all would submit without a struggle.

The "uncorking" began in the big corral, from which the main bunch had been removed, thus avoiding a wide open chase of horse and saddle in case someone got "throwed." George Jenson was the first ride, mounting an iron gray with a "glass" eye [a certain type of hard-looking eye] called Glassy Blue. Only a masterful ride kept George aboard as Glassy acquitted himself in glamorous fashion, bent upon dislodging the hated cargo. He finally gave up and was on his way to become a full-fledged cow horse.

One by one other colts were topped off with varying degrees of resistance. Some pitched a few jumps, others were easily held up, one fell over backwards, but on the whole no damage was done and the older hands took it in stride. To keep a horse from bucking whenever possible was company policy. But if buck he must, the idea was to rough him up good as a lesson for the future. Noche enjoyed a wide reputation as an expert trainer of young horses, and many a rookie profited from his help and advice.

Two riders were yet to go—Al Frost and myself in that order. By far the meanest, buckingest, most worthless broomtail in the outfit was Al's little bay called Liz—after the LIZ brand he carried. The old song, "That Strawberry Roan," gives a good description of Liz except for color. Narrow between the eyes, little pig ears, and a long Roman nose, he had none of the characteristics that draw admiration from judges of good horseflesh. Well, Liz did his stuff and was hard to ride. But Al stayed with him, not only through the corral session, but off and on all the forenoon. As fast as Liz got his wind, he would try again until Al was so beaten up and sore he could hardly saddle and mount a gentle horse at the midday change. Charlie Gillespie and George Jenson helped me saddle Skunk. Named for his blue-roan color, black and white mane and tail, Skunk acted the wildest of all. He would throw his head high and blow a shrill half-snort, half-whistle that echoed back from Stinking Springs Mountain and shook anew my shattered nerves. His looks were those of the Devil himself. Fear and trepidation overcame nonchalance, and I pondered what to do, but fast. I came over to punch cows didn't I? To chicken out right off the bat was unthinkable. On the other hand, this monster looked capable of throwing me off and stomping me to death. There was no telling what degree of calamity awaited. There came a shout from Noche, friendly but with purpose, "All right, Kotch!" This was it.

The boys had Skunk "eared" down by now as he stood all straddled out, as scared as I. [To ear down a horse meant to grab the horse's ears, which are tender, and use them to pull his head down in order to saddle or mount him]. All at once I threw caution to the wind, swung into the saddle, got my stirrups, told the men to turn him loose, and "socked 'em in 'im." The impulse came not from bravery but a strange characteristic of trying to drown fear through the element of bluff. It must have worked, for Skunk left the score in a dead run, never attempting to buck. Before it was over, however, I was wishing he had. He developed such speed across the big corral that I thought surely he intended to jump the seven-foot picket fence.

Instead, he set his feet and slid to a sudden turn in the opposite direction. The question to be solved in a split second was which way he would turn back. Already shaken loose by the impact, this was important in the matter of keeping my balance. I guessed right and withstood the reverse action. The bridle-hackamore combination was of little use on this cold-jawed runaway and merely served as an aid to equilibrium. Back he flew across the corral as the men gave him room to operate. Not until about the fourth go-around did he start slowing down, with each turn a problem as to whether he would come back to the left or right.

Out of puff and white with sweat, he finally gave in and I felt as if I had gulped up an elephant. Although tough to go up against, it turned into a valuable experience that bolstered my confidence. I had grappled with a formidable foe and conquered. Noche and the older hands were quite amused, knowing I had expected the horse to buck. Had he not mistaken bluff for the real thing, it might have been different. Old heads in the business will tell you never to let a horse know you are the least bit afraid of him.

Thus all set, we drove the remuda northwest across Greer Valley to an early camp in a small pasture lush with native salt grass and sacaton. Joe Knight had preceded us with the wagon and a helper. Beds had been unloaded and Joe was busy cooking our first meal over an open fire. He was well equipped with Dutch ovens, frying pans, gauchos (pot hooks), eating utensils, the usual rear-end chuck box and other paraphernalia common to the trade. Dinner over, we caught up fresh horses—everyone kept a horse saddled around the clock—but spent most of the evening fixing saddles, adjusting stirrups, lariats, bridles, hackamores, and spurs.

Many people of today are not familiar with the old method of catching up horses from the remuda where built corrals were not available. A rope enclosure was formed by men standing in a circle with lariats held tight between them. Every man caught his own mount, being careful not to swing his rope unduly and thus "booger" the more wary individuals through the barrier. We used a one-half, backswing only, called the "Julian" (Hoolyan) catch, quite different from roping a running critter on horseback. Daily practice produced expert ropers and a minimum of spooks.

Horse Wrangler

There had been some speculation as to who would be horse wrangler. Apparently, Noche was taking time to size up his secondary cowboys. When offered the job, I readily accepted. Actually, my experience had been more with horses than cattle, and while a wrangler was not rated on the same level with top cowhands, to be a good wrangler under those conditions was no small challenge. In fact, many of the better cowboys were graduates of that position as a stepping stone in their chain of experience. To say the least, I have never regretted the role of wrangler for the Long H, nor the exerted effort to do a good job.

In addition to knowing every horse in the remuda, a hundred or more, and counting frequently to make sure none were missing, it was important to make it as convenient as possible for the hands to change mounts at the right times and places. It did not take a man long to ride a horse down when chasing wild cattle in rough country. Such days were anticipated and the wrangler given instructions accordingly. He was expected to know what horses were wanted and at about noon have them at the most strategic location for all concerned. It could be done either by maneuvering the whole remuda to the spot where the country was favorable, or by having a helper look after the main bunch while the wrangler proceeded with needed horses only.

In rough, wooded country, such as Mesa Redondo, the latter method was both necessary and hard to accomplish. Horses are gregarious and if separated from their cronies try constantly to turn back. Others, raised in the wild, could hardly be blamed for sneaking away through the woods. With that division of horse instinct, there was no time to waste in keeping them together and heading in the right direction. Once at the "holdup," where the cattle had been gathered that morning, the men took turns guarding cattle and changing horses—a neat piece of coordination. The return trip with tired animals was much simpler. They lined out for the remuda water, grass, and a day off. Thus the wrangler carried heavy responsibilities, to be met without fail.

Time came for the first saddling of Crook. We were camped on the Little Colorado below Greer Valley. Noche took a kindly interest in his freshmen, not wishing to see any of us get hurt. He thought we might ease Crook off without incident if we took great care. Had not my confidence been bolstered by events thus far, I should have feared Crook equally with Skunk or worse. Wild from a winter and spring of freedom, he was the picture of ferocity, vitality, and action. He had been freshly shod, however, which toned him down in some small degree.

Changing from my night horse that early morning, I roped out

Crook for his first stint of the season. A more skittish saddle animal was nonexistent, although he had been well broke and actually ridden through three summer works. I was glad when Noche proposed snubbing him to his saddle horn. So, with my saddle "screived" down tight and everything set, I mounted cautiously and caught the off stirrup. Nor did I yell or "sock 'em in 'im!" Crook squatted with front feet forward as if to rare over backward. Instead, he leaped forward with great force, only to be reversed in midair by Noche's dally on the hackamore.

The unexpected neck-popper diverted his attention somewhat from the notion to place me in orbit around the moon. But he snorted and fumed, diddled up and down, jumped this way and that, watching me at all times—especially boots and stirrups—for half a mile or so before showing submission either to being snubbed or once again carrying a dreaded man and his gear. Noche handed me the snub rope and I thanked him for the lift.

For the next several hours it was touch and go between Crook and me. Each watched the other too intently for comfort. Only hard riding could reduce his skittishness to reasonable docility, for which there was plenty of open country and a hundred horses to look after. Before the day was through, we had raced many an extra mile in furtherance of that exigency. Once used to the bridle again, he handled like a cuttin' horse, reined well, and could be stopped "on a dime" with a smooth slide that jarred neither horse nor rider.

This slide is one of the fine points of a first-class cow horse, to which a good trainer pays particular attention. Unless a young horse slides naturally on his hind feet, the trainer sets about making him do so. The big reason for this is that a horse using his front feet preponderantly in the quick stop not only stoves them up unduly, but jars the daylights out of himself and the rider. The trainer may have to shoe the hind feet, leaving the fronts bare to become tender and sore under the extra weight and numerous sudden stops. Gradually, the horse will throw more weight on the shoes and eventually it will become second nature. What a pleasure it is to watch the well-trained quarter horse in rodeo work today, making that instant squatting slide the moment the calf is caught, then actually backing up to keep the rope tight while the rider makes the tie. The latter was too much to expect from the early trainers for actual range work, but they were just as particular as those of today in teaching a young horse to slide on his hind feet, using fronts more lightly for brace and balance.

Riding from the remuda to the wagon one day near Rock Corral east of Mesa Redondo, kidlike, I raised my right foot to admire a new spur only to find myself in midair with nothing under me but hard ground. The earth's gravity being what it is, several minutes elapsed before I could catch my breath from the impact. Crook ran off a hundred yards, turned around facing me, and with split reins hanging, stood there until I could make it over and remount. Exactly what he did is still not clear, as the movement was so quick and powerful I had no time to realize what was going on. We proceeded on to camp as if nothing had happened. The cook was asleep and had not seen the show, for which I was glad.

Horses, like men, have different personalities. Some men are referred to as individualists, or having characteristics all their own. Crook was such a character in the horse world. For instance, he was trained entirely from the left side and would not let you up to him on the right. After a calf, he expected the rider to make the catch within range and showed disgust if he missed. Swinging a lariat to rope something was part of the game, but just to be swinging was taboo. In other words, he drew a sharp line between duty and tomfoolery as he saw them.

Then came time to put the saddle on Little Z, a straight bay weighing little more than eight hundred pounds, but very much horse in other respects. We were at Newton Corral in thick cedars northwest of Hunt (named for Grandfather John Hunt who homesteaded a place on the west edge of Greer Valley). It was Z's first time up. I roped him out, led him to my night horse, off whom I switched bridle and saddle. His name derived from an oversized letter Z brand on the left thigh that made him look smaller by contrast. He was gentle enough in the saddling and I expected no trouble. But what if he did buck after being idle for months? My self-confidence had built up to where it didn't matter much either way.

Here was a small pony that anybody should be able to ride—I thought! Without bothering to "untrack" him (leading him around to take the kinks out of his back), I tightened the front cinch another hole and got on him.

Well sir, he leaped at the sky and changed ends in midair so quick and fast that I lost both stirrups, both reins, and grabbed the horn with both hands. Again I was learning a valuable lesson, this time much to my chagrin and onlooker amusement. Most of the hands were present, changing horses for the morning run. Z put on a show, with my ungainly assistance, never to be forgotten. He sun-fished, changed ends, and each time he hit the ground I lit out of mesh with the saddle. It was either on the pommel, the cantle, or to one side, while keeping a death grip on the horn. He bucked into a young juniper, which I supposed he would clear. Instead, he whirled back to the right, throwing me wide to the left. One more jump to the right would have finished me off, but luckily it came left and had the effect of pitching me up.

After a few more jumps of the twisting, crooked variety, he bucked in a straight line through a patch of wind-blown sand, thus enabling me to get set in the saddle and slowing him down in heavy going. In this situation, there was no pickup man, or ten-second limit, as rodeos provide. It was man against beast to the bitter end and nothing could have pleased me more than when he made his last jump. He stood still and snorted, as much as to say I had won. I gathered up reins which had dangled loosely from the first jump, caught the stirrups with feet that were doing a jig and knees that trembled as if with Saint Vitus' dance. What an ordeal!

Little Z reined nicely back to the corral where to my deep chagrin, all hands and the cook were rolling in the sand, emitting loud guffaws of laughter. It was a free show they would not have missed at a substantial fee. When Noche recovered sufficiently he yelled, "By golly, Kotch, you must have wanted to stay on that horse. I never saw a man throwed so many times and still wind up in the saddle!" He continued laughing with the rest.

Rolling a Bull Durham cigarette with fidgety hands and allowing time for the shakes to settle some—we both had them from near exhaustion—I let out the remuda and headed for grass while the hands went their way after cattle. Needless to say, I craved no more of Z's monkey business if it could be avoided, as much to save face as to protect bunged-up bones and muscles. He too was well trained as a cow horse but needed and got a hard first ride. I had in mind the next saddling two days hence. He was full of life, quick, alert, and well reined. Next to Crook, he turned out to be the most likable horse in my string.

We rode our grass horses half a day every other day. When I caught Z for his second heat—still at Newton Corral—the whole crew was noticeably on hand. Even Joe Knight, the cook, sneaked up to a vantage point, not wishing to miss any excitement. I pretended not to notice winks and gestures indicating the boys were not averse to watching another sloppy ride at my expense. "You S.O.B.'s," I thought, "are not going to be favored again with any such mirth-provoking entertainment, providing Z will cooperate!" Besides, a bucking horse here and there was so common, especially early in the morning, that only passive attention was given the matter by and large. So why all the interest in Z and me?

The saddle tilted menacingly upward toward the rear, indicating a decided hump in Z's back and what he would do if not handled with care. A changed wrangler was now prepared to do just that. Still sore as a boil from the beating he gave me two days before, I was forced to respect this half pint as though he weighed a ton. In other words, I untracked him, being careful not to show fear or nervousness while leading him around. The spot called for nonchalance, treating the matter as nothing more than routine preparation for the work at hand.

In the meantime, I had relived the first performance many times over, pointing out to myself the errors made. In the first place, it seemed probable that Z would never have bucked a jump, had he been handled properly. Secondly, if buck he must, I should have reared back in the saddle, taken a firm leg grip and made every effort to hold both stirrups, going for the horn as a last resort only. It can make the difference, but jerks the rider to pieces, so to speak. Without it (the horn), he is freer to balance himself with the horse's movements—which good riders develop to a science—and gets bruised up much less in the process.

The next few seconds would test my reasoning. It was time to get going. I checked the bridle and went aboard, being careful not to "sock 'em in 'im" this time, or give him other cause to act up. He sort of swelled out and hesitated that split second which would determine his intentions. Would he let bygones be bygones or try to finish the job so nearly accomplished day before yesterday? Holding his head up, I nudged him gently with the spurs, and he started off without a hitch, much to the relief of my pent-up nerves. After riding him around to make sure he was not going to buck, I turned to the disappointed onlookers, thumbed my nose in a wide semicircle to cover them all, and rode away.

Seriously, being in the saddle from daylight till dark that summer and fall, could not help having some effect upon a husky nineteen-year-old (twenty in October). We were practically glued to the saddle and an occasional bucking spree was taken in stride. On being spooked by a rattlesnake, or some other startling thing, many of those cow ponies would buck in two as a matter of course. Before the season was over, even I could rear back and "ride him pretty," in most cases.

These experiences proved invaluable to me in later years as district ranger and forest supervisor, before motorized equipment came into general use. All rangers kept extra horses for visiting inspectors, usually assigning them their slowest, laziest mounts as a matter of safety. In showing a preference for younger, snappier steeds, I was often cautioned against their skittish ways and admonished to play it safe. But with joking insistence, this preference brought me many a fine mount as compared with the "stick horse" type that had to be spurred or switched along in order to stay up with the leaders.

Perhaps this Z narrative is already overdone, with all the side angles and conversations invoked by our dual performance at Newton Corral. But he had gained notoriety by teaching a neophyte cowboy who deliberately asked for it, a few facts of life he never forgot, then turned right around to become a first-class cow horse, limited only by size. Often throughout the season at his saddling time, someone would banter, "Give him his head and sock 'em in 'im." I was satisfied with the status quo, however, and chose not to oblige.

My only direct experience with a cattle stampede came one night about 2 A.M. when I was riding night guard on Croppy. We were on the east edge of the Long H range near the New Mexico line, north of Zuni River. Some two hundred head of extremely wild cattle had been collected for shipping, and for lack of corrals it was necessary to guard them night and day. Each man took his turn at night guard, including the wrangler. Day herding was assigned the less experienced brush hands, with additional help when needed. In either case they worked in pairs.

On this particular night in July, young Don Nichols and I were on duty together. We rode opposite each other around the bedded herd, "singing" in subdued tones such as had been developed as a psychological soother for these wild creatures by older heads in the business. All was peace and quiet until Don struck a match to light a cigarette. In a split second all hell broke loose. Every critter was on its feet and running straight at me on the opposite side. The futility of trying to stop them was at once apparent. So I wheeled Croppy in that direction and took the lead, singing the same chant in a shout. Sacaton grass bumps were everywhere, a test for sure-footed horses, let alone Croppy who sometimes would "stump" a front toe and stumble. I looked for him to fall any moment to sudden death for us both. The leaders were within fifteen feet, running in compact form and with terrific momentum. I could picture the whole center column piling over us. But Croppy, holding his feet perfectly as we raced on at full speed, would have none of it. Skirting thick cedars to the north, we might have lost them all but for one or two things: wild cattle or wild horses in a state of stampede frenzy instinctively follow a leader, even if it's a man on horseback. It became noticeable in this instance as we dodged around trees barely visible in the darkness.

Instead of their scattering in all directions under ideal cover, with slight exception, they followed me back to the open flat. By leading them in a narrowing circle they soon ran out of steam, enough to stop them on the same bed-ground. Don did the right thing by crowding the rear all the way, thus keeping the herd together and reducing the loss to a fraction of what it might have been.

Nervous and jumpy, we milled around until morning—cattle, men, and horses alike. A careful count by Noche and day herders revealed a loss of not more than ten head, mostly mossback steers. No doubt they took off as we entered the wooded area, but as I recall, they were all recaptured before we left the vicinity. Noche complimented us on a good job of containing the stampede, but chided Nichols for smoking on night guard. He recommended Star Chewing tobacco as a substitute, several plugs of which were kept at the wagon.

An important lesson and unique experience! We had gained first-hand knowledge of what a stampede is really like. Old-timers had told about them, various accounts had been published of larger and more disastrous ones, but here was the real thing as far as it went, with all the factors surrounding this strange phenomenon present for study and analysis. As for Croppy, he had become the hero of an outstanding event. I could have kissed him when it was over, realizing his tendency to stumble and the lurking danger at our heels as he raced faultlessly in lead of the thundering herd. May his bones be yet intact, and horse heaven his home!

Little Ike Joins Up

We had worked considerable country the first two or three weeks and were back at Johnson Corral on the Zuni, a few miles northeast of Stinking Springs. Camp chatter had often included the name of "Little Ike," who rode for the Long H in 1906 but was then attending a speech correction school in Oregon. Considered by his mates an outstanding young cowboy, it was a matter of interest to the whole crew when Noche first hinted Little Ike might join us soon.

The nickname was in keeping with the fact that Isaac Isaacson,

Sr., an early pioneer of Apache County, had come to be known as, "Old Man Ike" so was a means of distinguishing between father and son. Far from being little, Ike was six feet tall, broad-shouldered, muscular, and as brawny as they come. Coupling those attributes with a nerve of cold steel and years of teenage experience, his qualifications were everything that range foremen looked for in the cow business. No account would be complete, or do Ike justice, without mentioning his speech impediment, a moderate stutter, which strangely enough heightened the respect in which he was held. It wouldn't be Ike without its mixture into his many exploits and daring adventures. He took it in stride, was not self-conscious, but talked on with frequent pauses for words.

At last Noche returned from a trip to the headquarters ranch with word that Ike was on his way. Everyone was pleased and looked forward to his arrival. My own acquaintance with him was scant. I had met him on dance orchestra trips into Apache County. Within a day or so, here came Ike with his bed, saddle, and traps. His hands were white and soft for lack of rough use during the school term. Nor had he been on a horse since the fall before. His twentieth birthday, June 21, 1907, was yet a week off, but he set about his duties with the know-how of men years his senior.

The first evening was spent around the campfire at Johnson Corral. Ike related his school experiences amid expressions of pleasure at being back on the range. To the astonishment of all, he spoke naturally, if slowly at times, not once reverting to the usual stutter. His buddies were pleased, yet sensed certain absence of the color that was usual for Ike.

On completion of the morning wrangle, Noche turned to Ike and said, "Catch old Tony for the morning run and I'll cut you a string later. You'd better hold him up if you can. He don't buck very often, but when he does he bucks like hell!" Tony was a pretty thing, fat, about eight years old, a rich brown color, weight around one thousand pounds, with good conformation of head, body, and legs—an object of my admiration in the remuda from the start. He and several other good mounts had not been used pending this very occasion.

Ike nodded, but said nothing. A certain expression indicated, however, that he was not averse to a few dry jumps if Tony were so inclined. Not having been ridden for months, Tony was one of many veteran cow ponies that, in like circumstances, would buck at the drop of a hat, just for the hell of it. Put together, these attitudes between horse and man were bound to create the excitement anticipated by the waiting crew.

Saddling was routine and Ike went aboard. He made no effort to hold him up as Noche had cautioned. Instead, he put the spurs to him, come what may, and Tony did his stuff! About the third crooked sunfishing jump—bucking like hell—Ike's right spur strap broke and he wound up on the ground with a thud that would have jarred the grandmother of a weaker man. On catching his wind, he rose unhurt to a sitting position—his long legs raftered in front—brushed off some dirt, and for the first time reverted to the stuttering vernacular that sent his pals into gales of laughter. "Heeyooo, if that's the first one," he began, "I wonder... heeeyooo... what the... heeeyooo... next one's gonna be?" So, scholastic restraint had lost to the occupation he loved, and his coworkers liked it better that way. Breathing normally again, he got to his feet, laughing the while, and we found the missing spur, believe it or not, some seventy-five feet from the nearest point of Tony's nefarious activities, probably kicked there by a hind foot as it broke loose. The spur was fixed and the undaunted youngster was eager for a second try, berating himself to our delight as a "tenderfoot schoolboy."

Sometime later, we were camped near the headquarters ranch in wild country thirty miles north of Stinking Springs. At a distance from the buildings was a large water lot, one of several like enclosures used in dry periods for trapping cattle too wild to water in daytime. The gate had remained open all spring, giving free access to water in the back end. There being no other water for miles, it attracted range cattle and horses from a wide area. No matter how wild, they must have water. When thirst became unbearable, they took the desperate chance of making it to the troughs and out again, always at night.

At trapping time the day herd was placed in the lot for the night.

Two guards were stationed out of sight from the open gate. The antics of the wilder clan in approaching the lot were interesting to observe. They sniffed the air, jumped and scattered at imaginary boogers, collected again, and moved slowly forward. Once they decided to risk it, each animal would jump and kick high in the air as it entered the gate. When all were inside, the guards converged on foot, throwing up sand or otherwise impressing the new arrivals that danger beset any attempt to escape. They shot into the luring herd with such fright that in some cases it is doubtful if they even ventured to the troughs for water.

Under these conditions Ike and I were paired for "gap" duty that first night at the ranch, and we relieved the previous team around midnight. Ike was riding a young bronc, while I rode Sampson, the old reliable. They were tied out of sight some distance back of our stand behind a juniper tree. Snuffy cattle came in small bunches for precious water they had long been without. Each group maneuvered as above set out. In turn we spooked them into the herd.

We began noticing the outline of a large steer silhouetted on a low ridge, around the point of which the trail led into water. The steer would start forward with each bunch that passed, only to retreat when instinct told him all was not well. He scented enemy man, perhaps for the first time since his branding and alteration some ten years before. Famishing for a drink notwithstanding, he would never knowingly be trapped. An hour went by with no new cattle showing up for water, yet the big steer stood around, torn between thirst and danger. Finally Ike whispered, "Let me have your horse and I'll see if I can rope that old hooo. . . . mossback." I answered, "Are you crazy or something?" Far from it, he didn't wait to change saddles, but cinched mine tight and took off in the darkness. I could hear the race as it thundered through thick cedars a half mile with only breaking branches and a dim outline for Ike and Sampson to follow. But neither was new to such hazards, their being part of the game in this primitive region.

Thirty minutes passed as I sat amazed at such daring, doubting its merits against insurmountable handicaps—or so they seemed in that darkest hour before dawn—and pondering my own lack of nerve to try such a thing. But the deathly stillness broke into sounds of Sampson's jog trot in rhythm with low whistling of a popular tune. The tone was evidence that the steer did *not* get away. Loosening cinches and tying Sampson to his tree, Ike walked back to our stand as unconcerned as if he had gone for a drink of water. In usual parlance I asked, "Where did you leave him?"

Ike replied, "Over in that hoooo.... flat east of here." He had found roping room beyond the cedars and made a horn catch the first throw. Sampson jerked old mossy down so hard there was ample time for "work on the ground" before he made a struggle. ["Work on the ground" meant hobbling the hind legs as previously described, with a piggin' string so that the animal could not go far and next day's pickup could bring him in.]

The cook's "Rooooll Out" signal could be heard in the distance as faint rays of light made discernible the Zuni Mountains on the eastern skyline. We closed the gate [to the water lot] and went to breakfast. Ike's pony bucked a few jumps for morning exercise. By sunrise the wrangle was over and each man had his best rope horse ready for action. From my vantage point in charge of the remuda, it was more exciting than having a box seat at a modern rodeo. When they turned those cattle out from the trap, the fun began. Fifteen or more newcomers made a break for freedom through a cordon of riders prepared for the emergency, and each wound up with its hind feet tied together. The remaining night's catch could be contained with extra help from day herders.

In place of the morning circle, everyone kept busy branding new calves and gentling down the catch so that day herders could take over. Hobbled critters were given several hours to wear out before release to a group of gentle cattle cut off from the main herd. The first of these would logically be the ill-fated mossback who refused to water and then fell captive to Ike and Sampson. My curiosity ran so high as to what this monster looked like in daytime that I arranged for a substitute wrangler and went along.

We followed Ike to the place where he left the steer and there he was, not a hundred yards away, the maddest cow brute that ever yielded to a rope. He charged the nearest horseman while his swollen hind legs were still lashed together. Ike roped his mottled head and once again slammed the red monarch down. Another caught the heels by which to hold him so, while a man on the ground untied his legs, removed the head rope, and got back to his horse. The heeler gave slack, Big Red (so dubbed from there on) kicked his legs free, got up, and stared at his captors, the quintessence of hate exuding from his eyes.

It is unforgettable that while we were nudging Big Red toward the gentle cattle, I suddenly realized that Crook—my fastest horse—and I were objects of a ferocious charge of blood-letting intent. Despite our instant getaway and high speed, that fiercest of beasts hooked at Crook's tail for thirty yards, barely short of a posterior goring. Nor was this his last dive at man and horse. Remaining in the herd through all the rounds to eventual delivery at Holbrook stockyards, he never ceased making a run at any rider who perchance got near him.

In one of our more recent conversations, Ike rated Big Red the meanest, most cantankerous critter he ever knew, in light of which his capture in black of night by this intrepid youngster is the more spectacular to me. Big Red was whipped, jerked down, and otherwise manhandled for his wickedness, all for naught in his aim to eliminate the barriers to freedom. Weighing around eleven hundred pounds at the start, he must have shrunk to seven hundred by loading time at Holbrook, not a serious matter moneywise since cattle were sold by the head. True to form, this reprobate showed fight at the chute and hooked and kicked gates until electric prods convinced him the enemy had won. Once headed for market by rail, the whole crew had a feeling of good riddance for the Bovine Satan of the Year—Ike's prize, Big Red.

The Mesa Redondo area and its foothills, where the thickets were the densest of all, were a hotbed for cattle as wild as animals can be. This southwest extremity of Long H territory was worked from Rock Corral several miles down a grassy valley to the east. Rough to the point of inaccessibility, with cedars so thick a horseman could scarcely ride through them, Mesa Redondo stood defiant as the protector of its bovine habitants.

Often riding two horses down per man per day, the hands came in at night with bloody scratches and torn clothing from speeding through cedar branches too thick to avoid. Legs and feet fared better under leather breeches and *tapaderos* (chaps). Cattle tracks were plentiful, but of no use once the animals were located. Cues were taken from the warning "blows" of outlaw leaders and the sound of breaking limbs in their sudden flight, signifying the enemy had been heard, or scented, and the chase was on. If lucky, the lead rider would be close enough at the first opening to swing his rope on the biggest steer or maverick bull within reach. He settled otherwise for a cow in the short time available. Men in the rear came on in stride, each succeeding leader making his catch as circumstances allowed. Barring a fall or tree injury, each cowboy wound up with one or more wanted critters floundering about with their hind legs tied together. No further attention was given them once tied, but as fast as ties were made the rider took to the trail for more while they lasted and while his horse could take it.

It was usually possible to hold up remaining cows and calves, hot and winded, after the leaders were caught out. They would be taken to the nearest open country, branded, marked, and all set free or driven to the day herd for later handling. Leg-tied individuals along the course were left overnight to generate varying degrees of exhaustion until the morning pickup. Gentle cattle (a relative term) were brought to the nearest open area as an attraction for those outlaws tractable enough to join them and stay put. For the few impossibles, it was a different story, and the following is a case in point. The pickup crew had failed to bring out three mossbacks that refused to be led or driven. They would only bush up and fight, or break for freedom. No alternative remained but to tie them each by the horns to a "gentle" cedar for later, more humiliating action. [The probable reference here is to a tree as a "gentler." As the animal struggled against the immovable tree, the rope wore the skin around the horns raw and made the animal more "gentle."] Adding insult to injury, they were dehorned with a small saw carried in a gun scabbard for the purpose, which left bloody stubs just long enough to hold firmly a rope around their base.

A most unique performance of its kind, within my personal knowledge, was yet to follow. What appeared to be excess baggage were several burros that followed the wagon for daily handouts of grain and other camp tidbits. On good grass as well, they stayed fat and lazy, utterly at peace with the world. But the time had come for them to earn their keep. The three monarchs of the backwoods, having spent one night with hind legs tied together, and another hideous twenty-four hours dehorned and tied to a tree, had to be brought to the day herd by the only remaining feasible means. Accordingly, two men, knowing where to go, set out, driving the burros in front of them, for the cedar breaks of the Mesa Redondo where the three animals had been left. A burro is seldom good to lead and our burros drove poorly that morning, having experienced similar ordeals in years past. They sensed trouble ahead and well they might, for each was to be necked up close to a bloody monster twice his weight and left at the spot on his own. One by one, tree ties were transferred to burro necks and the battle began. Vicious dives at the burro were quickly countered by severe kicking and biting as the rope sank deeper into flesh around the steer's stub horns. Thus the steer was soon humbled into strict obedience and yielded to the slightest tug on the rope as the burro's homing instinct came into play.

Three teams on the march! Slowly each donkey worked his separate way down the mountain while the cowboys scouted new territory for cattle as part of the day's schedule. By midafternoon, the first "team" emerged into the open draw leading eastward to camp at Rock Corral, followed at intervals by the other two. Quite likely there had been brush entanglements or straddling of trees in the thickets, but if so, the burros had kicked and maneuvered them clear. At any rate, here they came, slowly but surely, right up to the wagon, their charges looking helplessly askance at the enemy and his deadly works. Meek, totally subdued, and two hundred pounds lighter, they entered the herd resigned to their fate.

More than half a century later, I think of those burros and their place in the general scheme of things. Even now their kind is indispensable to the prospector, the sheep herder, and larger pack trains, yet very few people living today have ever seen or heard of the novel procedure related here, wherein his Royal Lowness functioned supremely!

Perhaps the best rider in the crew was Noche himself. At age thirty-four he no longer enjoyed the terrific churning and would not allow a horse to buck if at all possible. He admonished his men to do likewise. But one day at Rock Corral, east of Mesa Redondo, he had roped a calf for branding. Men on the ground released the rope which his prized bay, Paisano, got entangled about his ticklish hind legs, and the horse threw a fit. Noche straightened back in the saddle and made a beautiful ride of it. He exhibited perfect balance and the athletic grace achieved only by those of strong physique and long experience. Losing his patience at not being able to keep Paisano from bucking resulted in some excessive spurring, not ordinarily indulged in by our even-tempered patrón. Neither had we newcomers seen his reputation as a top rider put to test, and what a confirmation it was! As told elsewhere, this blood bay beauty was one of the few favorites to be fed grain at the wagon. Of good size and in excellent condition, his performance in point of difficulty to ride was unequalled for the season. It was no place for an amateur, and many a seasoned buster would have clawed leather to stay on.

Cowboy Humor

Wherever men congregate, a certain percentage are gifted dry wits, their quips hinging around the work they are doing. Everyone makes a try at something funny, but only the few put it over well. We had our share of humorous situations accompanied by wisecracks that broke routine monotony. Perhaps some were copies of previous authors, while others were natural firsts. In the latter category falls a wisecrack by Norman Bennett that topped them all for humorous ridicule.

One morning as we emerged from our bedrolls by the firelight near Seven Springs, Claude Youngblood was pulling his boots on from a standing, stooped-over position, with his bony rear pointed toward Bennett. The only sound to be heard in the predawn quiet was the crackling of Joe's fire when Norman bellowed: "By golly, Youngblood would make a good wasp if he had a place big enough to put a stinger." Of course, no insult was intended, and the group roared from the boss down.

Claude was well built, if on the slender side. In quick repartee he 'lowed there was always someone with nothing better to do than belittle a man's anatomy, though it be the only one he owned and not such a poor excuse at that. Bennett was content to say no more, but the "stinger" incident lingered on in our memories and brought chuckles at its frequent recall.

It is said the meat of wit is brevity. This may not always hold, but it did figure in a case at Newton Corral. Youngster Don Nichols was having trouble snaring a big brown horse called Bug. He had thrown several futile Julians as the remuda dashed around the corral, somewhat infringing the rule to catch your mount with as little disturbance to other horses as possible. Being the last man to catch for the morning change, the boy had us waiting with some impatience at his inability to throw an accurate loop, the resulting delay, and extra chousing around the corral.

As the remuda slowed to a clockwise walk, another loop lit across the horse's neck and over a post in the corral fence. At that moment Joe Knight yelled, "Back, Bug!" to the instant delight of all. The wagon was nearby and he had been watching the proceedings with the impatience of an old hand at the business. At any rate, his command that Bug back up so the loop could be flipped over his head released the tension with hearty laughter and left as unimportant how many throws it took for the final catch, or whether a more experienced roper came to the rescue.

But Joe started something. Thereafter when any throw lit back of the head, someone would shout, "Back, Bug!" And the full significance of Joe's wit is only apparent when one realizes that "back" is a command used on draft horses. Since Bug looked the part in size and bearing, Joe's burst took yet a deeper meaning—for instance, why use a rope at all, why not walk up and bridle him? To the boy's credit, however, none of these horses, no matter how gentle, would let you walk up to them at change time, if for no other reason than force of habit. They all had to be roped, and the deadheads were best at dodging a loop.

To mention Ike again, whose sense of humor was among the keenest, a sorrel horse was missing and he was trying to tell me where he had seen him. After several attempts to enunciate a needed word, he said disgustedly and without stammer, "What the hell! You could go and get 'im in less time than it takes me to tell you where he is!" Another prize remark came from Youngblood while griping about his breaking-in aches and pains. He blasted forth with, "Old Job just *thought* he had boils!" What could have more vividly described his own misery than this piece of wry wit!

Prospect

No story of the Long H and its wild cattle would be complete without inclusion of our first morning at the water lot, known as Prospect, four or five miles east of Long H Ranch. Gates had stood open all spring and no cattle had yet been worked there. In consequence, large numbers of outlaw steers, maverick bulls, cows, and calves watered there, some only by night, which we must not miss. We pitched camp back out of sight, and the horses were hobbled a mile away, having been watered already at the ranch. At dusk the day herd was placed in the enclosure and gap duty set up for the night. There had been insufficient rainfall to put out temporary water, which forced all animal life for miles around into Prospect for survival.

Following precedent, the front gate was guarded through the night by cowboy pairs working in shifts. They kept out of sight, emerging only as each wild bunch entered the gap, to booger them into the herd. Of the more than one hundred head thus captured, a big majority were extremely wary. Sensing something was wrong, they sometimes took an hour to build up sufficient courage to enter, while a few fled the scene unquenched. They smelled that precious water a mile away, but closer in, the taint of man corrupted its sweetness.

Cows with young calves must have water. They went in after a day or night. Steers, bulls, and dry cows took less chances of being trapped, their unbearable thirst notwithstanding. The cowboy term "moonshining" was applied to this type operation, including the rope-and-tie method for recalcitrant individuals refusing to be trapped. As in the case of Ike's Big Red, the latter came close enough for the roper to get a run at them as a last resort to effect capture.

The remuda was wrangled and put in the rope corral by sunrise. Noche ordered that each man change to his best rope horse, saying, "It'll take all hands and the cook to let them cattle out." And how well he knew. Distinct unrest was evident among overnight captives as we approached the trap. Several tried jumping the fence as a rider went inside to point the herd toward the open gate. About twenty cowboys took positions outside with loops and piggin' strings at the ready.

Here they came! Hell itself broke loose into one of the wildest scenes in frontier history. Mostly steers, bulls, and dry cows, they broke for freedom in all directions. They ran into us, between us, around us, snorting and sniffing, hooking at anything in their way. Patrick Henry's determination could have been no greater when he uttered those famous words about liberty or death. A moving picture would have been priceless. Beyond this impossibility was the fact that none of the crew had time for a look at the overall spectacle. Big steers were the prize. Each roper took the nearest one to him. As fast as he could throw, tie, and free his rope from one, he hustled after another, taking bulls and cows in next priority.

Norman Bennett on his big Black Beauty did the impossible by tying three mossbacks with piggin' strings manufactured from his throw rope. These important items had been overlooked as he left camp. His first steer blacked out from the terrific jerk-down, allowing time to cut his rope the right length for three strings—one for each strand—and make a new horn tie of the shortened lasso. Despite the delay, he equalled the take of other top ropers and drew their praise for resourcefulness in an emergency.

For my own part, Crook did himself proud on a big steer and a dry Hash Knife cow, perhaps acceptable for a lowly wrangler. A more experienced hand could have done better, what with Crook's speed and power. He took delight in the performance, albeit my anxiety ran high lest something go wrong. A foot over the rope, any number of things in fact, could have touched off a fiery tantrum, his greatest drawback as a rope horse.

It took courage to dab your loop on those monstrous critters, cantankerous to the ultimate, and heavier than the horse you rode. Difficulties often arose as part of the game, a broken rope or cinch, to name a couple. When a rope snapped—hard Manila twist, not to be compared with nylon material now in use—the steer simply got away dragging the loop end. The exceptions were the times an extra rope was carried, another rider was near enough to make the rescue, or the saddle end of the broken lasso was long enough to make a second loop.

But for real trouble, let a snuffy steer get to its feet while the man is on the ground cut off from his horse. That happened occasionally before he could get his rope off, or even tie the hind legs. Fighting mad, the steer charged the man but was stopped or thrown by the horse at rope's length. All lariats were tied "hard and fast" to the saddle horn and the older horses, as part of their training, had learned how to conduct themselves tied to a steer without a rider. At first they jerked each other down one or more times, with perhaps some hooking damage to the horse. Since no self-respecting steed wants any part of being swept off balance by the saddle horn, or tickled posterior-wise by the horns of a cow brute, his protective instinct started working fast.

In a short time any tightening of the rope found him facing the steer with feet braced for the impact. Conversely, when charged he whirled and ran out of danger, soon to hit the end of the rope and throw the steer. A cowboy thrilled at such a performance, especially when executed by a young horse for the first time. In due course there would be an opening for the rider to rejoin his mount, and from that time on they would function as a coordinated team in the business of gathering wild cattle.

"Well, we made a purty good haul," said the boss. The crew had finished branding and cutting the herd. Fresh horses were being caught for that purpose—and to fill up on water—in the trap where the remuda had been placed. There could be no afternoon circle as all hands would be needed to round up hobbled cattle and consolidate the new day herd. A special light lunch was served at the wagon during an hour's time-out, a pleasing departure from daily routine.

In the mop-up that followed, ropers led manageable segments of the herd to their respective catches as lures in which to contain them. The process was not as simple as it sounds. Despite their half day of torture and struggle against hind legs bound together, a good portion of the outlaws when footloose ignored the lure and broke for the wilds. There was nothing to do but rope and bust them all over again, and perhaps again, until submission had no alternative. No tender feelings actuated the ropers in this situation. It was as if they meant to kill the outlaws, which actually was done on occasion by means of a broken neck, leg, or other injury.

A cowboy took the hazards of the routine under open-range conditions in stride as part of the profession and made little ado about them. It was no life for timid souls, man or beast, yet as experience increased it all became commonplace, if not actual fun.

Cowboys in Town

Typical cowhands of that era looked upon a town primarily as a place in which to carouse and raise hell. Long H men were no exception. Although hardly comparable to the tougher elements of the Hash Knife and other large outfits of the Southwest, that reckless spirit of the wild was in evidence on those rare occasions when towns were invaded and liquor flowed free. While none of our crew could be called ornery at heart, there was still a rowdy poten-

tial on the part of some in given circumstances. A case in point
would be an evening at St. Johns from our camp below the Meadows
ten miles to the north. Eight or ten of us rode in for a little diversion
from roundup routine. First off, we must have a round of drinks at
Jake Armijo's (Jaramillo's) saloon, followed by another and yet another of rather low-grade bar whiskey. In the usual pattern, one
man spoke at a time, up to around three or four. Thereafter
speakers increased and the audience dwindled in proportion until it
appeared everybody was talking at once. Bad horses were "rode,"
big ornery steers were roped and tied, favorite friends—horses and
men—were praised to the skies as inhibitions gave way to alcoholic
exhilaration.

Jake Armijo was a character. Obese from long years of patronage
of his own business, he nonetheless commanded a polite friendliness
that brought customers to his door. You seldom see an "on the
house" round of drinks anymore, but it was common then. An old
pro in customer psychology, Jake knew when and how often to "set
'em up" for his best interests. His heavily mustached fiddler, Santa
Cruz, with guitar accompaniment, livened up the atmosphere, augmented by our own alleged harmony as barbershop singers. Charlie
Gillespie, Claude Youngblood, and I did produce strains less rau-
cous than some, while others less known for operatic fame chimed
in. Such was the power of Jake's "licker" on into the night.

Sometime after midnight, Straw Boss George Jenson began
rounding us up for the trip back to camp. Not that he had abstained
from the hilarity himself, but a sense of responsibility still domi-
nated his degree of inebriation. He wanted all hands to leave town
together and rightfully so. Some of the boys were becoming
boisterous, perhaps a bit unruly, contrary to the peace and dignity
of the community. It was time to call a halt before something serious
broke loose. A few had wandered across the street to other saloons,
further to complicate the gathering-up process. Jake's adobe building stood on the north side of East Main Street. The idea was for
everyone to collect at his hitching rack where the horses were tied.
To convince them all that the evening was *not* "still young," how-

ever, proved quite a chore. To leave unfinished favorite yarns, pet grievances, "important" discussions of the cow business, "Sweet Adeline" encores, or just the revelry in general seemed unthinkable to some. Even once together, there had to be "one more sociable before we go," followed by flamboyant handshakes and farewells to Jake and his staff. He had profited well from the sore heads and butterfly stomachs that would be ours before the new day was over.

Our mounts were mostly night horses, used to standing with saddles on, and therefore quite unconcerned with their lot. They could not, however, be expected to remain so while being mounted and spurred at this early hour by reckless, whooping riders who, by horse reasoning, must have lost their minds. Several responded as if pounced upon by a mountain lion from an overhanging limb. Others pranced and chewed on bits as someone fired a Colt .45 in the air just for the hell of it. When all were set, Jenson yelled, "Let's go," and we took off west along Main Street out of town at full speed, whooping and shouting like so many drunk Indians. A lane led north to open country through which we raced at unnecessary speed, arriving at camp around 2 A.M.

Nor was the younger set in any mood for sleep. They scuffled, roped each other, and otherwise cut up until breakfast was called just before dawn. No one slept while this went on, neither those who had remained in camp nor the few who crawled in bed on arrival from town. Yet no gripes were heard over loss of sleep in this wild and woolly atmosphere, where "anything goes," so long as no meanness ensues. What remained of Jake's whiskey in our bloodstreams was soon neutralized by copious helpings of sourdough biscuits, heifer beefsteaks (yes, for breakfast), and black coffee. It was time to pay the hard way for our tomfoolery.

Of an entirely different nature was a later visit to a local town. We made an early camp near the lake a mile east of Woodruff, en route to the railroad twelve miles beyond. Claude Youngblood, Al Frost, and I were well acquainted with Woodruff townsfolk and reasoned correctly there must be a dance scheduled for that Friday evening, as was weekly Mormon custom. What a pleasant time we could have if our attendance could be arranged. Excuse from night-guard duty was readily granted, but there remained one formidable barrier. We were *barred* from Woodruff dances!

Several months previous, Youngblood and I played for a dance there. Although wrong from every point of view, we had brought liquor up from Holbrook. Occasionally, while one fiddled the other took friends, including Frost, out to our cache behind the church recreation hall for a snifter. Now these dances were strictly supervised by the church, whose rules prohibited any form of strong drink, and properly so. They were, and are now, models of group recreation worth following wherever dances are held. They are even opened and closed by prayer. Knowing all this, we were deliberately asking for trouble.

Nor could the fact that no one got out of line in any way right the wrong. When the authorities discovered what was going on, they took immediate action. An hour or so before regular closing time, their venerable bishop, Levi M. Savage, a fine scholarly gentleman, addressed the congregation in this fashion: "Due to the fact that some unkind persons have seen fit to bring and consume liquor on the premises, contrary to church rules and regulations, it becomes necessary to bring our ball to a close, and furthermore, to bar those responsible for this violation from participation in our future dances."

Our two-violin, banjo, guitar orchestra was quite popular with the dancing set, and all were disappointed at this turn of events. For lack of honor—at least mature judgment—we treated the matter lightly and went our way, making no effort to square ourselves with the authorities. We seldom played at Woodruff anyway, and its loss on our circuit would be slight. We broke not only church rules, but those of common decency in not formally apologizing for the trespass.

Our chickens were coming home to roost. We very much wanted to attend another Woodruff ball, not as musicians, but to dance and have a good time. The privilege was not ours, however, pending appropriate amends for our misdeeds. Since the latter would be humiliating at best, the other two, on second thought, called the whole thing off. For my part, an added reason impelled me to ride into town, whether to the dance or not. Miss Effie Smithson, who had been my date on several occasions, lived there with her folks. I would call on them if nothing more.

We exchanged friendly greetings at the James D. Smithson home on the southeast edge of town and, yes, there was to be a dance. Moreover, Effie would be my partner, providing I got permission to attend. As time was short, that meant calling on Bishop L. M. Savage forthwith. Different approaches raced through my mind as I rode across town to his home. Perhaps the other boys were right in backing out, I thought. Supposing the bishop would hear to nothing short of asking forgiveness in public? At the dance, for instance?

The bearded man of high calling answered the door and bade me come in. Addressing me as "Brother Kenner" was a far cry from just plain "Kotch," by which I was known on the range. The hearty handshake, the dignified cordiality, the piercing but friendly gaze commanded immediate respect. Coming directly to the point in the best language at my command, I expressed regret for having violated church rules, explained that it had been more thoughtless than deliberate, that he could rest assured it would not be repeated, and finally, that I wished very much to attend the dance that evening.

His furrowed brow portrayed the thoughts turning over in his mind. Seconds of silence seemed so many minutes as each of us looked the other in the eye. He began his reply by pointing out how much more apparent my good faith would have seemed had I not waited until the eve of a dance I wished to attend before offering any apologies for the incident. A good point and hard to face. My only defense was isolation for months on the range. And being camped nearby on a dance night was an unforeseen coincidence. Of course, there was no real reason for not making amends before hiring out to the Long H, except carelessness.

The deciding factor was to come from an erudite study he had conducted from the outset, of my bearing, mannerisms, and probable sincerity. His education and long years of handling people had made of him a master of human psychology, all too apparent in my humble situation. Sneaky feelings were overshadowed, however, by ad-

miration engendered on that momentous occasion of a mind and personality superior to my own. In turn, he believed I was sincere, that
he and the people could depend upon my word of honor, and on that
basis my good standing was "hereby restored." We shook hands, I
thanked him fervidly and strode out to my horse, hitched to a
sidewalk shade tree.

A very pleasant evening it was. I spelled the local fiddler a few
numbers, but otherwise danced every set. Effie was a nice partner,
an excellent dancer, and full of fun. There was no liquor on the
premises, and the thought struck me how much better time could be
had without it. Closing at midnight, I walked Effie home—where
my horse was tied—fully satisfied with the day's events. She had
been curious to know what happened at the bishop's office, which I
related in detail.

As I think back, that meeting with Bishop Savage had considerable effect upon my young life. That I raked up the nerve to bring it
about, open and above board, has been a source of satisfaction, as
has the fact that my word was never broken insofar as Woodruff
dances were concerned. A lifelong friendship ensued between us,
even if our later contacts were somewhat infrequent while he lived.
The world could use more Bishops L. M. Savage in any generation.

In camp, the wrinkled suit, dress shirt, tie, and dancing pumps
went back in their cardboard valise alongside dirty underwear, a
shaving outfit, and sundry items. Two hours remained for sleep,
thanks to being relieved from night guard on this special occasion.
They seemed more like minutes as Joe's familiar "Rol-l-l-l-l Out"
shattered the predawn stillness. By sunrise we were on the move.
Crossing the Little Colorado below Woodruff, the herd was strung
out to the northwest a mile long. The remuda drove poorly nearby,
due to homesickness for the upper country.

Joe Knight took the wagon around on the main road, across the
bridge into Holbrook, and a mile west to the Santa Fe stockyards.
Cars waited on the siding, and the day's work would not be over until we had loaded them with our summer's harvest bound for the
Denver market. Noche had ridden several days ahead to complete
the arrangements, giving Paisano his first taste of life in a livery

stable. Sensing trouble crossing the river below Holbrook, he met us on the south bank.

But first, by midday we were two miles from town, hungry, hot, and dusty. With straw boss sponsorship, at least consent, a hand was dispatched to the Pioneer Saloon on a fresh horse for liquid refreshments. Pocket money contributions had been sufficient to buy four quarts of "good stuff" at $1.75 per quart, an unbelievably low price by present standards—even for fifths, which were then unknown. Having orders to let no grass grow under his feet, he was back within the hour.

How crazy could we get? Here we were, swigging hot hundred-proof liquor, about evenly distributed from front to rear of the trail herd, and the remuda to one side, all on stomachs devoid of food or water since early dawn. The effects could only be many times worse than if we had eaten a square meal beforehand. For my part, the pledge to Bishop Savage was still good, but it did not include activities away from Woodruff. Even so, being responsible for a hundred horses, and experienced in what liquor will do to an empty stomach, I chose a moderate course along with older heads in the business.

Between us all, we made short work of the gallon, soon to result in various stages of drunkenness on the job. The river was in partial flood from recent rains up the Puerco, which heads at the Continental Divide east of Gallup, New Mexico, and joins the Little Colorado three miles above Holbrook. As the Spanish word *puerco* implies, its water was little more than soft red mud, not potable for man or beast, which increased the difficulty of crossing the herd. Dry as they were, the animals showed disgust at not being able to satisfy their thirst on reaching the water's edge. "Too thick to drink, and too thin to plow," the stuff even stunk of carcasses and debris washed down from the Puerco watershed. Cattle wanted no part of it, even to wetting their feet. And the fun began.

High as a kite on hundred proof, riders dove into the fray with reckless abandon. In close formation they literally shoved a few leaders into the stream with their horses' breasts. They whooped, yelled, and cussed, only to fail in several attempts at getting the outfit started. Steers fell and floundered; horses did likewise, dousing riders in slimy silt, so treacherous was the quicksand footing. At slightly less than swimming depth, the water was nonetheless swift and turbulent.

Thirty minutes of such chaos passed before an old steer started following a leader horseman. Others followed suit as riders pushed them off the bank from each side, making sure there was no break in the procession. Too wide a gap at any point would mean another mass rebellion. Whipping chaps and rumps, screeching cowboys brought up the rear in tight formation, and before long "Operation Puerco" had been accomplished. Corralling them at the yards a quarter mile beyond was reasonably simple. Troughs in each section had been freshly filled with clear water from tank cars that cattle could sniff for some distance. We were at trail's end.

Joe Knight had placed the wagon in the shade of huge cotton-woods between river and railroad and prepared a big feed. He also revealed a fresh stock of company liquor intended as a treat to the boys apropos the occasion. Having exhausted the effects of earlier imbibing on the trail, the hands were more interested in a recharge than taking on food—at least for the moment. Some restraint was necessary, however, for we were behind schedule and the herd must be loaded that evening.

With help, I had crossed the horses in advance, watered at the yards, and was holding them near camp. Nose sacks hung on the few that were grained while I grabbed off half a dozen biscuits, several beefsteaks, and black coffee—still not a total abstainer, yet holding the line until the last horse was hobbled for the night. Noche was jovial but insistent that all hands eat their fill and start loading. To save time, we strung ropes between cottonwood trees to form a catch corral from which the boys changed to night horses, one or two at a time, as they could be spared from the chutes.

Using steel-tipped prods on backward cattle, our loading went fast enough. A switch-engine crew stood by to move the cars up a length as each was filled. A chorus of yells went up as doors clanged shut on the last loaded car. Cowboys raced to camp where company liquor was yet in good supply, feeling it was time to relax and make merry. Noche figured it a part of the trade. He shouted a pleasant

adios and boarded the train for Denver with his charges, leaving
Jenson as boss. Jenson checked to see that I had the horses well in
hand before joining the revelers as an equal.

Hobbling was purposely delayed within available daylight to give
homesick horses less time to hop the back trail. Meanwhile, the boys
grew wild and boisterous as generous amounts of free liquor were
consumed. They bragged on pet horses, on their buddies, and indulged in various forms of horseplay. One hand bantered the lot for
a pulling match, his night horse being larger than most. Of course,
Ike would be the first to accept the challenge, having had some experience with the fine points involved and less alcohol to blur his
timing. The rest took sides to give it the importance of an Olympic
Game. A throw rope was tied fast, horn to horn. They started rump
to rump and raced in opposite directions. At impact, Ike was leaning
forward to take full advantage of his weight. The rope broke, but
not until his rival's larger horse was jerked squarely over backward.
Yelling in terror, the challenger was barely able to fall clear of his
mount and thus avoid serious injury. Other such antics continued
for a time, pending the ride into town.

The sun was getting low, with my big job yet to come. Hanging
gunny sacks full of rope hobbles on the saddle horn, I set to my task
of rounding up loose horses, pointing them back across the river,
and hobbling the whole caboodle. Joe Knight rode up eventually to
make good his offer of help. The expression on his face told me
something had gone wrong, so I asked him how everything was going. He said, "We had a little run-in at camp and I almost killed a
man." One of the hands with whom he had gotten along poorly on
the works took offense at some remark, charged him as he was in
the act of opening a fresh quart of whiskey, and promptly got south-
pawed over the head with it. Joe was left-handed, it will be recalled.
The two of us finished hobbling before he continued with details. It
is nature's dictum that differences evolve between certain people
who are brought into close association. Bits of sarcasm here and
there and designs on the part of one to discredit the other gradually
create a storehouse of grudges that must explode sooner or later.
Demon rum equally magnifies likes and dislikes and produces the in-

centive to make them known. Such was the background here with
respect to a pent-up aversion of the principals, each for the other.
Staying down a minute or so while his head cleared, the cowboy suddenly ran toward a bedroll containing a gun. George Jenson
anticipated the move and got there first. He also maneuvered between the two, preventing further physical contact. Profane invec-
tives and recriminations rent the air as the cowboy mounted his
horse and headed for Holbrook, vowing to even the score.

Camp had quieted down noticeably when Joe and I rode in. Of the
two sobering factors, the fight was one, and bellies full of beef the
other—all to the good, for an evening in town was yet in prospect. It
had been anticipated for weeks, not only by the crew, but saloon-
keepers and merchants as well. Fall business was estimated largely
in terms of paydays at shipping time for the various cattle outfits.

In our case, we received bank drafts, negotiable at the Pioneer
and Bucket O'Blood saloons and Frank Wattron's drugstore, with a
bar in back. Merchants who also stayed open late for their share of
the trade were A & B (Adolph and Ben) Schuster, the A.C.M.I.
(Arizona Cooperative Mercantile Institution) and Harry Scorse, all
in the same block on Front Row, south of the railroad. Sam
Chinaman's Restaurant completed the Row at its east end. Sam,
too, profited when cowmen and their hands were in town.

Washing up at our crude facilities, we proceeded on our mile ride
into Old Holbrook and hitched our horses at waiting racks in front of
the saloon trio. Inside, the hands bought a round of drinks, each in
turn as his draft was cashed in gold and silver. Genial Joe Woods, a
cowboy himself later to become one of Navajo County's most famous
sheriffs, operated the Pioneer. Small of stature but big of heart and
character, he enjoyed a wide circle of admiring friends. His sense of
humor and genuine welcome made of his place the natural headquarters for range men. Liquor business elsewhere was largely
overflow from the Pioneer.

We wondered about our buddy who had ridden ahead after his encounter with Joe, but not for long. We met his horse at the edge of
town, all confused, but instinctively headed toward camp. He had

been unsaddled and turned loose in the street. We caught and kept him with our own mounts. At the Pioneer bar was his rider, mad and well oiled. Having heard the details, Joe Woods was prepared for any emergency. Joe Knight had tended bar there in times past, and the two were close friends, happy to meet again. The hands cooperated with Woods in keeping the rivals well apart for the evening, lest the fight be resumed. None could see the point when urged by the aggrieved to cut our horses loose in the street, as he had done, and wipe the dust of such an outfit forever from our feet. On this note the incident was closed, if not entirely forgotten.

As a whole, our boys behaved well enough. Much better perhaps, than if we hadn't started hitting the bottle early in the day, worked it off, and filled up on Joe's heifer beef, Dutch-ovened to a queen's taste. Shirts, hats, Levi's, underwear, and socks were purchased at the stores and put to use after baths at the Santa Fe pump house east of the depot. Few are left who can recall this old facility, for years the only one of its kind open to the public. Thus cleansed, togged out, and freshly barbered a la Bill Cross, our general appearance was so improved we began calling each other "Mister."

A certain amount of hilarity could be expected from any group converging on Holbrook's front row after months of back-country isolation, and ours was no exception. Here was a central meeting ground for cowboys, ranchers, farmers, freighters, and others. Old and new acquaintances were greeted over friendly nips at the bar, in a din of multiple conversation and boisterous laughter. Even the teetotalers, and there were a few, dropped in for relaxation or an occasional business transaction. Gone were the roulette wheels and dice games of former years, banned by the legislature that spring of 1907, and, no doubt, it saved a portion of our paychecks.

All who craved music crowded around Frank Wattron's Edison phonograph, one of the few thereabouts, to hear popular songs by Ada Jones, Billy Murray, and many other recordings of the old cylinder type. "The poor, lovesick S.O.B.," was one cowboy's reaction to a male singer's sensual moan, and the laughing series of Uncle Josh scattered mirth to all within hearing. We enjoyed that old machine, totally oblivious of its stereophonic counterparts the ensuing half century would bring, and only a witch would dare predict television, or some kind of nut that actual color would be added.

Our crew milled around from bar to bar, some taking on a big feed at Sam Chinaman's before heading for camp. No effort was made to round them up, as previously at St. Johns, since the immediate work was over and breakfast would not be gauged by the morning star. They trickled back to the wagon on their own from midnight to three or four in the morning, ready for that deep slumber which only cowboys know after a long, hard day and night. For my part, it had been two nights in a row. Old Sol beat down from a high angle as I awoke to the realization that my horses must be scattered from hell to breakfast. Grass was all but lacking for miles out from the shipping pens. They would cover more ground in search of it, not to mention their natural instinct to back-trail for home. Five or six of us, energized on steaks and coffee, combed the countryside, until by noon every horse was found. Watering them at the yards, we caught fresh mounts and turned the remuda over to Ike, Charlie Gillespie, Norman Bennett, and others who dead-headed back to Stinking Spring and the Long H Ranch, with a substitute driver on the wagon for Joe Knight who remained in Holbrook.

George Jenson accompanied Youngblood, Frost, and me the twenty-eight miles to our homes at Snowflake, each with a packhorse for his bed and personal effects. Lodging and meals were arranged for George, and pasture for the eight horses. Meanwhile, we persuaded George to stay over for a dancing party in his honor the next evening at the old Flake Brothers' hall, a sort of homecoming for us three natives as well. George was not much for mixed company and would have been more at home by a campfire, but we fitted him out in go-to-meetin' clothes and got him a date in the person of Miss Martha Hunt. She had been tipped off concerning his bashfulness and did her part well in making him feel at home. He was having the time of his life, no less. Next day he rode through to Stinking Springs with the eight horses, deeply impressed by a somewhat different "town" experience.

The tendency of range men to act up on those rare occasions when they could visit a town having liquor establishments and other lures for their patronage has been given rather wide coverage in this section. To their credit, however, our boys of 1907 failed to furnish material of a sensational nature. Only one row, no killings, no actual gunplay or scandal. With slight exception, lifelong friendships were formed wherein chance meetings among them have brought mutual delight over the years. By contrast, the giant Hash Knife and other contemporary outfits employed cowboys whose real names and backgrounds were known only to themselves, men wanted for various crimes, including murder, by states they had left "between suns," men who were listed on the payroll merely as Shorty Smith, Slim Jones, or some other brief alias. Brawls and shooting scrapes were to be expected from these undergrounds, in towns full of booze, as was witnessed to by old newspapers and tombstones. "Cowboys in Town" for this class often spelled trouble, *bad* trouble, whereas one could hardly ask for better behavior than that exhibited by our Long H crew at Old St. Johns and Holbrook's "Hell's Half Acre."

The Long H in Retrospect

Little did I realize at the time how valuable my hitch at the Long H was to be in later years. It could have been the deciding factor in my passing the forest ranger examination in the fall of 1911, the only successful candidate from the Snowflake group of six. The Long H experience was a builder of character. Roundup efficiency depended upon the self-discipline of the cowboys. Orders were orders, though tactfully issued, and their strict observance was a tradition, a code of the range, with no questions asked. Do your utmost, the code went, to accomplish any task assigned. Ride any horse, rope any critter, no matter how big or ugly, and take your turn standing night guard. To show weakness was fatal to one's prestige. Do your damndest, no matter what, and failure was no disgrace. Courage and honest effort commanded the respect of boss and hands who would "go to hell for you" in any emergency.

Never will I forget help received from Noche if he thought I needed it. This was mostly because I didn't ask for it, but instead tackled anything I was told to do; the older hands were the same. The wrangler was always to know where the holdup was to be. Where possible, he would have part of the remuda nearby so men could change horses. If the holdup was close to the wagon, the cowboys came in for the change. If there was plenty of room, the wrangler would graze the whole remuda slowly out to the holdup, and then back after change. To be a good horse wrangler was no simple job, and I felt good when Noche told me he appreciated the way I had taken hold and put it over.

Something of note was the way men and horses adjusted to working in a dry climate. As a general rule riders drank no water on shift, nor would they allow their mounts to fill up on those rare occasions when water was available. The idea was to not "spoil" either to the habit of requiring water when it could not be had. In like manner, no midday meals were served. Men gorged themselves night and morning but carried no lunches. An occasional midafternoon "oyster" feed, while a rare treat with salt from chaps' pockets, was not to be counted upon.

Beefsteak was standard for breakfast, for hard riding creates unusual hunger. We started out with sowbelly for breakfast until a fat heifer was found for beef. From then on it was fresh beef every meal, and what beef! The grass fed is the best flavor of all. You crave fruit to go with it, and dried apricots are ideal. Baking powder, or better yet, sourdough biscuits, plenty of Dutch-oven beef, potatoes—but rarely green vegetables—and tapering off with boiled, dried fruit was the ideal menu. And the volume each healthy man could put away night and morning is unbelievable to the inexperienced.

The old open-range breed of cowboy was wild and woolly, come what may, wind, rain, or shine, but he is gradually vanishing from the western scene. He marked an era in forming Western civilization. He is now portrayed in Hollywood mockery by literally thousands of so-called westerns, with cheap plots enacted by soft-handed drugstore punks, with their two six-guns hung low for quick draw. Real hands of half a century back must turn over in their graves at such antics, or, if still alive, explode with indignation at the way the silly stuff is put on the screen from pens of glamour-seeking scenario writers, most of whom never "turned a cow." Actors ride like a sack of mush and yell "Whoa!" to stop their mounts. Old cow outfits got rid of any horse that reared up on his hind legs, yet this is great stuff in the movies. Cowboys did sing, but not while at work, except sometimes while night herding. Few could twang a guitar, at least not in the Hollywood style.

Worth mentioning in passing were the miscellaneous itinerant cowboys who visited our camp. Some worked a few days for their keep, and they knew the trade. Others stayed overnight and went their way, some laying over a day to rest their horses, usually two mounts and a pack. It was custom not to ask their names, where they were from, or where they were going. A few volunteered being from Texas, Oklahoma, or elsewhere, even giving their names. One could draw his own conclusions on whether the names were real or assumed. But it was up to the traveler to divulge what he would, and more often than not, little or no information was given. Under range-code procedure they were always welcome at camp. The cook fed them anytime, early or late, with no questions asked. They left with the usual, "Much obliged," and the reply, "You're welcome, Podner. Come again." One or more remarks were heard aside from our crew, "Wonder what that guy's up to? Who's he runnin' from? Where's he headed?" There was no answer.

Yes, there were outlaws among the cowboys, but only a small percentage. How many more outlaws are there today in other fields? Average cowhands carried guns, yes, but mostly for defense against Indians—before that hazard ceased—or to put hopelessly crippled animals out of misery, kill rattlesnakes, or just practice on jackrabbits. The cowboy was peaceable and accommodating and would go the limit for his friends. Unfortunately, liquor brought disaster to many a young, innocent man. Cowboys were not trained in good behavior and proper restraint in town. They looked upon it as a place to let their hair down and "make whoopee." There was a period in some frontier towns when they were not required to cache their guns. After so much rotgut, tempers flared more quickly, and on the spur of the moment guns were brought into play, to their everlasting sorrow. The point is, barring spur-of-the-moment incidents with liquor involved, cowhands of the period were just people as we have today, with good intent and not at all hard to get along with.

And what of the old-time cowboy? He is no more! His modern counterpart drives a pickup with pliers, wire, stretchers, and post-hole diggers used in keeping up the fences. When horses are needed, they too ride in pickups to and from work. When range feed is scarce, ranch hands spend much of their time trucking hay, grain, cottonseed cake, or meal to field mangers built for the purpose. The professional cowpoke of yesteryear worked from the back of a horse. To work on foot cramped his style. His grandson is transported by motor vehicle and, for the most part, works on the ground.

Cow-country conditions described here have largely vanished from the American scene. They are now history, and if this account serves in some small way to preserve their memory, the writer will be glad it is written. Long H and contemporary spreads had their day. And what a day it was!

CHAPTER SEVEN

Selling Horses
The Globe Venture

Georoge Elmer Richards was an individual often referred to as a "character." We have already seen evidence of it in the account of our leaving home together in February 1903. Born July 16, 1885, and raised in Saint Joseph—now Joseph City—twelve miles west of Holbrook on the Little Colorado, Elmer followed in the pursuits of his pioneer father, Joseph H. Richards, and four older brothers, raising cattle and horses on adjacent open range. He thus developed into a full-fledged cowboy at an early age and enjoyed every minute of the wild, rough work it entailed.

But his venturesome spirit craved other things as well. Dull periods on the range would find Elmer riding the rods—or perchance the cushions by arrangement with the railroad conductor—headed for new country, anywhere in the West from Canada to Mexico. When necessity dictated, he accepted employment of any kind, but only long enough to earn grub money for the next segment of his travels. Of medium size, sinewy, and athletic, no physical labor was too much for him. Nor was he at all lazy. Only his insatiable desire for new scenery prevented his holding a given job for long. He must get on his way.

He was a born gambler, and this occupation often altered his schedule. "One day big winner, next day no dinner" was his pace. Losing his paycheck at poker brought forth no change of expression or visible evidence of concern. It merely meant a delayed itinerary that could wait. Conversely, a streak of luck would see him cornering the game, but with the same stolid expression as if he had lost. True to type, his winnings were spent lavishly on drinks, often for the house, expensive wardrobes, T-bone steaks, and whatever else suited his fancy.

Elmer was smart, quick-witted, much man physically, a hale fellow well met. There was nothing really mean about him. He meant no harm to anyone and would go out of his way to help the unfortunate. His sympathies went to the underdog, even if it spelled backing him up with his fists. In such circumstances, a few days in the county jail for disturbing the peace were taken in stride as he cheered his fellow inmates with nonchalance and witty good humor.

In late October 1907, following our stint with the Long H cattle outfit, Al Frost and I were contacted by Elmer Richards regarding a trip to Globe, Arizona, with a bunch of horses he planned to sell. He was under bond to appear there at the fall term of district court, and the horse venture would kill two birds with one stone. As hired hands, Al and I were to receive forty-five dollars per month and expenses, including some fancy living once the money started coming in from the sale of horses. We were to live on T-bone steaks smothered in mushrooms, dress in style, take in the local dances for which the area was famous, and live it up in general. A bit reckless ourselves, and with nothing to lose, we fell for the idea at once.

Around the first of November, we met in Holbrook at a country dance for which the Youngblood-Kartchner stringed orchestra furnished music. Elmer brought along extra horses for Al and me, and another on which to pack our beds and traps to Joseph City the following day. My violin was sent back to Snowflake by the team and buggy that brought us to Holbrook.

At Joseph City we bought groceries and supplies for a "greasy sack" outfit [an outfit that includes sowbelly, which supplies cooking grease as well as food], packed them and our beds, pots, and pans on two gentle horses and took off for range country to the south. Sometime after dark we pitched camp at a corral where water was handy and centrally located for the work at hand. The day had been long and hard, what with a dance and about three hours sleep the night before.

For the next several days the trio rode hard in rounding up twenty-five head of good saddle horses, a few half broke, including a pair of well-bred three-year-old mares. When the fall works were over, it was customary on the open range, so long as feed was plentiful, to turn saddle stock loose to shift for themselves. Good grass was everywhere that year, and all the horses gathered were in excellent condition.

We shifted camp to Mud Tank, west of Heber, where the nightly howl of now extinct lobo wolves ran shivers up our spines. These were the original Mogollon species, larger and more deadly than the Mexican variety, which to this day occasionally cross over into Arizona. To describe the howl of a lobo is difficult. One who has heard a tied-up bloodhound give vent to his loneliness can get some idea of what it was like by imagining a 100 percent increase in depth and volume. In any case, it struck terror to man and beast. It meant danger to wild game, to calves and colts, even grown animals as the mood of the wolves became desperate. Sheep and goats were easy prey when not fully protected. Even so, a woodsman once familiar with the blood-curdling bawl of the lobo has now a certain feeling of nostalgia at its absence from the original scene.

We rounded up additional horses in the Mud Tank area, where the total for market was cut to twenty-two head. With grub running short and bedding inadequate for mountain temperatures, we headed for Globe. Our first day's drive was over the Mogollon Rim into Pleasant Valley and down Cherry Creek to a point near the historic Ellison Ranch. The owner, J. W. Ellison, rode over to camp and spent the evening with us—one of the most interesting in our experience. After giving us directions on the best route through to Globe, he told about Tonto Basin and its history, the Pleasant Valley War in particular. We had heard of his daughter, Duett, and her exceptional skill as a ranch hand. It will be recalled she later became the wife of Governor George W. P. Hunt. Her father spoke of her affectionately, saying he wouldn't trade her for any cowboy in the area when it came to handling livestock on the range.

In answering or commenting on our many questions concerning the Pleasant Valley War, Mr. Ellison was noticeably careful not to be drawn into details, or to mention names, which might possibly get back to people concerned. Many were still living who had taken sides with either the Grahams or the Tewksburys, and bitter feelings were yet a long way from the vanishing point. Only twenty years had elapsed since the thick of that bloody feud, and Ellison had barely been able to remain neutral in the eyes of the warring factions.

"Those were mighty anxious days for me," he said, leaving the impression that at first his sympathies were with the Grahams who represented cattle as against the prospect of sheep in Tonto Basin. But when Billy Graham, youngest of the Graham brothers, was killed, August 17, 1887, the war changed from a struggle between cattle and sheep to a bitter, personal vendetta between the Graham and Tewksbury factions—too hot for active participation by himself or his fellow settlers. The three of us were mere infants when all this took place; however, the war was of such lasting interest we had heard it re-fought many times by contemporary people in the general area. But here was a man speaking at close range from personal knowledge, and it was only natural for us to ask many pertinent questions once the subject came up. We took a good lesson in ranch country diplomacy from the manner in which he measured his words, lest they be carried to and misunderstood by persons saddened by the conflict and hence having deeper than ordinary feelings toward the matter.

After a scanty breakfast, next morning found us hunting horses on the back trail. Their homing instincts were evident as we picked up stragglers hopping along several miles from camp toward their home range. Had they not been hobbled by the front feet, all except our three night horses would have been back over the rim by morning. In view of the impending sad fate at Globe, we reasoned later that perhaps it would have been better had they all gotten away except a mount apiece and the two packs.

By the time all horses were accounted for, fresh mounts saddled, and packs placed in order, it was around 10 A.M. The three-hour

delay was largely made up, however, by hard riding over rough terrain without stopping for lunch. We arrived by nightfall at Wheat
Fields northwest of Globe. We had to cross the Salt River somewhere en route, although I can neither recall the occasion nor its
location. No doubt the water was low that time of year and the
crossing mere routine. Roosevelt Dam was under construction some
twenty-five miles downstream from the mouth of Cherry Creek, in
which vicinity our crossing was probably made.

Overnight pasture was procured from a Wheat Fields rancher, as
were some eggs, butter, and other food items of which we were
greatly in need. Along with Al Frost's Dutch-oven biscuits, no king
ever enjoyed a meal more than we did that late supper. With no
worry about the horses back trailing, as they had attempted all day,
three tired young men hit the blankets around midnight for a long,
sweet sleep undisturbed until a high sun shone down upon another
day. Recuperative powers of our youth are amazing to look back
upon. In this instance and in events to come, they served us well.

By midafternoon, we reached our goal—the city of Globe. Elmer
rode ahead to make arrangements for the horses while Al and I held
them at the edge of town. Upon his return, we drove them to a large
livery stable on west Main Street alongside the city arroyo, where
adequate feed, water, and corral room were available. Alex DeWitt,
an old friend of our families, worked there. His vouching for our integrity brought about favorable relations with the stable and prospective buyers.

Storing saddles and packs at the stable, the "Three Horsemen"
strode uptown, dirty, unshaven, in cowboy clothing saturated with
sweat and grime. Having sold three or four horses right off, we had
funds for immediate needs in the form of scrip issued by the banks
and mining companies but negotiable at all places of business. Thus
was our introduction to the "Roosevelt Panic." Teddy was having
trouble with a slump on Wall Street, which in those days could
throw the whole country into a depression. Government controls of
today's stock markets make this impossible, at least its happening
overnight. Men walked the streets out of work. Mines were largely
shut down, prices of cattle and other livestock sank to low levels,

and hard money was virtually unobtainable. Such was the outlook on Elmer's disposing of his horses at anything like reasonable prices.

In any case, we checked into a rooming house over the Sanders Saloon on the south side of Main Street, paying a week or so in advance with our scrip. Barbers were glad to see us as they, too, were having a hard go of it. Merchants were eager to sell us complete sets of clothing—underwear, sweaters, socks and boots, black cowboy hats, fancy shirts, all and sundry. Thus decked out, we drew some attention among the crowds of unemployed and other habitués of a dozen saloons and eating places along front row, all complaining about the panic and resultant poor business. Lon Sanders and a younger brother, "Red," ran the Sanders Saloon. They were tall, sinewy men from Texas cow country whom we found to be genial hosts for a central headquarters.

Since the main object of our trip was Elmer's appearance at the fall term of court, he left us to report at the newly constructed Gila County courthouse up the street. Completed in January 1906, this stone building was still very much in use in 1969. Elmer did not return, and upon investigation we found him in jail! Sheriff Edwards had locked him up forthwith upon his appearance, an action which stunk from two points of view. Not only was Elmer still under bond until his case was called, but it so happened the plaintiff, Buff Edwards, was a younger brother of the sheriff. Acting as spokesman, I pointed out the illegality of incarcerating a bonded defendant, but it got nowhere with the cocky sheriff. He did suggest that we see the presiding judge.

Getting through several minor officials, we were pleased that Judge Frederick S. Nave, fifth judicial district, Territory of Arizona, consented to hear the story. We explained the situation: that we came from prominent families in Navajo County; that we two had accompanied Richards to Globe for the sole purpose of his appearance at court; that after taking such pains to be on hand and reporting to the sheriff on his own volition, it seemed quite absurd to suppose he might have any notion of skipping out; that the action was thought to be illegal since the defendant was still under bond and entitled to freedom until his case was called; and, finally, that the sheriff's action smelled badly in the fact that he and the plaintiff were brothers, suggesting the possibility of malice or even a conspiracy to intimidate the defendant.

Judge Nave was a scholarly gentleman and gave full ear to our plea. He asked a few questions to clarify minor points and checked his record of the Richards's case. "This does seem a bit irregular," he turned to us and said, "and the best way to correct it is to release the defendant at once." He signed and handed me a note to the sheriff, which, to be sure, was delivered with considerable satisfaction. Edwards scowled as he opened the jail door. Elmer walked out with a broad grin on his face, notwithstanding a mood to scramble the countenance of anyone by the name of Edwards. As calmer emotions prevailed, however, we set about the business of selling horses and having a good time.

Grand larceny, in the theft of a high-priced saddle, was the charge against Elmer. It seems he had been on a cattle works with Buff Edwards south of the Mogollon Rim, quite likely to pick up strays belonging over the mountain to the north. Such a hand was known as a "Rep" (representative of owners in a given area). They were common at all roundups before the open range was fenced off. In this instance Elmer was riding a bronco with Buff's saddle, the reason for which is not known. Nor is it clear at this writing how the horse got away with the saddle still on. But that is what happened, and neither horse nor saddle had been heard of since. There might have been other factors in the case not within my knowledge. In any event, Buff Edwards filed suit and Elmer posted bond for appearance the fall session of district (now superior) court for trial.

He remained on notice until the case came up about December 10. His defense attorney handled the case well, we thought, but the verdict was guilty and the fine around two hundred dollars. The court refused to take local scrip in payment, and it became necessary for Elmer to wire his older brothers in Joseph City for the amount in solid money, which they sent at once by return wire. His case thus terminated, Elmer was now a free man with ten or twelve horses yet to sell at pitifully low prices due to the panic. Why, in common sense, we did not take them back the way we came to avoid the virtual giveaway that followed can only be described to a devil-may-care attitude of reckless youth. Allen Frost grew understandably restless following the trial. He caught a ride back to Snowflake with an old man by name of Reidhead, a peddler he knew from Woodruff, who was heading back empty after selling his produce and had plenty of room for Al's saddle, bed, and extra clothing. Al was good company, and the old gentleman was pleased to have him along for the trip.

By this time I had gained some popularity as a saloon and dance fiddler. We had been having good times at dances since our arrival and fiddle music was much in demand at Sanders Saloon. In fact, business at the bar was bolstered on this account to the extent that it brought liberal tips from the management without a fixed wage. Texas boys Frank Dawson and Charlie Radford played violin and guitar, and we became close friends through this medium. Our hoedowns, rags, two-steps, and schottisches were much on the same order, both in keeping with popular dances of the period. Frank, like other Texas fiddlers I have known, was less adept in the waltz department. By contrast, a series of my old-time tunes, such as "Over the Waves," "Mansion of Aching Hearts," "Old C Waltz," "Lost Goose," and others, were soon in great demand.

When the last horse was sold and the scrip used up, Elmer and I sold our saddles, beds, and other gear, thus to meet continuing expenses. "Ribs" Henderson, a cattle foreman, paid me three ten-dollar gold pieces for my good-as-new saddle made by Gallup of Denver. Gold money was hard to come by, just as in this case where it represented a mere third of full value. Although gambling had been prohibited by Arizona law since April 1907, it played a part in our diminishing assets. We played illicit poker, bet on wrestling matches, pool games, or whatever came up in the way of a contest. One of our heaviest losses was on a wrestling match between Elmer and a young bruiser, George Rustin. Outweighed by twenty-five pounds, Elmer still believed he had the agility and experience to win. He made a noble effort, but the weight factor was too great and it took a horse or two to square the bets. Occasionally we won, only to lose later. On the whole, we batted far below .500 at games of chance. As a sidelight, two widely different characters come to mind as having some part in our experiences around Globe. One was a mining engineer from Louisiana, Oscar Shane, with a beautiful tenor voice. He seldom drank or gambled but loved to sing with our "Whiskey Row" quartet. This handsome young bachelor was always neatly dressed, spoke and sang a musical southern brogue—an attractive gentleman in any company. His presence in the evening signaled requests for some barbershop harmony, and but for a few sour notes not of his making, we furnished near stage-worthy entertainment. Oscar's tenor rang out mellow and clear in such songs as "Old Black Joe," "Sweet Adeline," "Carry Me Back to Old Virginny," and "You Tell Me Your Dream and I'll Tell You Mine." We even sang the old hymn, "Softly and Tenderly Jesus Is Calling," with its excellent harmony parts. It was one of Oscar's favorites.

The other character, Jack Mankins, was a skid-row drunk kept perpetually pickled with responsive treats at the bar for his natural wit and showmanship. He played the guitar and sang songs, some of whose obscene lyrics could be tolerated only in a saloon atmosphere. Some others were nice enough. One such was "San Antony Antonio," then just out, on which the quartet climbed for a pretty good number. We memorized this one, both to sing and to play as a two-step at the dances. Jack had to be just so tight to sing and play, and it was surprising how patrons, sometimes the management, would supply his needs in order to get him started. He slept on a pool table, but only when "business" was dull. His retiring admonition to anyone near was always, "Be sure to wake me up if a 'live one' shows up," meaning, of course, a spender for drinks and amusement.

Dance Music to the Rescue

Time and funds were running out. I borrowed a fairly good violin from a widow woman, tuned it up with new strings, and began playing for dances on my own. Our best customer was a young man named Gibson, sporty son of the owner of the Gibson Mine, fifteen miles into the high hills south of town. He fell prey to my type of music and gave twice-a-week dances in the camp recreation center. He specially loved to waltz with his fiancée to the tune, "Mansion of Aching Hearts," and made repeated requests for that number during the evening. Standard price for a fiddler had been ten dollars, whereas Gibson paid me fifteen, with an extra five for a guitarist, plus team-and-buggy transportation from Globe.

Elmer was having a grand time dancing and learned to play guitar with certain pieces. He chuckled at the turn of events, wherein I borrowed an instrument and fiddled our way out of financial difficulties. "From hired hand to boss," he would say with his usual nonchalance. We had other engagements—at Copper Hill dance hall, the grade-school—and were doing right well considering the hard times.

Dawson and Radford came to feel we were unduly invading their territory, going so far as to claim the widow woman wanted her violin back. This proved to be false. It was only a cheap ruse to eliminate competition, whereupon I scolded them for resorting to such tactics, at the same time reminding them that no one has a corner on dance territory; moreover, I was being paid some 50 percent more than they charged, which might inure to their advantage when we were gone. It left a scar on our friendship, but no serious harm was done.

Nostalgia Overrides

As Christmas holidays drew near, our feet grew itchy for the good times bound to be had at Snowflake and vicinity. Gibson offered us well-paying jobs in the mine—knowing nothing about mining was immaterial—to keep us from leaving. There would be a guarantee of two dances a week at increased pay, a place to eat and sleep, all and sundry. In reality, such an opportunity was not to be frowned upon, especially in my own case. With a little frugality, I could have done well there on a permanent basis.

But it was time to go. We could not be dissuaded. The livery stable had profited from the horses they kept and a few they purchased at giveaway prices, and was willing to accept Elmer's note for the hire of two other horses with saddles for our trip home. We cleaned up a few bills about town and returned the violin, for which there was no charge, to its owner. In fact, the lady was pleased to have it in good playing condition after years of nonuse since the death of her husband. Other rounds were made to say good-bys to saloon owners, bartenders, and friends, a finale to a rather reckless sojourn in Globe, Arizona, historic mining town on the western frontier.

On the afternoon of December 21, 1907, Elmer Richards and I rode twenty miles east from Globe to Rice, on the San Carlos Indian Reservation, putting up for the night at a Mr. Tuttle's forage station. With "fiddle" money saved for the trip, we purchased food for ourselves and horses. Mr. Tuttle gave us blankets for a hard bed on a granary floor. The lonesome sound of an Apache medicine man's all-night chant comes back to me now. We wondered if the ordeal were not more of a kill than a cure for the ailing subject.

The tiny cafe at Rice was open by daylight next morning. After a hearty breakfast, with sandwiches to go, we were in the saddle by sunrise headed for the mountain. We lunched at Casadora Spring, some twenty miles out, and gave the horses oats brought along for the purpose. Elmer's horse had developed a decided limp in a front foot, the cause not being apparent. It looked as if we were in deep trouble, with no other mount at hand. After the noon rest, however, as if by magic, the limp disappeared, somewhat to our amazement.

We followed the old military wagon road up over the summit past the sawmill (inactive) and down into Black River by late evening. There we met Pat Duke, an old-time cowhand in charge of the army forage station at that point. We were happy to accept his invitation to spend the night with him, which included a sumptuous supper, breakfast, and beds for ourselves and forage for the horses. Pat was living alone and seemed to enjoy our type of company. For years he had been a famous bronc rider on the professional rodeo circuit, and now, though all bunged up as a result, he was still able to carry on his duties as station master. We swapped yarns into the night. He was interested in our recent goings-on and wished we had a fiddle, being himself a typical Texas cowboy who loved hoedown fiddle tunes. In turn, we listened intently as he related his exploits as a rodeo performer, which took him from Arizona and New Mexico as far north as Calgary, Canada, in season. During the late nineties such bucking horses as Steamboat and Midnight had thrown or disqualified riders considered tops in the business. "The best ride I ever made," said Pat, "was aboard old Steamboat for first money at Pendleton, Oregon, in the year 1900. To conquer that old demon was a great satisfaction, even if he did wind up my career as a saddle-bronc rider with a permanent sore in my side from the terrific pounding he gave me." Pat had also "stayed with" big, black Midnight on a previous occasion for a good share of the prize money.

In early morning of December 23, we took leave of our genial host and reined our well-kept mounts to the north. Crossing beyond White River, we left Fort Apache off to our right and rode northeast through the White River Indian Agency to Cooley's Ranch, arriving by late afternoon. En route we passed through Indian camps and wickiup villages, typical of the Apache way of life. The inhabitants peered at us with what looked to be a mixture of curiosity and suspicion. Several conversations were had with riders along the way, who were friendly enough, though anything but talkative.

Col. C. E. Cooley was a fluent talker, interesting and hospitable. Upon learning our identity, he insisted we rest our horses and have a bite to eat. It will be recalled he married two Apache squaws, sisters of White Mountain Apache Chief Alchesay, and raised a unique family of half-breeds. We were acquainted with Charlie, Bert, and Don, high-type young fellows, intelligent, educated, and well-mannered. An ex-army officer, Cooley gained fame as an arbiter of differences between the Apaches and the federal government in those hectic days of Geronimo, Cochise, Victorio, and the Apache Kid.

Much refreshed, both man and beast, we rode on to Pinetop for the night, arriving after dark. Eph Penrod ran a saloon, a boarding-house, and way station of sorts. He welcomed us to all the facilities, including a warm stable, hay and grain for the horses, food, drink, and lodging for ourselves. We shivered with the cold by contrast with Globe's pleasant winter climate. On the inside, however, pot-bellied heating stoves burned around the clock for the comfort of everyone.

I was well acquainted with these people, especially the Penrod families, having played with Youngblood, et al., for several dances there in times past. After a good supper we exchanged anecdotes with Eph and a dozen other local residents gathered in the saloon section. Also, an old violin was kept behind the bar, and nothing would do but that we have some hoedown fiddle music to liven up the wintry calm. Your pseudodistinguished author of these lines, being in good practice, was happy to oblige, perhaps as much for his own satisfaction as that of his audience.

We had covered near forty-five miles that day through mountain-ous country, a sizable feat considering the uphill distance made the day before of about forty miles. But the horses were holding up well as we fed and rested them at every opportunity. A lover of good horses, it has always amazed me what one can stand as a beast of burden when properly taken care of. All he asks to start a hard day's work is a bellyful of hay, grain, and water, to be well shod for stony terrain, and, by no means the least, kindness from his master. Our two mounts rewarded us well for such treatment on this memorable journey where horse stamina was put to a severe test.

December 24, 1907, Christmas Eve, found us on the home stretch. Leaving Pinetop before sunrise, we rode the 35 miles into Snowflake by 2 P.M., having covered a distance of 140 miles in three days' time. The homefolks were in gay holiday spirits, staging dances, social gatherings, and other yuletide activities. Elmer stayed over for several such occasions before journeying on to Joseph City with the two hired horses and saddles. And thus was history made, of sorts, by a young, reckless trio, only one of whom remains alive at this (1969) writing, he having reached the age of eighty-three in good health.

Meanwhile, my old fiddling partner, Claude Youngblood, awaited
my return. Based on assurances by mail that I would be there by
Christmas, he had advertised our popular two-violin combination
and was booked weeks ahead for dance music at Snowflake and surrounding towns. It was thrilling to play again the old, rich-toned
Stainer violin as we practiced harmony pieces and hoedowns for
coming events.

CHAPTER EIGHT

Time to Settle Down

Despite the Youngblood–Kartchner popularity as dance musicians, the occupation by itself was inadequate to make a decent living. We also tired of its shiftless nature, loss of sleep, and the tendency to overimbibe free liquor. By October 1907, we were planning along more serious lines and had gone our separate ways, though we did continue to play together occasionally, as noted in the last chapter.

Up to that time I had worked at other jobs as well, notably, punching cows at the Long H Ranch or the seasonal job of shearing sheep. As if the variety of occupations to then had not been wide enough, I now took a job on Cal Stratton's sawmill in Water Canyon, southeast of Pinedale. There were those who said I must be crazy when there were dances to play for and the easier life to lead. But a deeper motive was involved than met the eye. I was going to be married. That meant providing a place to live, or else "throwing in" with the folks. Dad proposed that an addition be built to the family home at Snowflake, which I accepted. I needed several thousand feet of cured lumber for the purpose. So, why not work for it in a slack period, handling green lumber at the mill in exchange for the finished product?

Wages and prices were agreed upon, and I went to work. Snow covered the ground that January 1908, and night temperatures sank below zero. Off-bearing green lumber up to ten thousand board feet per day could hardly be rated as child's play, but "Aunt Laura" Stratton's cooking and regular hours made for physical vigor the equal of any task. In a few weeks enough credit accumulated to more than fill the order. Hauling lumber eighteen miles by team and wagon was slow, but within a week it was on the ground—together with shingles, nails, hardware, and lining material from the local stores. For lack of cement foundation, I quarried stone a mile away, hauled it, and cut it to fit. What? Me a carpenter? A stone cutter? You know, it's surprising what one can do if he sets his head to it. Dad gave advice and did some of the work as time allowed. Younger brother, Lafe, at age fourteen, was good help after school hours and on Saturdays. With an ordinary handsaw, square, spirit level, hammer, and stone chisel and maul for tools, there soon emerged quarters quite suitable for a bride and groom. The whole thing was a work of joy, stimulated by romantic anticipation, which is part and parcel of human life.

Culminating a beautiful romance of several years standing, the wedding was set for March 25, 1908. On that Wednesday evening, at 8 o'clock in Flake Brothers' hall at Snowflake, Miss Electa Adlee Lindsey and one Kenner C. Kartchner were united in marriage. Officiating could be none other than Grandfather John Hunt, in his twenty-ninth of thirty-one years as bishop of Snowflake Ward. A program and dance followed the ceremony, headed by the traditional grand march. We were showered with presents, congratulations, and typical goodwill of the townsfolk, among whom we were raised from childhood. No more joyous occasion could be imagined by which to inaugurate a new era of adult responsibilities. In my own case, some of the latter had been lacking, but now we could face the future as a team with confidence and determination.

Our first home was not to be occupied for long. There were several sheepshearing runs that spring and summer—the most immediate source of badly needed income. By fall we could finance a trip by rail to the October general conference of the LDS Church in Salt Lake City, which we considered a delayed honeymoon. With us went the bride's esteemed mother, Elizabeth Fair Lindsey, a widow of long standing, who had made her own way and raised three children under difficult circumstances. Her justifiable skepticism toward me as son-in-law vanished on closer acquaintance, and we became great friends. I was always intrigued by her quaint sense of humor, as expressed in the accent of her native Mississippi.

On boarding a Santa Fe train at Holbrook, I proposed that we procure Pullman berths on the sleeper to be set aside at La Junta, Colorado, and picked up there by the Denver and Rio Grande. But Mother Lindsey would have no part of it, explaining that if she had to die in a train wreck she wanted "to know about it." So, rather than separate, we sat together in a chair car. The La Junta depot was crowded with transferring men, women, and children during the two-hour layover between trains. Midnight snores and groans punctuated the din of switch engines and crying babies. One elderly grandmother kept repeating to her daughter, "I tell you that child wants milk!" And so went the berthless night.

Aboard the D. & R. G., our trip up the Arkansas River valley into the Rocky Mountains was one to remember. At Pueblo, Colorado, we stretched our legs and thought of the Mormon pioneers who spent the winter of 1846–47 there en route to Salt Lake City. Among them were Grandfather William D. Kartchner and his wife, Margaret Jane Casteel, to whom was born their first child, Sarah. On Mother's side, the Hunt family was also represented. Great Grandfather, Captain Jefferson Hunt of Company A, was allowed to take his family along with the Mormon battalion, which arrived in Santa Fe, New Mexico, in October 1846. At that point, women and children and disabled soldiers were sent to winter quarters at Pueblo, leaving only the fittest for the perilous march to the West Coast. Accordingly, Grandfather John Hunt, a lad of thirteen, who had driven the family wagon all the way from Leavenworth, Kansas, drove the same to Pueblo with his mother, Celia Mounts Hunt, and seven other sisters and younger brothers. The oldest brother, Corp. Gilbert Hunt, was placed in charge of sick and disabled soldiers, thus also joining the Pueblo group and leaving Captain Hunt and his second son, seventeen-year-old Pvt. Marshall Hunt, with the battalion.

Farther west through Canyon City, we marveled at the Royal

Gorge of the Arkansas, the beautiful scenery up through Leadville, across the Continental Divide at ten thousand feet and down through box canyons of the Colorado to Grand Junction. Beyond Green River and up over Soldier Summit of Utah's Wasatch Range—again at an elevation nearing ten thousand feet—it seemed incredible to be riding on continuous threads of steel, thanks to a gigantic engineering feat of the times. On major winding ascents, extra coal-burning locomotives were added to put us over the top. Not used to mountain travel by rail, vibrant youth thrilled with adventure, while Mother Lindsey looked on in terror. Convinced we were to meet our doom, she denounced those responsible for building such a monstrous deathtrap.

At Salt Lake City we took one of many horse-drawn hacks to our hotel. We saw for the first time several small, electric automobiles cruising the streets between battery recharges and now and then a primitive Ford or Buick bumping along with internal combustion motors inadequately cooled, as shown by steam emitting from crudely built radiators. Trolley cars grinding their way through the streets made money for the company at five cents a fare. All this must be the ultimate in modern civilization, we thought, having no idea of the tremendous change in our way of life to be brought about within the next fifty years by the machine age.

Some fifteen thousand people attended the LDS semiannual conference that fall, many of us from out-of-state. The great Mormon Tabernacle's seating capacity was less than ten thousand; hence, an overflow of thousands stood around the outside hoping to hear sermons, by President Joseph F. Smith and other high officers of the church, interspersed with hymns and anthems by the famous Tabernacle Choir and the soul-stirring accompaniment of perhaps the largest pipe organ in the world. Thereafter, we would attend many such occasions, but none were quite so impressive as the first. Nothing more worthwhile could have been fitted to a honeymoon, which included going through the magnificent temple nearby, which took forty years to build. Those early pioneers, masterminded by the greatest organizer of his time, Brigham Young, had left their marvelous works for oncoming generations to see, to enjoy, and to serve as solid foundations for greater achievements to come.

Getting back to personal matters, my mother's youngest sister, Lois Hunt, had married Joseph A. West at Snowflake and then moved to Salt Lake where he operated a gent's furnishings store and mail-order house across the street from Temple Square. After talking it over with the wife and mother-in-law, I accepted Uncle Joe West's offer of a job in the store [as already alluded to earlier]. Mother Lindsey returned alone to Arizona, and we looked for a suitable place to live. John Collett, a friend of the Wests, had recently lost his wife and was batching at his home, Number 5 Church Street. He got us to move in with him, rent free, in consideration of two meals a day and keeping up the house. This arrangement proved ideal for his work as a printer at the Salt Lake Telegram and mine at the store. We grew fond of John as a man of high principle and pleasing personality, and we hated to move eight months later at the approach of our first increase in the family.

My work at the store as salesman and bookkeeper was both interesting and educational. The only drawbacks were the long, eleven-hour shifts, six days a week, and a low salary of forty-five dollars per month. The latter would have been totally inadequate but for wholesale prices obtained through the store on clothing, groceries, coal for fuel and many other items in the family budget, and the income from the annual spring "vacation" shearing sheep. Gottlieb Van Gunten was head store clerk. By reason of his fluent native tongue, we had quite a trade with German immigrants who spoke little English. Learning my name, some thought it odd that I spoke no German. Five generations in America had not only wiped out its use but mixed us up with English and other blood until the name Kartchner represented but a small fraction of a composite lineage.

Sales over the counter were substantially augmented by mail orders from a wide area reached by the *Deseret News* and other advertising media. Winter underwear was especially profitable, with low overhead and the Salt Lake Woolen Mills close at hand for stock. Thus, packaging and mailing took up spare time from the local trade.

One of our toughest assignments in slack periods was collecting bills. My first attempt was an eye-opener. Not knowing any of the parties on my list, I approached them unsuspectingly, only to find that in most cases ill-feeling existed concerning amounts due. In fact, I had fallen heir to the more chronic accounts, mostly outlawed by the statute of limitations, and their mere mention brought immediate resentment. Some of the sarcasm was hard to take, but in that business one learns to take the bitter with the sweet. I accused the management of deliberately setting a trap for a green hand of which there was no denial as we laughed it off. A tighter credit policy resulted from these losses, and little difficulty was had with later accounts.

Bookkeeping was added to my duties—checking the cash register, handling bank deposits, posting charge accounts to the ledger, and getting out monthly statements. In time, I had sole charge of the shoe department, which did a lively business. About twice a year eastern drummers, the erstwhile moniker for traveling salesmen, set up sample rooms at local hotels. My job was to keep ample stock on hand, yet not overbuy. Such trade names as Watson–Plummer and Endicott–Johnson come to mind. Retail markups were purposely high, with discount allowance on the slower moving items. Drummers were a breed apart. Funny stories and wisecracks for any occasion accentuated the lure of their products.

Once we got used to the big city, it was nice living there. We went to church on Sunday, to shows that only made the big towns, and resorts nearby, such as Wandamere, the Salt Palace, Lagoon near Bountiful, and Saltaire on the west shore of Great Salt Lake. Big circuses made their annual visits—Barnum and Bailey, Sells Floto, and others. Charlie Irwin brought his huge Cheyenne, Rodeo to the state fairgrounds one year, the Salt Palace or Wandamere another, which to me meant "the call of the range." A cowboy, surnamed Vernon, bulldogged a steer, my first to see (although a common rodeo stunt in later years), and Art Acord rode the famous bucking horse Steamboat to a finish, hitherto seldom accomplished by top buckaroos. The great Houdini did his miracles at the Salt Lake Theater. Legitimate theater—*Ben Hur*—played there for weeks with actual horse teams running in the chariot race on a broad-belt

treadmill gauged to their topmost speed. In those days when wrestling was on the level, Frank Gotch beat the Russian giant Leone at
the Colonial, Helen Keller lectured at the Orpheum, and actor-gone-
alcoholic Willard Mack packed the old Majestic for weeks on end.

Other events are mentioned in passing. In November 1908 we
spent Thanksgiving with Clayton relatives at Provo bench (now the
city of Orem) in a blinding snowstorm. At the grand ball that evening, Mrs. Kartchner and I entered the waltz contest along with
fifty other couples. A series of eliminations found us still on the floor
with but one other contesting couple, that of Cousin Donny Clayton,
Jr., and wife. The judges scratched their heads, ordered us to dance
again and again, amid cheers about equally divided, and finally
awarded first prize to the Claytons. It was great fun in any case.
Donny's mother was Dad's older sister, Marinda. The Claytons
raised fruit and grain there on the bench [a level to sloping land area
above the Provo River west of the City of Provo].

In 1909, at the Utah State Fairgrounds, we saw our first man-
made "flying machine" in flight. Less than six years following
Wright Brothers' famous first flight at Kittyhawk, North Carolina,
on December 17, 1903, Louis Paulhan, (the Frenchman) exhibited a
rickety biplane in action, circling the grounds in separate flights
over a large enchanted gathering. Who sponsored the undertaking
is not clear, but it might have been the French government since it
awarded several medals to the Wright boys and took an early interest in aviation possibilities. Thus, man learned to fly on the heels of
establishing automotive transportation on the ground.

Two totally unrelated events took place in 1910. Halley's Comet
appeared and James J. Jeffries lost to Jack Johnson, then the
heavyweight boxing champion of the world. Named for Sir Edmund
Halley, the comet streaked across the sky, plainly visible to the
naked eye, for about two months that spring. We watched it in
wonderment, especially around the first of May at its greatest brilliance, and wished we might live to see it on the next round seventy-
five years hence—an unlikely possibility. For over two thousand
years astronomers have recorded its appearances without a break,
every seventy-four to seventy-nine years. They told us the tail of

this one actually brushed the Earth on a certain day, but if so it was not discernible.

Jack Johnson was heavyweight champion from 1908 to 1915. White fighters and fans resented the title being held by a Negro. Accordingly, James J. Jeffries—champion from 1899 to 1905—was persuaded to try a comeback and if possible restore the championship to the white race. Both fighters stopped in Salt Lake en route to training quarters at Reno, Nevada. Johnson's Caucasian wife and Pierce-Arrow car drew more attention than he. By some coincidence I was in a group of fans that swarmed around Big Jim Jeffries—by then fat and flabby—as he walked south on Main Street. Something told us his five years of inactivity since abandoning the title in 1905 could spell trouble from the nimble first Negro champion who had been felling opponents right and left.

On Sunday, July 4, 1910, we joined a large crowd on the city and county building lawn to hear telegraphic returns of the fight direct from Reno, round by round. Willard Bean, a Salt Lake sportsman, megaphoned the summary of each round from a second-floor window. His personal quip of "nobody hurt" died down in the later rounds when it was evident Big Jim could not find his target, but, in fact, was taking a terrific beating from the bragging champion. At one point Johnson stuck out his abdomen and bantered, "Ain't that a pretty belly? Why don't you hit it?" Popular Big Jim couldn't make it, losing by a knockout in the fifteenth round. Gloom and disappointment spread across the land at a time when the Color Line was yet to be forgotten.

By far the most exciting event while living in Salt Lake City was the birth of our first child on July 30, 1909. Announcements were mailed far and wide that a daughter had arrived, weighing six pounds, fourteen ounces; she was given the name of Merle. All the joys and thrills of initial parenthood were present as our new center of attraction took over the home on East North Temple Street. Anticipating this event, we had moved to the latter location from Number 5 Church Street.

As time went by, we leased the rooming house over West's store as a means of increasing the family income, we thought. The venture proved unsatisfactory, however, and after six months of barely meeting expenses—aside from dealing with a clientele of drunks and night prowlers at all hours—the lease was sold to a Doctor Middleton, and we moved to an apartment in the old Cannon House two blocks from the store on West South Temple Street.

In passing the store late one Sunday evening pushing the baby carriage, Mrs. K. and I noticed the front door was slightly ajar, although I had been there earlier to turn on night lights and check the locks. Wrecking-bar dents indicated how it had been pried open. Inside, I found two or three dozen suits of clothes were missing, along with a lot of shoes, shirts, neckties, underwear, and socks. The back door was also open, a heavy bar having been removed from the inside. A stone-monument concern occupied the back yard, in which most of the loot was soon located, neatly piled on gravestones for further handling.

I rushed to the telephone and called police who responded at once. Plainclothes detective Flaherty took charge with the help of three uniformed policemen. Following Flaherty's instructions, we sat at a round table in the office, where we could barely see the clothing through a back window, and left everything about the store exactly as I found it. Knowing his burglars, Flaherty predicted these would come for their loot around 11 o'clock when the police changed shifts. Uncle Joe West was kept abreast of the situation by phone and agreed everything was being done that could be.

Sure enough, at 11 P.M., three men drove into the yard with a team on a light hack. Two got down and walked cautiously to the cache. Satisfying themselves that all was clear, each grabbed an armful of clothing and started for the buggy, not realizing this was to be the signal for Flaherty and his men to close in. With guns drawn, they burst out through the large back door in rhyme with Flaherty's sharp command to "drop it and reach." Totally surprised, they meekly obeyed and were handcuffed by two of the policemen, while the third joined Flaherty in subduing the driver. None of the three was armed with anything more than a pocketknife.

The culprits had taken time somewhere along the line to fit themselves out in our new clothing, which added mystery to where the night watchman had been all this time. He was later fired for lack of satisfactory answers. Meanwhile, the burglars were jailed and their livery outfit impounded. I telephoned developments to Uncle Joe, also the wife who sat worried at home, brought in the contraband, and turned the place over to a special police guard around 1 A.M.

Our prisoners turned out to be members of a ring operating between Salt Lake and Ogden. Stolen goods from one city were disposed of in the other. At the ensuing trial, I learned a few fine points on being a prosecuting witness. The district attorney had known about the gang for some time, and this was his chance to break it up. But he warned that plenty of money was behind it, that witnesses would be harassed in cross-examinations by tricky defense attorneys as far as the court would allow, and I soon knew what he meant.

Flaherty and company were experienced witnesses on their end, but even they were forced to admit they had not actually seen the defendants carry the clothing from the store, and therefore it could have been done by someone else—even me! All this despite the fact they were wearing new store clothing and were caught trying to haul away the cache. The spokesman of two defense attorneys ripped into me with deliberate aim, hoping I would fly mad and perhaps cross myself on some salient point. He could not help making me wish we were outside the courtroom for a brief spell, but I had been warned of these very tactics and held unswervingly to a simple set of facts. The trio was found guilty and sentenced to eighteen months in the state penitentiary.

Back to Arizona

By and large, our three short years in Salt Lake City were well spent. Living under city conditions, merchandising and bookkeeping experiences were all to the good in preparation for the future. The mercantile experience proved invaluable over the long haul. It brought me in contact with all classes of people, from hand laborers to bank presidents, from agnostics to high-church authorities. It developed a smoother flow of language, taught the fine points of diplomacy and salesmanship, and made possible a certain degree of polish to a country roughneck, which had previously been lacking. Despite the hard work, long hours, and low pay, I have never regretted tending the store from October 1908 to July 1911.

It had been necessary, as noted elsewhere, to revert back each spring to the sheepshearing trade for reasonable family support, a goal which the store salary hardly met. Moreover, in 1911, following the usual thirty days shearing at Milford, Utah, I went to Montana on the northern circuit with my partners Bill Jenkins and Pete Greenhalgh, thus more than doubling the usual spring vacation, and probably quintupling income of the same period at the store. Under these circumstances, neither the wife nor I favored going back to store routine at a paltry sixty-five dollars per month—a raise from the original forty-five dollars! Just to make sure we were not making a mistake, I canvassed numerous other stores in town for something better but without success. The few openings that fitted my experience paid little more, if any, and our nostalgia for home range to the south grew stronger. Regrets at not having straddled a horse since leaving Arizona in 1908 came into sharper focus at a time when the new U.S. Forest Service was advertising for men with range experience to facilitate placing the national forests under administration.

These and other factors actuated our move back to Snowflake, Arizona, in July 1911, while there was money to pay off debts, for railroad fares, and a small nest egg to boot. Dad met the train in Holbrook with a team and buggy to convey us the remaining twenty-eight miles through pleasing scenes of our youth. Younger brother Lafe, now approaching age eighteen, caught a ride out to meet us, and never before had we realized such a change could come over a teenager in so short a time. He had jumped from a runty fifteen-year-old to a tall, deep-voiced adult, seemingly overnight. Between him and Merle the mutual curiosity was amusing—her only uncle on my side, his only niece not quite two, but an inquisitive chatterbox as to where new faces fitted into her life. "Gampa" had earlier established his place on the family tree through the same, rapid-fire interrogation, and exhibited great pride in his first grand-child.

To greet us at the front gate of their new home stood not only my mother and three sisters, but Mother Lindsey as well, who lived next door. All the hugging and kissing, especially showered upon Merle, left her thoroughly confused, but not for long. New members of the clan opened a wide field for her young inquiring mind. By nature she loved people, especially *her* people, and with rare exception was always—as Mother once said—"bubbling over in the joy of living." Nor was she alone on this joyous occasion. Such reunions of immediate relatives accentuate the closeness of family ties.

During our absence, Dad had sold the Webb place west of town and bought the Peter Lundquist lot on what is now West Freeman Avenue, which was next to Mother Lindsey's home. He had completed a new house alongside hers, thus bringing within talking distance the two families involved in our marital union. Wife Adlee's only sister, Carrie, had married John T. Flake and moved away, while her only brother, J. Arthur, about twenty, was living in Holbrook studying telegraphy and the duties of an agent with the Santa Fe Railroad. Thus left alone, Mother Lindsey had room and wanted us to move in with her. For the next year-and-a-half we shared her home, far more congenially than is often the case in like circumstances. We bore all the food and household expenses, at times over her protests, and still profited by the convenience. The proverbial discord associated with a mother-in-law relationship was proven a myth in this instance, thanks to the good-heartedness and high motives of Mother Lindsey and a showing on our part of due appreciation.

Examination for Forest Ranger

The firing in 1910 of Gifford Pinchot, chief of the U.S. Forest Service, stirred up a nationwide controversy between forest conservationists and politicians. Pinchot, although in the Department of Agriculture since 1905, engaged in a bitter dispute with Secretary of the Interior Richard A. Ballinger over national forest policies, resulting in his dismissal by President Taft for insubordination. I became interested in the pros and cons as covered by the press, particularly the aims and purposes of the Forest Service. Somehow they made sense to me.

At the local supervisor's office of the Sitgreaves National Forest in Snowflake, I got a general idea of subjects to be covered in the ranger examination scheduled there in September and secured appropriate literature for study. No one knew in advance, of course, what the written questions would be, and only the civil-service examiner knew what the field tests would cover. However, it stood to reason that both would bear directly upon the various duties of a ranger then in practice, and I proceeded to learn as much about them as possible.

When the time arrived, Hugh Calkins, a college-degree forester with abundant field experience, was on hand from the district (now regional) forester's office in Albuquerque to conduct the examination. Of the six candidates I recall the names of five: Phile Kay of Lakeside, who had spent that summer as a forest guard; Ellis Stratton; John T. Flake; John Miller; and myself, all of Snowflake. A soldier from Fort Apache made up the half dozen.

We sat at tables in the forest supervisor's office upstairs over the Bank of Northern Arizona, each in ominous anticipation. Calkins broke the wax seal that guarded their secrecy and passed out the examination papers, a set to each man. One look at mine made clear this was no child's play, that my very best efforts within the time allowed could easily fall short of a passing grade. Had it not been for the knowledge gained in two months of strenuous preparation, I might just as well have called it off and gone no further.

One by one the other examinees turned in their papers, some in less than half the time limit, while I studied each question carefully before starting an answer. I took plenty of time and finished last. Fortunately, one had his choice of exam areas between forestry and the grazing of livestock on public ranges of the West. Naturally, I chose the latter, thereby escaping scientific terms and equations of technical forestry, and drawing upon experience as a cowpuncher.

The field day was yet to come. Gathered next morning on the hill south of Snowflake, Calkins took us through the course, one by one, making notes to become a part of the written exam. To bridle, saddle, mount, and ride a horse was routine for all. The rest was more complicated. Strewn over the ground were miscellaneous fire tools, pots and pans, a tent, bedding, a pack saddle, two panniers, a pack cover, and lash rope. A gentle mule stood by on which to make the test of packing ability. My thoughts turned back to three months as a packer at Grand Canyon in 1903, which now were to come in handy.

Calkins flunked the first entry for imbalance, loose cinching, and a poor hitch—an odd version of the diamond. When he pulled the whole pack down under the mule's belly, I vowed this would not happen to mine. He might jerk the mule down, but the pack would hold, I figured. The soldier did very well until he ran out of lash rope, throwing what he called the army hitch. We never knew whether Calkins passed him or not after being shown where a longer rope would have gone en route to the final tie.

A veteran pack mule will invariably swell up at the first cinching of the saddle—an item not contemplated, at least by the first man up. At my turn, the front cinch was drawn extra tight at the start and let stand. (The rear cinch is not so important, needing only moderate tension.) Starting from scratch as had the others, I reassembled all items, loaded and hefted the two panniers for equal weight, and tightened the front cinch for two or three more groans from the hapless mule.

Being allowed no help, the first pannier that was hooked over the saddle forks swayed low to that side. The second balanced it up. Long-handled tools were placed lengthwise on the panniers, half and half by weight, in such fashion as not to touch the animal in motion. Over all came the tent and bedding, adjusted for balance, and canvas cover. An improved diamond hitch, evolved at Grand Canyon, was ideal for this simple pack, drawn tighter than necessary to make sure the examiner could not jerk it loose. And it paid off. Of course, an experienced packer would hardly take time to read such details.

Our most difficult test was a metes-and-bounds survey by courses and distances of an irregular piece of ground staked off for the purpose. We were given a standard Forest Service compass, a Jacob's staff, a Gunter's chain with pins, and a head chainman. When received, the compass setting would be purposely incorrect. Our job, each in turn, was to make the correction, assuming a magnetic declination of 13°30' east of true north for that area, and proceed accordingly. One candidate failed to start for lack of knowledge along that line, another failed to finish, perhaps both having taken preparation too lightly. Three others went all the way, but how they fared I never knew. For my part, a refresher course in land surveys must have done the trick as my readings and measurements closed within the allowable error.

We waited several months for the ratings, not without suspense. The same examination was held at 150 locations throughout the country and the Civil Service Commission in Washington, D.C., had its hands full. Word finally came that I had passed by the narrow margin of two points—72 against a minimum passing grade of 70. Although elated over success, the low rating was disappointing. Then I learned at the local office that all the other applicants failed, and I realized the screening process was tougher than expected.

Baling Hay

Passing the examination carried no guarantee of appointment. In any case, the certification of eligibles would take additional time, and this left the immediate outlook uncertain. My enthusiasm for a career with the Forest Service had greatly increased, however, and I continued reading books, documents, and official reports on the general subject, incident to other activities that kept the family going.

Dad and Frank Campbell (remembered as railroad grade foreman for B. B. Crosby in 1904) operated the only motor-powered hay baler in the area. I worked for them as feeder and bookkeeper through the fall and winter of 1911–12. Whereas ten tons per day was about average for horse balers, we sometimes baled forty and were in good demand among farmers around Snowflake, Taylor, and even Hunt (Greer Valley), thirty-five miles distant, where some five hundred tons were processed.

Upon returning from another sheepshearing tour in July 1912, I purchased Campbell's interest in the baling outfit and, at Dad's request, became manager of the Kartchner Baling Company. We had a good run over much the same circuit as the previous season, operating on a cash basis of three dollars per ton. We hired four of the best hay hands available, paid them twenty cents per ton rather than a daily wage—an incentive for maximum output—and fixed each man's duties at moving time. Once in full swing it was a pleasure to see them in action. Dad and I made up the six-man crew as bale-bucker and feeder.

As manager, bookkeeper, and paymaster, much of my work came after hours. Totaling weight sheets, collecting bills, buying supplies, and contracting work ahead were about all one man could handle on top of eight hours feeding the "plant." Some farmers with a background of frontier hardship would haggle over pennies, to which we acceded as a matter of standard policy.

Conversely, our largest single contract involved three hundred tons owned by David K. Udall, Apache County pioneer leader and an uncle by marriage, who masterminded the old Hunt irrigation project in Greer Valley. On completion, I handed him twenty or thirty long weight sheets showing column totals, grand totals converted to tons, and the amount due, so that he might check them in detail. He complimented us on a job well done, said he was confident the weights and totals were accurate, and would have a check ready next day for the full amount, which he did. Uncle David was discerning, in fact, a great man, as borne out by his posterity of today. The name Udall is closely identified with the progress of Arizona and the nation.

Sunday School Superintendent

In the fall of 1911, Silas L. Fish, bishop of the Snowflake Ward, paid me a visit. We had gone to school together and were always good friends, but something told me this was not strictly a social call. He wanted me to take over and reorganize the Sunday School. I declined on grounds that I smoked cigarettes, contrary to the Word of Wisdom by which good Mormons live. Although surprised, he still wanted me to take the job on condition that I would quit smoking and observe all other tenets of the faith. I was on the spot.

After pondering the matter for several days, I notified Bishop Fish I would accept the appointment on his terms, subject to the customary approval by the people. But there was a second call, this time by the president of Snowflake Stake, Samuel F. Smith. He had heard of the impending appointment and came to tell me he would oppose it. Of course, that was his privilege, I told him, but I related the conversations with Bishop Fish (his nephew, by the way), covering the tobacco issue and the understanding reached that I had not asked for the job, and only accepted the offer because of Bishop Fish's urgent plea and his confidence in my ability to make good. He was not impressed.

While Brother Smith was acting only as a member of Snowflake Ward, his prestige as president of the stake—containing six such wards—was bound to carry weight with the townsfolk at voting time, and who wants to be the subject of a public controversy anyway? I reported to Bishop Fish, expecting him to accept my summary withdrawal. Quite to the contrary, he smiled and said, "You gave me a promise. Can I depend upon your making it good?" Thus struck down on a point of honor, I had no other course than to say, and mean it, "Bishop, if this matter means so much to you, if you have such confidence in me, that you are willing to go up against this kind of opposition in my behalf, I am with you all the way."

At Ward Conference where such matters are presented, a number of other appointments were sustained without a dissenting vote. But when Bishop Fish proposed that I be sustained as superinten-

dent of the Snowflake Sunday School, he added to the usual word-
ing, "Are there any comments?" As expected, President Sam arose
in opposition. He recounted our conversation and the issue involved. He made the point that a nonobserver of the Word of Wisdom should be required to demonstrate for a reasonable length of
time his full compliance with that sacred teaching before being considered for this important position in the church. I thought so, too,
as a matter of fact, but couldn't turn back now.

"Any other comments?" the Bishop went on. There being none,
he made some of his own, recounting my proposed withdrawal, his
holding me to the promise, and added that he was thoroughly convinced from our various discussions that I was the man for the
place. He called for a vote, saying, "All in favor of the proposition,
please raise your right hands," and boosted his own high. The
response was overwhelming. "Those of a contrary mind," the word-
ing went, at which seven hands were raised. "The ayes have it,"
said Bishop Fish, whereupon President Smith, as leader of the opposition proposed that the aye vote be made unanimous, and it
carried.

Thrilling indeed was the first count of two hundred to seven, yet
the responsibility implied—and the touching confidence of membership—produced a feeling of profound humility I had never known
before. With such wholehearted support, however, further
amplified by the minority's spontaneous action to make it unanimous, I could not—must not—fail. My inward vows to that end were
never more solemn. On adjournment, President Smith was among
the first of many to offer congratulations. He had done his duty as
he saw it, which I admired, and I told him as much.

The decks were thus cleared for the work at hand. Bishop Fish
pointed out various weak spots in the organization and procedures,
but gave me wide latitude in the selection of new personnel and
other measures designed to improve the school. To fill positions of
first and second counselors, I chose Brother Ira Willis of middle age
and young Marshall H. Flake, respectively. Both came from Latter-
Day Saint pioneer families and, it must be said, were genuine,
dependable workers from start to finish. We met time and again on

organizational matters before taking actual charge, thus laying the groundwork for a systematic program which, with thorough preparation, would largely operate itself.

Had we set out to find an issue that would stimulate new interest in the Sunday School, none better could have been found than the controversy surrounding my appointment as superintendent. At our first session the assembly room of the old district schoolhouse was filled to overflowing. Adults and some youngsters who had not been to Sunday School in months seemed curious to see the new regime in action. At least the huge turnout was reassuring and bolstered our hopes that good attendance would continue.

On the premise that preparedness, punctuality, and system are key factors to success, we met with the complete staff fifteen minutes ahead of opening time to make sure the teachers, new and carry-over, were prepared with their lessons and other assignments. Ushers took charge of seating arrangements by classes, and all was in readiness to convene sharply on schedule. Although an opening statement was in order, expressing gratification for the large turnout and inviting suggestions for betterment of the school, we did away with program announcements. Each performer knew when his time came and proceeded without formal notice. Hymnbooks were distributed in advance and collected at the close. Song numbers were posted in the order sung. And thus clicked off the twenty-minute program in general assembly.

Separation for class work was signaled by the organist, who followed with march music for each class in planned sequence. Our three-man superintendency rotated in classroom visits, making mental notes for discussion at the regular Thursday night teachers' meeting and lending our moral support. Reassembly for the final song and closing prayer was also accomplished on the minute and without verbal announcement. Our first attempt had been a success beyond expectation and laid the groundwork for a most interesting fifteen months of progress in an atmosphere of cooperation and goodwill.

Our most important function to assure complete preparedness for the following Sunday was the Thursday night teachers' meeting.

Here we called upon each teacher to discuss the church prescribed lesson for his or her class and the manner in which it was to be conducted. Class participation was stressed over the less desirable teacher's monologue, the fruits of which were soon apparent in stimulated interest and better order. The preliminary fifteen-minute session just prior to opening Sunday School served as a last-minute check on program readiness, and, once these procedures were well established, rarely was any staff member late or unprepared.

No originality is claimed for the principles involved. The important thing was carrying them out to the letter and on time. This took constant leadership and drive. Returning from an extended absence in the spring of 1912, I was pleased to find that the two counselors had carried on at their usual high level of excellence and that every phase of school management was in good working order. First Counselor Willis has long since passed away, but his memory is revered by all who knew him. Second Counselor Flake has been an active church worker throughout his life, which includes serving as tourist guide at the Mesa Temple. He resigned in the fall of 1912 to fill a church mission in the Netherlands and was replaced by another young man, Burton R. Smith. The latter, too, has held various church positions through the years, including the important role of president of the Flagstaff Stake.

If asked today what has been my most interesting experience over long years of public service, I would have to say superintending the Snowflake Sunday School. A certain wholesome spirit permeated the organization and our best efforts were generously rewarded in the satisfaction that accompanies a job felt to be well done. Moving away to enter the Forest Service in January 1913, my resignation naturally followed. Our annual report for the year 1912 was read in the next stake conference by none other than President Samuel F. Smith, who elaborated at some length upon its format, thoroughness, and the favorable statistics it contained. When he held us up as a model for the other wards to shoot at, our gratification swelled to the bursting point. We had done our best and not altogether in vain.

CHAPTER NINE

Seventeen Years in the Forest Service

My first two offers of a position, as a result of passing the ranger's examination, were declined. One came from the Carson National Forest in northern New Mexico, the other from Supervisor Harold Green of the Tusayan (now Kaibab) in Arizona. The new supervisor of the Sitgreaves at Snowflake, Charles H. Jennings, had told me a new position was soon to be set up on the Sitgreaves forest, which I could have as soon as it came through. Otherwise, I would have accepted the Tusayan appointment out in the Williams area, where as a teenager I became somewhat familiar with the lay of the land.

Although civil service records show it as the twelfth, I took the oath of office January 13, 1913, as assistant forest ranger attached to the Sitgreaves National Forest at a salary of eleven hundred dollars per annum. A field auditor with a southern accent was present. He was going over the books in the Snowflake office. Never have I forgotten his comment when the oath was completed. It ran: "Boy, you've got more nerve than I have. The year 1913 is bad enough, but the thirteenth of the month for such a step is unthinkable so far as I am concerned." Had it been on Friday the thirteenth instead of Monday, no doubt he would have "stood in bed." Despite our friend's misgivings, however, it marked the beginning of seventeen years with Uncle Sam's Forest Service, working on five different forests of the Southwest in capacities from assistant ranger to forest supervisor, with no apparent ill-effects from a spooky takeoff.

My first assignment was acting district ranger for three months on the Park district, with headquarters at Willow Wash Station, twenty-five miles southwest of Snowflake. The incumbent, Osmer D. Flake, had been granted leave of absence for the period. I sold my interest in the hay-baling partnership to John Ramsey and used the proceeds to purchase saddle horses, riding equipment, and supplies. A miserable wintry day was spent with a hired team and wagon moving the family and personal effects out to the ranger station in late January. Muddy roads and an uphill drag made travel slow and arduous. The horses, to say nothing of us, were nearing exhaustion upon arrival around 9 P.M., and what little enthusiasm Mrs. Kartchner might have held for the new venture had about reached the vanishing point.

The one-bedroom house wasn't much, but was tight and comfortable. We were used to coal-oil lamps and no running water, the latter being drawn from a shallow well with a wooden trough alongside for the animals. A log barn lay fifty yards from the house, complete with stables, hay mow, and train room, a pleasant spectacle for a worn-out team. The two small children were no worse for wear. Merle was three-and-a-half years old and curious to know what it was all about. A little brother, Lindsey Vernon, at five months of age, took it all in stride. We got to bed by midnight after a strenuous day for man and beast.

Learning on the Job

Once settled at Willow Wash Ranger Station, I began studying maps and records of the Park district—named for Phoenix Park ten miles to the southwest—and riding its ninety thousand acres to become familiar with the country and what it contained. What a great treat it was to be back on the range. What I had been looking forward to was now a reality, this time in a role more important than just "turning a cow." I visited the few ranchers, mostly old acquaintances who were not spending the winter in town and got their ideas, and some complaints, on Forest Service regulations then in force. The one thing that impressed me most was the consensus of opposition to the government "coming in and telling us how to run our business." Of course, this meant their having to secure grazing permits for their livestock on forest range, and paying a nominal fee per head, with "nosy" rangers around checking cattle by brands against permits on file.

The service was still young, and the Sitgreaves was not alone in having to cope with this adverse sentiment. All over the West, pioneer stockmen had long enjoyed free use of public rangelands, making understandable their resentment against regulation in any form. As early as 1891, Congress authorized the setting up of forest reserves under the General Land Office of the Department of the Interior. Many were established in following years, but, for lack of personnel, they were administered largely on paper, with little or no effect on the ground.

In 1905 the reserves were changed to national forests and transferred to the Department of Agriculture. The Forest Service was given full bureau status and charged with management of the national forest system for "its most productive use for the permanent good of the whole people." Funds were appropriated for an effective field organization to carry out rules and regulations promulgated by the secretary of agriculture, which, by authority of Congress, had the force and effect of law. Their enforcement had been so long delayed, however, that timber operators, livestock graziers, and other users treated them as a joke. Not until the cowpuncher-type ranger appeared on the scene, and several major trespass cases had been upheld by the courts, did stockmen, for instance, begin to realize that the grazing regulations were here to stay and had to be observed.

Many sore spots remained, however, and vast numbers of excess cattle, horses, and sheep were yet to be removed from heavily overgrazed forest ranges, including the Sitgreaves. For the Park district, whose primary use was grazing at that time, the picture began to clear as contacts were made and the permittees' viewpoint considered in light of case histories on file. For cattle and horses, the grazing year began April 1, by which date all permits were to be issued, with letters of transmittal to accompany the payment of fees. This meant the taking of applications by March 15, a tremendous undertaking in so short a time for an inexperienced ranger.

Using two borrowed saddle horses and two of my own, well fed and shod, I rode the district rain or shine, checking topography with the map, and all livestock found by brands and earmarks. Knowledge of the country and data thus gathered were invaluable at application time, when every phase of each man's status as a grazing permittee was discussed. Some applicants were cooperative, some indifferent, while others were clearly hostile to the whole procedure, bemoaning the fact that we no longer lived in a free country. For a raw recruit, however, my first two months in the Forest Service were crammed with responsibility and action such as to bring about the earliest possible understanding of the district and its problems. Before it was over, I suspected Ranger Flake of timing his leave partly to miss the grazing application season, although I was benefactor in experience gained.

For a clear understanding of the somewhat chaotic grazing situation on forest land at this time, and the strained relations between its users and the federal government, one must go back to the initiation of regulated control. Because they ran in herds, sheep were no problem to count. Cattle and horses, however, ran at large, and, for lack of fencing or other means of control, their numbers were difficult to ascertain. In either case, a call was made for all users to declare the size of their outfits as a basis for prior-use recognition, the top scale of *preference* classification. (No actual *rights* have ever been recognized.) A liberal deadline was set, after which all stock not so declared and placed under permit was considered in trespass.

Sheepmen, readily vulnerable to accurate counts on the ground, were quick to see the writing on the wall. In many cases they over-declared their numbers to provide leeway for increases, whereas certain cow outfits turned in far fewer numbers than were actually grazed in order to hold down fees, in the belief that the service would be none the wiser. But a day of reckoning was inevitable as they might have known, yet learned to regret.

By 1913 on the Park district, sheep permits for summer months had been pared down to actual use and a good start made on ridding the range of excess or unpermitted cattle and horses. Pool roundups—always the rule on unfenced range—were attended by the ranger, who tallied all animals gathered, whether turned loose after branding, as in the case of calves, or retained for market. Seasonal cowboy help was provided in case of need. Sanitary Board shipping records were copied at the railroad in Holbrook as a check against roundup data and acceptable ratios set up between yearling steers sold and the approximate total numbers remaining in a given brand.

With such data at hand, owners were required to remove stock in excess of their permits after payment of damages, as long as forest boundaries were properly posted, even though unfenced. All these and other measures were taken as preliminary steps toward sound range management that called for equitable distribution of the grazing privilege within limits of the forage resource. Cowmen who turned in low figures for prior-use status found themselves disposing, in some instances, of half their cattle—mother cows and all—in order to come within numbers for which they had been recognized. Having agreed in advance to this procedure, and since the range was still considered overstocked, they were left without recourse.

Concurrent with these events came the removal of wild horses from forest and outside ranges. Following the disastrous drouth and resultant cattle die-off of 1903–4, King Brothers, in cooperation with known owners and the State Sanitary Board, systematically gathered and shipped out thousands of these worthless animals to eastern soap factories. They infested ranges from the Mogollon Rim to the Little Colorado, and from the White Mountains to Flagstaff. Their ultimate extermination was indispensable to a stable livestock economy and of great assistance to the Forest Service in reducing the drain on its lands to authorized use.

From Willow Wash to Lincoln

Ranger Flake returned from leave in mid-April, necessitating our moving from Willow Wash to the Lincoln guard station five miles southwest on the head of Decker Wash. Other than a good horse pasture and telephone communication—through a mine-set metal instrument attached to a pine tree—the place was unimproved. We lived in an improvised box tent and cooked on a campfire. Incidentally, those who have never eaten "frijole" beans buried overnight in a bed of coals, or Dutch-oven beefsteaks and biscuits, have been sadly neglected.

Our immediate project was construction of a forty-five-foot pole tower at Deer Spring Lookout three miles east by trail on the Mogollon Rim. The family stayed in town. Charles H. Kissam, forest engineer from New York, and Pennsylvania-born Lynn Henderson, ranger on the Show Low District, camped with me. We from Lincoln and Ranger Flake from Willow Wash rode horseback to and from work each day. Tools, bolts and nails, and platform lumber were packed in. Handy pole material was felled, peeled, and snaked into position by saddle horn. Kissam had completed a one-hundred-foot structure at Promontory Butte on the Chevalon District and knew his wooden towers. We find him again in the narrative nine years later on the Manzano Forest of New Mexico.

No sooner was the job finished in May than the fire season began. My role that first summer was a combination lookout, smoke chaser, and telephone lineman—always by horseback, seven days a week. A normal run would be to arrive at the tower by 8 A.M., scan the country for smokes and report to Flake by phone. If all was clear, I worked on painting the tower, smoothing ground for a cabin, or trail maintenance—all in hearing distance of the telephone, interspersed with frequent tower observations. In case of smoke in our area, according to its location, either Flake went directly to it or came to the tower while I handled it.

Such limited manpower and transportation for controlling forest fires on a ponderosa pine area of that size would be totally inadequate today. At that time, however, the stands were open as a result of natural and Indian burning of ground cover through the centuries. Only tolerant trees matured, and dense thickets of young pines were rare exceptions to the rule. Therefore, fires that started seldom got off the ground and burned mostly grass and weeds at a slow pace. Effective fire control had been practiced less than a decade, during which pine seedlings gained in mass survival but were still too young and thinly spaced to influence the status quo. Under these conditions, one man with a take-down rake and hoe (specially designed for carrying on horseback) and an axe could extinguish the average spot fire within the Class A limit of one-fourth acre. If delayed in reaching it, or in case of high wind, he might not be able to control it before midnight, or under five to ten acres of burn, but such cases were infrequent, and little or no damage was done to standing timber. Control meant raking a fire line to mineral soil around the perimeter and the felling of any dead snags burning inside. Back firing from the line was often possible and most effective.

Our most critical hazard came (and still does) in June, just prior to the somewhat uncertain rainy season. High winds blew up storm clouds accompanied by "dry" lightning that struck tall trees by the hundreds. Dead ones usually ignited at the base, and we had a lightning fire. Arrangements were made with certain ranchers to meet this emergency. They were connected by telephone and furnished fire tools, and their horses stood by, saddled for instant use. Secondary lookouts, including Deer Spring, were manned around the clock to augment the primary system and furnish additional cross readings in locating smokes on the map forestwide.

Working under a fire chief at Snowflake, district rangers remained in constant touch with the lookouts and directed operations within their districts. On one or more peak days at this critical time, as many as one hundred smoke reports were turned in, after allowance for duplicates. On our district, six or eight fires burned at the same time. I went to the nearest from Lincoln, while Flake sent men to others. Flying sparks from high, daytime winds made suppression difficult, but they usually subsided by nightfall, giving fighters a chance to comb their lines. In some cases, mop-up crews were sent back next morning before the wind came up to make sure there were no break-overs.

In this fashion we struggled along, making the best of available manpower and facilities until the July rains brought welcome relief. It had been a hectic first fire season for me. When not on fires, there were always stretches of telephone line to be maintained. So much depended upon this means of communication that it had to be kept in working order. In case of a break—which occurred frequently in periods of high wind and lightning—my job was to drop everything else, find it and make the splice. On excellent pasture and heavily grained, my two horses were well ridden down after thirty-five straight days on one or the other activity.

The original ground-circuit telephone line has long since been replaced, but, like the Model-T, it served its purpose. A single No. 9 wire was strung loosely the full length of the forest in the pine belt below and roughly parallel to, the Mogollon Rim, with laterals connecting the various stations and lookouts. Except for an occasional pole in an opening, the line was anchored to live trees by means of five or six swinging insulators to one solid. Enough slack was thus provided to prevent breakage, which in most cases was from falling timber or swaying anchor trees in a strong wind.

Becoming a "tree" lineman from scratch was tough and scary business as I learned working alone on the spring overhaul of some twenty miles of line. We had good equipment—climbers with double-length spurs for heavy pine bark, leather belt and long wraparound strap, pliers, cutters, splicers, wire stretcher, and a test-set telephone. Adding wire, an axe, insulators, brackets, a hammer, and spike nails to the saddle with a man aboard presented a monstrosity that only the gentlest of horses would tolerate.

Climbing a large limbless pine tree with spurs and belt is an art by itself that must be carefully observed if one values his neck. You first splice the bracer, or wraparound, belt with wire to a length that permits standing out from the tree so the spurs will hold firm. Then you make sure it is fastened solidly to the main belt at both ends around the tree and keep it so. You flip it up the opposite side, lean back for tension, climb to that limit, ease tension, and flip again, repeating until the desired height is reached. Sounds simple, but try it sometime!

My first lesson on big trees came the hard way. The climb was made without incident, but in working on the connection my knees gradually moved so close to the tree that both spurs cut out, leaving me dangling thirty feet in the air, with a couple of cracked ribs and a skinned-up face thrown in. Our telephone manual cautioned against such an error, but it took the real thing for it to sink in. And, if you think it easy to get back in correct posture from a snug position against a three-foot heavy-barked pine tree—held tight by your weight on the belt—you might try that also. Coming down, the belt flips and spur steps are in reverse, of course, but the whole procedure is routine with practice.

This all took place in the spring and summer of 1913. Over half a century later, there is now no such thing as the Park district, or Willow Wash Ranger Station. The pine belt has largely been cut over. Roads and truck trails are everywhere and horsemen seldom seen. Blackjack (young ponderosa pine) thickets have invaded former openings to the extent that one who knew "every rock and tree" fifty years ago is now lost and bewildered by the change.

Two-way radios are replacing the telephone; helicopters put trained men on fires within minutes; various chemicals extinguish spot fires before they can spread. But still and all, once a fire starts in this dense young growth—mostly germinated from the bumper 1919 seed crop—it crowns at once and destroys everything before it. Such tremendous heat is generated that a frontal attack is impossible, all vegetation is consumed to the deepest root systems, and the soil rendered sterile for years to come—a pretty bleak picture after a half century of total fire protection as Forest Service policy.

Nature does its own thinning, even without fire, but it takes fifty to seventy-five years of high hazard for weakling yellow pines to die out and make room for saw timber to mature. In addition, periodic ground fires speed up the process, perhaps overdo it here and there, as part of the general scheme. At least eminent foresters are taking a hard look at artificial, light burning as a better practice than all our fire intolerance. Experiments on Fort Apache Indian Reservation have already shown promising results. There is also the possibility of utilizing thinnings as pulp material in such plants as the new paper mill west of Snowflake.

District Ranger

Rains were sufficient in July to soak up forest litter and leave us free for normal administrative duties. As Flake's assistant, I rode the west half of the district, meeting appointments with permittees, checking cattle and horses, counting sheep under short-term permits, maintaining telephone lines and pasture fences, and so forth. The two of us alternated riding with the fall cattle roundup, and here is where disgruntled owners and hands aired their gripes, mostly at Forest Service grazing regulations, but in fact, at any form of control over the ranges. Such campfire discussions were valuable, however, in covering at grassroots the pros and cons of forest administration.

On a biweekly trip to town for mail and supplies, Supervisor Jennings made known the impending transfer of Ranger Flake to the Show Low District and his desire that I take over the park. Nothing could have pleased me more, being already familiar with the district and its problems. My move with the family back to Willow Wash to assume with a great deal of enthusiasm the heavier responsibilities of district ranger followed in October. We thrilled at the outlook in a profession I loved and in whose objectives I sincerely believed. Under civil service rules the appointment became permanent and cleared the way for investing in additional horses, a milk cow, furniture, and other needed equipment.

Good horses were a must. Grazing was the principal forest use and called for a cowboy ranger equipped to ride abreast of stockmen and their hands, to keep current on conditions throughout the district, attend all roundups, and, in fact, to make a hand himself, short of interference with counts and records. Eastern forestry school rangers had been found sadly out of place in these circumstances, which set the stage for employing western frontiersmen without college degrees but schooled in the lore of the open range.

A case in point comes to mind. A certain cattle permittee, suspected of running excess stock and other violations, gave me a somewhat colored description of his outfit and how he handled it "for the good of the range." When asked diplomatically where he thought I had been all this time, his reply was something for the book. He said, "You know, what we need here is a ranger like the first one they sent out. I came by here one day looking for a small bunch of cattle and asked if he had seen them. As he went to the well for a bucket of water, he said that a short time before he had seen two—a 'sorrel' and a 'bay'—which turned out to be his own milk cows!" He referred to a forestry graduate by the name of Campbell, whom I never met, but I understood he later found his niche in timber management.

In addition to an excellent pasture of three hundred acres at Willow Wash, the service allotted the Park district grain and usually a good grade of oats, sufficient year long for the two ranger-owned horses. With permission, I chose to furnish four to six horses, ration the grain between them according to seasonal need, and thereby have fresh mounts at all times capable of hard service, plus a buggy team for road travel. Only mountain horses raised here, or at least having sound "rock" feet, were selected for this rough country. Using a "clabber-footed" horse (raised on soft ground) in rocky country is dangerous to the horse and the rider, whereas one raised in the rocks will negotiate the roughest terrain at any speed with amazing skill.

My three best horses grew up wild along the Mogollon Rim. They were captured young and partially gentled by the time of purchase. With their training finished on hard riding and only the best of care, they developed into ideal cow horses for duty on their home ground and were the envy of neighborhood stockmen and cowboys. Two were bays, the third brown. Called "Browny," the latter was a real pet, although fiery in action and quick as a cat. His liking for Merle (during ages five through seven) was mutual and unique. If she got close to his hind legs he simply turned around carefully and nudged her with his nose, all the while uttering a purrlike snort of affection. We all loved him for it.

For the next year and a half we remained at Willow Wash. In many respects, administering the Park ranger district was the most interesting and enjoyable segment of my Forest Service career. There were many problems, complaints, and long working hours, but on the whole, good progress was made toward amicable relations with the local forest users. Gradually, they realized the service was here to stay, that its regulations were fair and sound, and in fact the only means by which the grazing privilege could be administered equitably and in perpetuity—within their carrying capacity— on unfenced community ranges.

As time allowed, I continued studying forestry and related subjects for a broader concept of the work at hand and nationwide. Included was the collection of a district herbarium containing specimens of two hundred representative plants—trees, shrubs, grasses, grasslike plants and weeds—to be found there. Of three specimens gathered of each plant in flowering season and cured in presses of service issue, one went to the supervisor and another to the Washington office for identification. With the returns came such economic notes as were available, along with Latin and common names.

While one or two species had no record of previous discovery, I do not recall a botanical-board name suffixed with "Kartchner!" Yet the collection and processing of each specimen, followed by official identification, enabled me to remember through the years practically every name—generic, specific, and common. It also stimulated an incentive to identify and memorize any strange species encountered on four other forests of the Southwest where I served. The knowledge thus gained was of incalculable value in grazing, wildlife, and timber administration.

One main difference between a lettered botanist and a memorizer of individual plants was amply illustrated some years later in association with Dr. W. W. Eggleston of the Bureau of Plant Industry. We were on a pack trip over the Mt. Taylor division of the former Manzano National Forest in about 1924. Its flora is almost identical with northern Arizona forests. Whereas I could name the genera and species of all trees, most shrubs, nearly all grasses, and many other plants found, the doc could identify the order, family, subfamily, a few genera, but rarely the species. He determined the genera and species by microscopic examination of dissected material and found the "key" that fit a given species from reference books carried in the field.

Complimentary, yet embarrassing, was Dr. Eggleston's direct question early on the trip as to where I majored for a degree. A hobby was paying off, but there was no degree, no knowledge of keys, very little of the minute parts of plants, just the knowledge of whole plants, their corresponding identifications, whether poisonous to livestock or good feed, and whether of other ecological importance. Perhaps its greatest value lay in spotting the earmarks of overgrazing, the succession of worthless plants where valuable species once flourished, and other factors that form the basis for administrative action. Eggleston's interest was botanical science per se, mine, the practical application of plant familiarity on the national forests of the Southwest.

Make Your Horse Do It

Along with other cowpuncher rangers, as much of my work as possible was done on horseback. Most homestead and pasture fences were provided with wooden gates with hoop fasteners at road entrances. A horse with normal sense can soon be trained to sidle up while the rider removes the hoop, walk around the open end and back up on the opposite side while the hoop is replaced. Some rated it downright laziness, but just the same it eliminated dismounting and easily cut the go-through time in half.

The biggest saving in time and effort came in running section lines. A horse, measured at a given gait, will actually pace more accurately than a man. First, a standard 4-rod (22-yard) Gunter chain is laid full length on the ground. With a walking start, the horse is ridden from one end to the other several times at a fast walk to determine the average number of paces he takes to the chain. If an odd number, say 25 paces, one must count them all. If an even number, like 14 or 26, you need only count one front foot 12 or 13 times, as the case may be, and punch a tally register for each chain.

Thus equipped, one rider to the nearest known section corner gets his compass bearing as far out as he can see, horse-pace the distance, take another bearing, and repeat the process as needed to tie in the object of his mission. It might be a special-use pasture, a stock tank or corral, none of which requires the precision of a chained survey. Another advantage was that on a horse one can often see twice as far as his focal point from the ground. He simply projects the line of sight and keeps going.

One particular incident illustrates this time-saving procedure. Lynn Henderson and I came to an unsurveyed township midway between its north and south boundaries. We needed to locate the section corner six miles due east of that point in gently rolling country. Taking bearings at about one-mile intervals, and knowing my horse's pace count per chain, we came out on course within two chains of the corner, all in two hours' time, or about one-fourth what it would have taken men on foot.

Another case in point is the reliability of a mountain horse in heavy snow. During the winter of 1915–16 our main-trunk telephone line was down somewhere west of Willow Wash. Ranger Clark Owens was holding down the station alone while I did duty in the supervisor's office. Eight to twelve inches of snow lay on the ground and the idea struck Clark to use a pair of bear-paw snowshoes that hung on the wall—purely for ornamental purposes—in repairing the break. Aside from his inexperience with snowshoes, there were several fat saddle horses at his disposal, but he was curious as to whether the snowshoes were of practical use under southwestern conditions. Certainly, they were in common use up Michigan way where all foresters traveled on foot.

Accordingly, he loaded himself down with telephone wire and equipment, donned the bear-paws and struck out. Mile after mile he trudged, expecting to find the break any minute. When he saw his mistake it was too late to turn back. At about eight miles out the break was found and repaired. Almost totally exhausted and sore all over, he longed for any one of those fat horses, wondered seriously if he had strength left to make it back, and cursed the maker of the so-and-so bear-paws.

Next morning calls came to the office from points west of the break, but no one answered at Willow Wash. By midafternoon we were considering sending someone out to investigate when Owens finally called in. He had barely been able to reach the station, far into the night, so utterly worn out that nothing disturbed his slumber for the next twelve hours. For a week he nursed blisters and sore muscles before being able to laugh with jokesters about the snowshoe experiment. But two things were sure. His curiosity had been satisfied, albeit the hard way, and his love of a good horse was enhanced tenfold.

A. O. Waha of the Albuquerque regional forester's office made an inspection of the Park district in the spring of 1915, principally of the Willow Wash Station, its files and records. His tour of duty covered inspection of one ranger district on each of the fourteen national forests of Arizona and New Mexico, to bring about uniform practices, in the office and the field. This inspection, by a man eminently qualified, gave me a broader picture of the service as a whole, of its aims and objectives in the national scheme. For lack of other accommodations, he ate and lodged at the station under a mandatory rate schedule during the four or five days involved.

Fortunately, although not by design, I had spent a lot of time setting up a new set of files in strict accordance with the service filing scheme. Day after day during inclement weather of the previous winter, papers were scattered in piles about the office according to classification. Material of the same designation had been filed in half a dozen different places, folders were dirty and torn, labels illegible, and no attention given to chronological sequence, or outdated correspondence.

When the job was finished there were two sets of files, current and closed, in new metal cases, new guides and folders throughout—requisitioned from the supervisor's office—filing by date in each folder from back to front, and typed labels done on the old-fashioned

Oliver No. 5. In addition, all material over three years old, of no reference or historical value, had been destroyed. The overall result placed at fingertips any document or case history since the forest was created. Incidentally, an old Washington circular among the contents bemoaned the increasing "paperwork" in the Forest Service, stating that it must be cut down in favor of more productive activities. In real fact, paperwork and red tape have steadily increased from that day to this, and no change is expected.

When Inspector Waha's mimeographed report came out, with copies for all supervisors and districts, I ran through it with some anxiety. While his comments were not all favorable, he extolled the perfection of the files and records in superlative terms, suggesting that all districts follow this lead toward greater efficiency in the transaction of forest business. Among unfavorable items were substandard headquarter improvements for lack of appropriations and faulty outdoor plumbing to be corrected without additional funds. Outside of grazing, where the inspector had little experience, his many constructive criticisms benefited my administration of the district. A. O. Waha transferred later to the Washington office of Forester Henry S. Graves (1910–20).

Deputy Supervisor

As action was completed on grazing applications in the spring of 1915, notice came that I had been selected as fire chief for the ensuing season. While I appreciated the honor, it would disrupt certain personal plans based upon remaining in the field, not to mention some misgivings as to how older rangers in years and service might react to my leadership. Such fears were largely groundless, however, as I found the entire force cooperative at all times, ready and willing to carry out orders typical of a firefighting organization. By comparison with some others, it was not a severe fire season.

During slack periods, I was given administrative work in the supervisor's office that served to broaden my understanding of the purposes and problems of the forest as a whole. By mid-July, the fire season over, I began thinking about moving back to the Park district, but each time there was a noticeable reluctance on the part of Supervisor Jennings to discuss the matter. As time went by, more and more of the daily flow of business came over my desk, and I began wondering about such an indefinite situation. Then when he took a field trip, leaving me in charge as acting supervisor, I could only surmise that perhaps my days as district ranger were undergoing a countdown.

I loved those days, the backwoods, the range country, good horses and equipment with which to keep constantly abreast of conditions throughout the district, and with just enough paperwork for a desirable balance between office and field. Moreover, living expenses were much less than in town, what with rent-free quarters, an excellent pasture for horses and milk cows, keeping a few chickens, a hog, and so forth. It became more ideal with the purchase in June of a new 1915 Model-T Ford, which did away with horse and buggy transportation for mail and supplies, pleasure trips, and social activities, and cut the time involved to less than one-third.

Then one day the word came. I was being appointed deputy forest supervisor. Jennings explained it had been hanging fire several months in Washington, but he had chosen not to divulge his recommendation for fear of its disapproval and my disappointment. In reality, I would have preferred the status quo. The few hundred dollars increase in salary fell short of the difference in living expenses and, of more importance, was small inducement to giving up range life for the more confining office routine. But it meant advancement in the service and was so accepted. Many times I have wondered if a lifetime career as district ranger would not have been better in the long run than to accept the various promotions and moves as they came along.

Ample time was given to clean up district odds and ends, dispose of animals and equipment no longer needed, and move the family to Snowflake by late fall of 1915. Partial familiarity with the supervisor's office came with the duties of fire chief, but now my responsibilities were so much heavier that for months, overtime and hard study were necessary to keep up with them. This proved valuable in view of rather frequent changes in supervisors that followed. Each new supervisor involved a get-acquainted period, office and field, during which the deputy must carry the office load, so that in time there was hardly a permit or other transaction on the forest with whose background and current status I was not conversant.

Charlie Jennings resigned in 1916 to take the Ford auto agency in Holbrook. His replacement was the genial, hard-working, technical forester from the Albuquerque regional office, Paul P. Pitchlynn. "Pitch," as he was known throughout the service, was so anxious to make good on his first forest that overwork, worry, and loss of sleep brought him to the brink of a nervous breakdown. Especially annoying were the numerous small fires that broke out from the dry lightning that June. He could envision the whole forest going up in smoke, and it was hard to convince him that in order to give one's utmost to the fire effort health-impairing worries must be shunted aside. I pondered my own future in this regard, resolving to guard against responsibility getting me down no matter how difficult its fulfillment.

Forest Users of Note

I recall several people, whom I met in the course of performing the official duties of a district ranger, who characterized the typical forest user. Zechariah B. Decker was one such sturdy pioneer who helped make the settlement of northern Arizona against odds of Apaches and outlaws. His ranch on the Day Wash lay two miles west of Willow Wash Station, where he, a widower, and his youngest son, Silas, aged nineteen, headquartered in their operation of some five hundred head of permitted cattle branded Quarter Circle Z. That was in 1913–14. In the 1880s Decker had grazed a band of sheep over the same area under something more than precarious circumstances.

One morning in December 1914, Decker rode to the station on forest business. A violent blizzard came up, so I stabled his horse and insisted he wait it out. The business over, we had lunch and discussed various topics of the day while the storm increased its fury. Despite his personal dignity that all grownups respected, I recall how the old gentleman enjoyed Merle's blunt informalities. Aged five, she was not one to shirk her responsibilities as a member of the ranger team.

At one point she gushed: "Say, Decker, do you know how to get to Heber?" (fifteen miles west by road). "Come here and I'll show you on this map" [of the Sitgreaves Forest]. He complied with a broad grin, listening carefully to her minute description of the alleged route and asking questions to make sure he would not get off on the wrong road. Little could she know that Z. B. Decker knew every road, trail, rock, and tree for fifty miles around, having run sheep and cattle there for the past thirty years, on horseback and on foot, all of which brings us down to the real highlights of his visit.

Gazing out the window at a spot near the well, he said, "I'll never forget the night of August 10, 1888. My tent was right there (pointing) and the sheep were bedded down close by. Lying in bed about 10 o'clock, I heard horsemen approaching. They halted and one called out, 'Decker!' I said, 'What do you want?' He said, 'There's gonna be sumpn doin' up the draw, come and go along.' I said, 'No. I'd rather not.' He said, 'Well, then, mum's the word.' I said, 'All right,' and they rode on to the Stott Ranch" [three miles south of the station, later (1914) owned by the well-respected, part Indian, George Bailey].

In a moment of stupidity I asked, "Who was it?" When the old fellow just stared out the window and said nothing, it dawned on me that this was the question he had been asked many times in vain. Mum's the word. All right. He had given his word, never to be broken. My uncle John A. Hunt went to Decker's bedside shortly before he died in 1939 and asked if he might be willing to divulge the names of those in the posse, now that all were presumed dead and gone. The answer was still, "No, I gave my word."

To break the tension, I hastened to ask other questions about the hanging on August 11, 1888, of James W. Stott, James Scott, and Billy (some say Jeff) Wilson on the Mogollon Rim southwest of Stott's ranch. His answers coincided substantially with details that may now be found in Forrest's book, *Arizona's Dark and Bloody Ground*, chapter 15. But to get the story from Z. B. Decker, so nearly an eyewitness, yet who seldom talked about it, was of special interest to me. He came directly to each point, using no extraneous verbiage, the easier for one to remember almost word for word what he said on this and other events to follow.

James W. (Jimmy) Stott "never did wrong in his life," went one version of the story of this young adventurer from Massachusetts. Another, "He was a horse thief." Still another, "He never stole horses himself, but was careless about the true ownership of those purchased from rustlers." There can be no doubt that he came from a good family, had a charming personality, and enjoyed the friendship of many upstanding citizens. But the following incident, as told by Z. B. Decker himself that snowy afternoon, leaves no doubt about Stott and his shady horse business.

"A bay mare of mine had been missing for several days," Decker said. "I suspected something wrong and dropped by Stott's place to inquire if he had seen her. He had not but was courteous as usual and invited me to stay all night. It was late and my horse was tired so I accepted. After a good supper we talked awhile, during which something told me he knew more about the mare than his gracious manners would indicate. He finally said he was going to leave early for the River (Holbrook) next morning, but for me to make myself at home and get up whenever I felt like it. This made me all the more suspicious, but I remained nonchalant. We retired early and both pretended to sleep soundly.

"About 3 A.M. Stott got up, ate a snack while his horse munched grain, saddled up, and rode off. I was wide awake but faked otherwise until the coast was clear. Just at the peep of day I took the trail which led down the wagon road half a mile or so, as if headed for the 'River'. Instead, the fresh horse tracks bore off to the left, around the north base of a knoll opposite the ranch. Soon I came upon fresh sign where a horse had stood for some time in a clump of trees. Boot tracks told me Stott had dismounted to untie the animal, and two sets of horse tracks from that point on explained why he started so early for the 'River'.

"I followed as fast as trailing allowed, west and south around the Knoll, up over the Mogollon Rim and beyond to the Deer Spring corral. Sure enough, there stood my mare inside with the bars up! I led her directly back to the ranch where Stott was standing in the yard, having returned by another route. 'Well, you found the mare,' he said, trying not to show embarrassment. 'Where did you find her?' he went on. 'Right where you left her. I wasn't far behind you all the way,' I told him."

Whether additional words passed between them, I cannot recall his saying, nor whether any legal action was taken or contemplated. But to meet the problem in such head-on fashion was a Decker trait, and it seems likely he would at least have given Stott some rather pointed advice. When the incident occurred is not certain, but thought to have been prior to September 4, 1886, when Sheriff Commodore Owens killed three and wounded another of the so-called Blevins gang in Holbrook. Allegedly, Stott had some connection with the gang and no doubt took fewer chances following that tragic event. Certainly, the next incident came before, since Andy Cooper was one of those killed.

The Pleasant Valley War was in full swing. Andy Cooper, a partisan of the Graham faction, had killed a Navajo sheepherder among others of the Tewksbury clan and was considered deadly and ruthless. Asked if he knew Cooper personally, Z. B. Decker had this to say: "I knew him all too well. One day I was riding along near Phoenix Park with my rifle across in front of me, when I saw a horseman partly concealed behind a tree. He seemed surprised when I yelled, 'Come on out, Andy.' Slowly we rode toward each other. At closer range Cooper said, 'Decker, how is it that you Mormons at Snowflake and Taylor lay it onto us whenever your horses come up missing?' I replied, 'When you quit stealing them we will stop accusing you.' He went on to say he personally had been blamed for a lot of things he didn't do. 'But,' he said, 'I did kill that Navajo, and I'll show you just how I did it,' making a grab for my gun! I jerked it out of his reach, held it directly on him, and said, 'Oh, no you don't. You're not showing me how you killed *anybody*, Andy!' (I had purposely kept him on the muzzle side just in case.)

The ruse having failed, and finding himself covered, he made a sheepish attempt to say that he meant no harm, which, of course, was not so. I told him to get on his way, not to try any funny business, and I watched him until he was out of sight."

My memory ends here of just what Z. B. Decker told me about the incident. However, his son Silas is authority for these additional items. His father shot at a squirrel a few minutes before spying Cooper behind the tree. After they separated, his father rode to the Phoenix Park log cabin and entered with gun in hand. Two Hash Knife hands inside panicked at this sudden intrusion of the man Cooper was supposed to have killed. One was making biscuits while the other played a fiddle, no doubt the latter noise being the reason they had not heard Decker ride up. Silas does not remember their names but says they were probably not in collusion with Cooper.

Regaining their poise, they informed Z. B. that Cooper had been there, but left with the brag he was "going out and get me a Mormon." When they heard the shot at a squirrel, they supposed he had made good his boast. Then when Decker burst in on them, they figured he had killed Cooper instead and was now after them. On the other hand, Decker sensed a conspiracy among them to get rid of him and his sheep and was determined to get to the bottom of it. They denied being parties to any such plot or having anything to do with Cooper except as a passing acquaintance. At any rate, the three reached an amicable understanding.

Decker continued grazing his sheep on government land in an atmosphere of constant peril, which may be noted in two other incidents he related while waiting out the blizzard. His headquarters cabin between the present Gibson and Joel Flake homestead patents on Decker Wash was destroyed by fire in his absence, by outlaws bent upon driving him out. On another occasion several armed horsemen—believed to be the same party—rode up and told him they had come to move his sheep. In his usual forthright manner he said, "Well, there they are; there you are; here I am and here is my gun (the rifle he always carried). When do you expect to start?" They didn't.

It was another case of would-be badmen realizing that if they forced a showdown, even with a four or five-to-one advantage in numbers, one or more of them would likely meet his fate, and none could be sure it would not include himself. The Decker sheep stayed on, but only by the sheer courage of an owner who stood ready to defend his claim of equal rights to the public domain. Born in 1850, he was thirty-seven—give or take—when most of his range troubles took place. That makes him sixty-four at the time of our ranger station visit. He died in 1939, at age eighty-nine, one of my most unforgettable characters.

Johnny Blevins

When I first went with the Forest Service in 1913, Johnny Blevins had a homestead on the Park district. I had known him for a number of years and we were good friends. He was the only male survivor of his family from the Graham-Tewksbury feud, which took place in the late 1880s at Pleasant Valley some seventy miles southwest of Snowflake, and was known as the Pleasant Valley War. It was one of the bloodiest cattle-sheep related feuds of the old West. His father and four brothers died during the war, and he himself was badly wounded in the shoot-out mentioned in chapter 5.

Johnny was a country fiddler, and when Youngblood and I used to play for dances in Holbrook, he often came up and offered to play a change or two of a quadrille while we took a breather. He had even done a stint at the Long H ranch. In fact, my first meeting with Noche, in the fall of 1905, was at Holbrook where he was shipping Long H cattle. Johnny was his cook. He had imbibed too freely at the Pioneer that night and Noche was there trying to persuade him he should go back to camp. A horse for him was among those tied out front, but the last I knew, Johnny was holding out for further delay. Sad memories weighed heavily upon him as the only male survivor of a family that fell victim to circumstances surrounding the Pleasant Valley War, and at times like this he sought to drown them in alcohol. His father, Mart, and two brothers, Hamp and Charlie, were killed at different times in Tonto Basin, the focal locale of that bitter struggle. No wonder Johnny once said to me while in his cups, "Kid, you have no idea what trouble is."

For Johnny's part in the fracas, he remained in the county jail at St. Johns a full year before a grand jury got around to his indictment for assault with intent to commit murder. In September 1888, he was tried and found guilty before Judge James H. Wright and sentenced to five years in the territorial prison at Yuma, none of which he served. Perhaps no other event of the period is shrouded in greater mystery. It appears that Sheriff Owens started for Yuma with his prisoner, taking a Santa Fe train out of Holbrook, only to be handed a telegram from Governor Zulick at Prescott ordering Johnny's release. There is no record of a pardon. Likewise, John Blevins's name does not appear in the Yuma prison records. Forrest suggests the pardon entry might have been lost when the state capitol was moved from Prescott to Phoenix in January 1889, only four months after the pardon, if a pardon it was.

Red Holcomb

Playing for dances around Holbrook and riding for the Long H ranch brought me in contact with a number of aging Hash Knife cowhands. Among them was "Red" Holcomb, who drifted west from his native Kentucky hills in the early 1880s, seeking adventure and fortune. He took no part in the Pleasant Valley War, 1886–1888, but was often in company with those who did. They told me Red owned and was living at historic Phoenix Park, and that is where I found him in March 1913, in the same old log cabin that served for many years as a Hash Knife side camp. Quelling his dogs with a yell that echoed through the pines, he bade me, "Giddown, giddown and come in."

Red held a grazing permit for thirty head of mostly gentle horses. I had ridden the ten miles to get his written application for renewal. Not until it was handed him for signature did I know he was totally illiterate—quite in contrast with a ready flow of cow-country English. A witnessed cross served the purpose and he started din-

ner, which he insisted I stay for. He parboiled pork from the brine
barrel before frying, dipped out biscuit material from his sourdough
keg—replacing the same with stirred flour and water—and ground a
batch of Arbuckle's coffee. Red was not noted for speed or sanita-
tion, but made it up in hospitality.

When the last dish was cleaned, I had been there three hours, had
the lowdown on Red's history, his stories and viewpoints long in the
telling, and was amazed at his wide range of knowledge based
entirely on word-of-mouth information. That he defended the cause
of early outlaws was not surprising, on which I passed no opinion.
My job called for diplomacy toward all remaining factions having to
do with forest use, and in Red's case we became good friends.

To illustrate Red Holcomb's sense of humor, on another occasion I
rode up to his place, his dogs ran out bawling as usual, and he hollered, "Shut up you SOBs. Gittin' to where ya don't give a damn
what ya bark at." When told there was no one home the last time I
came by, he chuckled out, "So, that's what happened to that sack of
potatoes I been missin'." But there was more to it than missing
potatoes.

During heavy snows of December 1914, or perhaps January 1915,
a report came that Red was snowed in, his horse had gotten away,
and his chuck must be running low. Next morning I rode by the
Newman sheep ranch and bought at the commissary twenty-five
pounds of flour, bacon, sugar, coffee, and a plug of chewing
tobacco—about all that could be carried on the saddle—and struck
out for Phoenix Park in a foot of snow that got deeper with each
mile. Over the last three or four miles, heavy drifts were encountered through which no one would ask a horse to carry him except in an emergency. But bay Billy was stout on grain, newly shod,
and did a magnificent job of lunging through them to our destination
and back.

But Red was gone! From all appearances no one had been there
for a week. The cabin door was unlocked as usual and I left the pro-
visions on the table, glad to be rid of their forty pounds. Whoever
brought Red home could read the note that I had been there and
why. The day was clear but cold. Little time was lost starting back

to avoid night crusting of the snow. Retracing our steps with less weight made easier going, yet the round trip covered the toughest twenty miles of my horseback experience in snow. Johnny Blevins and family looked after Red. They had taken him to Winslow for a much needed clean-up and vacation during the heaviest snow, and, of course, when they brought him back they found the groceries and read my note alongside. Thus, Red was all primed when I mentioned my last time there, and his "missing-potatoes" inference was just his way of concealing emotions of gratitude. Likewise, scolding his dogs for carelessness in what they barked at was a symbol of range tradition. Rougher the Joke, Better the Friend.

CHAPTER TEN

The Violin and Public Relations

During his early years as a forest ranger, Kartchner was still at his musical prime. Even when living out at the ranger stations from 1913 to 1915, he found time for fiddling, much of it for family entertainment during the lunch hour, or after the evening chores were done. He was often accompanied on the guitar by his wife, Adlee. Sometimes, they visited people at nearby homesteads and ranches, or friends dropped by the ranger station in the evening and they sang and listened to the fiddle around a huge bonfire. There was also dancing if there were enough for a "square." He played for dances at neighboring ranches and in Snowflake, or other nearby towns, as well.

Of interest to us in more recent times was a practice that developed involving the telephone. The lines strung throughout the area connected various ranches and homesteads as well as the ranger stations. While necessary for the work of the forest, particularly during fire season, the telephone also filled social-information functions as well. A number of telephones were hooked up to a single party line, each identified by a specific set of rings, for example, long-long-short. Whenever people heard the Kartchner ranger station set of rings they would pick up the receiver because they knew that sooner or later there would be a request for some fiddling over the telephone. Kartchner's telephone was in a box nailed to a tree in the front yard of the ranger station, which put it at just the right height to be fiddled into. While this practice may seem quaint to us, it underscores the yearning those people had for music, particularly the sound of the fiddle.

In Kartchner's social relationships with forest users his fiddling also had some very important practical value. In his younger days he had traveled widely throughout areas of northern Arizona playing for dances. Since these were occasions of note, they were well attended by the local people. Being the fiddler, he was the center of some attention and came to know and be known by large numbers of people. Many of the forest permittees were acquaintances from this time, and thus there was much common ground between him and them. This led to an easy rapport when sitting around the campfire discussing the pros and cons of Forest Service policies and their impact on the livelihoods of the permittees.

In the spring of 1919, Kartchner was transferred to the Coconino National Forest with headquarters in Flagstaff. Some twenty months later he was transferred to New Mexico.

During the three years we lived in Salt Lake City, Utah, from 1908 to 1911, I never played for a single dance, but I did take violin lessons under a Professor Nebeker. It gave me a broader concept of music as a science. He had me playing solos of the old masters, and he frowned upon ear music of any sort, especially hoedowns which he called "vulgar." Of course, such a doctrine could be classed only as hogwash by thousands of acquaintances in Arizona cow country. But the training was invaluable. Sight reading was accomplished by my proper observance of musical signs. My new appreciation of the classical broadened, and with profound apologies to the Professor's memory, it actually served to improve the playing of a hoedown! I developed a better understanding of harmony, and greater precision in playing. Defects in beat measurements of strictly ear pieces became obvious for correction.

Back at Snowflake, in 1911, a sheet music orchestra was organized late in the year comprised of first violin, cornet, clarinet, tuba, and piano. We pooled our money to buy the latest in popular numbers, and they added to many already on hand. Practice was mostly for our own enjoyment, intermittently pursued up to 1919 when I was transferred away. When we did play for local dances, the old pieces of bygone days were far more popular than the stuff we read.

The Fiddlin' Forest Ranger

During twenty months residence at Flagstaff, May 1919 to January 1921, little attention was given to the violin, other than keeping the Stainer tuned to standard pitch and occasional practice for home consumption. Lake Mary, as part of Flagstaff's water supply, had replaced Clark Valley, where George Rogers, Joe Robinson, and I sawed wood in 1903. The little schoolhouse struck a note of nostalgia in the memory of group dances we had played for there sixteen years before. Old acquaintances commented on my return this time as deputy supervisor of the Coconino National Forest.

A most interesting change was the move from Flagstaff to Alamogordo, New Mexico, headquarters of the Lincoln Forest, to serve in the same capacity under Supervisor O. Fred Arthur. The nearby Sacramento Mountains were commonly referred to as "Little Texas," from the fact that most of our forest graziers hailed from the Lone Star State. They brought with them its folklore and customs, not excluding country dances, hoedown fiddle music, and a decided antagonism toward the Forest Service.

One of my first field assignments was to represent the supervisor's office at a meeting of stockmen holding permits to graze cattle on the Sacramento Division. O. L. Coleman, of the Bureau of Biological Survey, and I rode horseback to Fresnal Ranger Station south of Cloudcroft where the meeting was to be held. His interest was predatory animal control by the bureau, which he explained in detail. Mine had to do with proper range management, seasonal distribution of livestock, and control of numbers within permit limits.

Our proposals went over rather lukewarm, but at the close we were invited to a dance up the canyon, which had been planned to coincide with the meeting.

After supper, Ranger Phelps, a fireguard, Coleman, and I agreed it might be fun to sit in on the dance awhile and listen to the music. When we arrived it was underway, to the fiddle music of a large raw-boned Texas girl, later introduced as Mrs. Jack Young. A young, local cowboy was playing guitar accompaniment, and the combination was very good for that backwoods environment. To me it brought back memories of the good old days in Arizona cow country. I felt thrillingly at home. Pretty soon a man, not the equal of Mrs. Young, took over the violin in order that she might dance. Later a third fiddler changed off the second, all of which gave me the same idea. When Mrs. Young's turn came again, I stepped up and offered to join in the relays if she wished me to. The look on her face, looking me over in my Forest Service uniform, and the hush that fell over the crowd, especially ranchers we had met with that afternoon, bespoke their utter astonishment at the thoughts of such a thing. Here was a "Guv'ment Man," maybe from Washington, D.C., so dressed, and with badge, choke-bore trousers, and leather puttees, offering to play the fiddle at a country dance! To make matters worse, I told Mrs. Young I would try, when she asked if I could play for the square dance coming up next.

The manager yelled, "All set." I passed the key of G to our right good guitar player and cut down on that old familiar Texas hoedown, "Leather Breeches." In stunned silence the crowd listened a moment. Once convinced they could believe their own eyes and ears, those cowpunchers whooped and hollered, stomped and laughed, the gals swayed in rhythm, and the guitar player bore down with added gusto. Such are the moments that inspire a fiddler to play his best. At the half-time intermission, Mrs. Young rushed over from her set and said, "Mister, I don't know your name, but you shore are a fiddler!" She wanted "Waggoner" [Tom Wagner] for the second half, named for the famous cattle ranch in the Texas Panhandle. We obliged in the key of C. Both hoedowns were, and still are, great favorites in square dance circles. Mrs. Young's violin was better than average, and although no two instruments note exactly the same, it responded well to my particular fingering and bowing.

The caller spieled off his last line, "Promenade all and you know where" (to their seats). Almost to a man, those present at the afternoon meeting gathered around to shake hands, congratulate, ask where I was from, and express amazement at the combination of deputy forest supervisor and country fiddler. We had reached a hearty common ground that I enjoyed as much as they. Frank Brown, an outspoken critic of forest regulations, was the most exuberant of all, perhaps as much from surprise as his love for pat-your-foot violin music. He sat close by between dances and talked fiddle. After an hour or so of waltzes, two-steps, a schottische, polka, and "Put Your Little Foot" (missuvien, but I can't spell it [varsovienne]), nothing would do but we have another square before I quit playing. They wanted the same pieces, but I talked them out of that on grounds there were so many other hoedowns in about the same class. Which two I played I cannot recall, but they seemed to like them just as well.

In taking over, Mrs. Young expressed her delight and thanks for the lift. She wished I lived in the area so she might learn some of the pieces that were new to her and perhaps improve her playing of others. A nice person of the raw frontier type, but we never met again. Walking back to the ranger station near midnight, Coleman remarked that our meeting would have been far more successful had the dance been held first. In terms of Forest Service prestige, Phelps averred it was the best thing that ever happened in Little Texas.

Sometime later, Supervisor Arthur conducted a field inspection of the Sacramento Division, conferring with cattle permittees on range management plans, and with other forest users. Returning to the office, he called me to his desk and said, "We've got this thing licked!" I said, "That's good—whatever 'this thing' might be." He went on, "We'll send you out through the mountains with that fiddle of yours and those stockmen will do anything we ask of them!" The Fresnal meeting and dance, he said, had done more to establish amicable relations with them than had otherwise been possible in twenty years of forest administration. Everywhere he went they inquired about that "Fiddlin' Forest Ranger" (using "Ranger" in its broader sense) and wanted to know when he might be coming back that way. It made an easy entree for more serious discussion of range matters on friendly terms.

My feeling of satisfaction went beyond the personal, for I was a firm believer in the broad, commonsense policies of the Forest Service and enjoyed getting them over to the permittees and the general public. If playing the fiddle helped, so much the better. Unfortunately, shaping events precluded further participation in dances of the Sacramentos, to which I was looking forward. Most of that summer and fall Fred Arthur kept me on pack-trip field inspections over the various ranger districts from Jack's Peak on the north to the Guadalupes at the Texas border. He made shorter trips while I ran the office and made up reports of inspections.

About the time a general inspection of the Sacramento Division was due, District (later changed to Regional) Forester Frank Pooler came down from Albuquerque on personnel business, part of which resulted in my promotion to Albuquerque as supervisor of the Manzano National Forest—separate from the district office—effective November 1, 1921. Suffice it to say, I left the Lincoln with many fond memories and some regrets, having served less than a year on the trails of Billy the Kid, and being denied further social contact with the good-hearted back-country people of Little Texas.

Two incidents occurred on the Manzano wherein playing the fiddle helped in breaking down opposition to Forest Service policies. South of Mountainair, New Mexico, east of the Rio Grande, lies the Chupadera Mesa Division, occupied by cattle and sheep under Forest Service grazing permits. Cattle owners were of much the same type and origin as those of Little Texas on the Lincoln. One such permittee was Jimmie Cooper, who had bought one of the older ranches and secured a waiver of the grazing privilege. He looked upon the red tape involved with some suspicion, obviously wondering whether he could operate satisfactorily under forest regulations, to which he was unaccustomed. Also, when the transfer was completed there and he had in possession a permit to graze three hundred head of white-faced Hereford cattle on a year-long basis, he could not understand our polite refusal of his offer to buy Claude Nave, my assistant, and me each the best Stetson hat to be found in Albuquerque.

In due course, District Ranger Louis H. Laney and I jointly inspected the area by Model-T Ford and horseback. Jimmie Cooper rode with us over his allotment as we made the rounds. At their palatial ranch home that evening, Mrs. Cooper served a T-Bone steak dinner of which only she and her kind are capable. Having our own camp outfit, we had intended to move on for the night, but both Jimmie and Mrs. Cooper were so urgent that we accepted their invitation to stay there instead. In the corner of the sitting room was a violin, which prompted me to ask Cooper if he played the fiddle. He said only slightly, but it was his favorite instrument and he had a good one that he sawed on occasionally. When I said the violin was my favorite instrument also, he opened his up for our inspection, believing it to be a genuine Stradivarius, from the inside label and claims of previous owners. However unlikely that may be—probably one chance in a million—it was a good copy, although poorly strung and maintained.

Of course, it was not my place to disabuse Jimmie's mind on an unofficial matter that brought him great pride. Before the evening was over, however, I had played about every hoedown with a Texas slant, plus several repeats by request. Although totally surprised at first, Jimmie was true to his breed of rural Texans who were born with hoedown rhythm in their blood. He shouted his pleasure and patted to the beats. Mrs. Cooper bemoaned the absence of three more couples for a square dance. Lou Laney was pleased with the newly created common ground between the Service and one of his important forest users, and the certainty of its spreading to others. He remarked that the Manzano was probably unique among 150 national forests in having a country fiddler as its boss.

After an early breakfast next morning, nothing would do but that I play "Leather Britches" once more before leaving. It seemed to be the favorite. Jimmie Cooper watched closely the fingering and bowing in a desire to emulate the technique, and, as we bade them

good-by, he made an unusual statement. Laney reminds me of it
when we meet infrequently to this day. It ran something like this:
"Now I tell ya! I've got three hundred head of white-faced cattle,
ten head of good cow horses, this ranch home, barns, corrals,
fences, and equipment, all in the clear, and the whole business is
yours if you will just teach me to play 'Leather Britches' like you
play it!" Resorting to the outlandish seemed the only way he could
fully express his feelings. At any rate, we had a "satisfied customer," largely attributable to a "Guv'ment Man" playing the fiddle.
My promise to bring the old Stainer with me on the next trip failed
to materialize, due to another transfer before it could take place.

The other incident occurred a few months later, about 1924, not
far from the Cooper Ranch to the southwest. Guy Hills of El Paso
operated a good-sized cattle outfit that grazed on and off the forest.
Homesteaders began filing on the outside portion, which Hills could
only interpret as a serious threat to his future welfare. Un-
beknownst to the Forest Service, he appealed to his close friend,
New Mexico Senator H. O. Bursum, who got through Congress an
act adding more than two townships of this critical area to the Manzano National Forest. Thus, it was dumped in our laps for administration and, in effect, closed to further homestead entry, effective
at once. To the credit of Guy Hills, this was probably the fastest
piece of work of its kind in Forest Service history. We were as surprised as the homesteaders at what became known as the Bursum
Addition.

Our first job, of course, was to post the new boundary line against
all forms of trespass, in the course of which Ranger Laney encountered bitter hostility, not only from inside nesters with claims
of record, but many prospective entrymen and sympathizers. They
were literally up in arms, carrying Winchesters at work and
threatening to use them. Rumors were afloat that all settlers within
the addition would be evicted, and the ranger was unable to convince them otherwise. He needed help to allay their fears. Accordingly, I picked him up at his headquarters in Mountainair for a
special trip to the area. We contacted key homesteaders and explained their true status, namely, that all entries of record were

held to be valid by the act itself; that up to ten head of domestic animals used on each claim could be grazed on adjacent forest land free of charge; that free-use permits were available to them for timber products used in buildings and fencing; that so long as they met minimum requirements of the Forest Homestead Law of June 11, 1906, they need have no fear but that patent would issue. We made some progress, but those people were still mad, feeling they had been double-crossed in any event. They were not sure but what we had a substantial part in it, despite our statements to the contrary.

Among the belligerents was a bachelor and World War I veteran from Texas, known as Red Pickens. Noticing a flock of chickens on his place, we stopped to buy some fresh eggs since our food supplies were getting short. He had been playing a violin that lay open on the kitchen table. Completing the egg deal, I asked him to play a piece, as we both were fond of the violin. It took some urging to get him started, but when I called for old-time pieces that should be foreign to "Guv'ment Men" his reluctance waned. A two-hundred pounder with red hair and freckles, he clomped his number twelves to the tempo on the kitchen floor. We voiced delight and he was pleased.

When Red Pickens inquired how I became familiar with old-time fiddle tunes, Laney said, "Why don't we have the supervisor play some himself?" "Why, shore thing," said Red, with some astonishment. His fiddle was not much and the bow was patched up with wire, but after a series of hoedowns, some he did not play, we became choice guests. "We must stay for lunch and play some more fiddle." Pickens thought he had seen everything now, expressing surprise that a "forest ranger" could be so down-to-earth and human, especially that a supervisor could also be, of all things, an accomplished hoedown fiddler.

The three of us pitched in, cooked lunch, ate, and washed up the dishes to the accompaniment of free and easy conversation. Pickens asked every conceivable question about his status as a homesteader within a national forest, thus providing the very opening we sought to clarify the whole situation. He knew everybody in the neighborhood, and what applied to his place likewise applied to all others within the addition. His contacts were frequent, both as the only local fiddler for Saturday night dances some distance to the west and through the sale of eggs and fryers to the local market. Furthermore, his speech, bearing, and forceful personality were such as to wield some influence in the community.

As if a heavy burden had been lifted from his mind, as though delighted with newfound friends, Red Pickens expressed appreciation for our visit, for the information given him on a vital issue—in which he now had full confidence—and last but not least, for his enjoyment of fiddle music played other than by himself. He had been misled by the rumors but now was in a position to put his neighbors straight, naming several who had told him he and others so situated were to be evicted from their homes. So far as we could tell, his representations did the job. At any rate, the hostility died down and little trouble was encountered thereafter.

Promising we would come back, as other duties allowed, and even try to attend one of their dances sometime, we chugged away in the government Model-T, feeling that our mission had benefited materially by gaining the confidence and friendship of Red Pickens— soldier, bachelor nester, and fiddler of the Bursum Addition. Lou Laney was to return as part of his work, but numerous problems elsewhere kept me from doing so. He told me, however, that Pickens made pleasant inquiry about the supervisor whenever they met. At a ranger meeting in Albuquerque, Laney told me also that he told his counterparts facetiously, "You guys should adopt my technique. Whenever I get into difficulties with dissident forest users, I just get the supervisor to come out with his fiddle and the problem is solved."

Before leaving the Manzano, whom should I meet on the street in Gallup but my old fiddling partner himself, Claude T. Youngblood. We both had families and by hard effort were far afield from our earlier joint pursuits. He operated two trading posts on the Navajo Indian Reservation and was in town for supplies. I was supervisor of the Manzano National Forest, making a field inspection of the Mount Taylor and Zuni divisions. Crowded schedules were interrupted while we recalled the past, its ups and downs, humorous incidents and otherwise. Each expressed a desire to meet sometime for a fiddler's reunion, which, incidentally, took place about three years later (1927) at Holbrook when veteran dance enthusiasts of the 1900–1908 era got us to converge there for an old-time shindig. They whooped it up as in days of yore and our pleasure was just as great in playing together again the many old pieces suited for two violins. Before it was over, we recovered somewhat from nineteen years' lack of practice, but with sore fingers and arm muscles that had lain dormant for so long.

In September 1925, I was sent to Springerville, Arizona, in charge of the Apache Forest. What struck me most in this quasi-home territory was that permanent residents seemed more interested in the Kid Fiddler of twenty years ago than the new supervisor. They remembered a team-and-buggy trip through the area in May 1905, made by Claude Youngblood, Edgar Gardner, and myself, and the several dances for which we played. B. B. Crosby, railroad contractor and sheepman, brought me a clipping from the *Saint Johns Herald* he had saved on the subject.

On that 1905 tour, we had met Curt Maxwell at Springerville, one of the best hoedown fiddlers of his time. He was still playing for dances, from 1925 to 1930 during my stay there. Occasionally, I would drop in to listen or dance, sometimes spelling him off for a piece or two. He made a number of very good records, some of which are doubtless still being played. My last meeting with him took place in Phoenix about 1941, when he called at the Game Department for a friendly visit. Learning he had his violin with him and two accompanists—guitar and banjo—I invited them to the house for an evening of old-time string music, to the delight of all concerned. Curt died a few years later and now, I dare say, heads up a procession of top fiddlers on a reservation especially set apart for their breed. Claude Youngblood moved back to Holbrook in the late twenties, and our trails crossed again. Including the above Holbrook dance of 1927, we came together every few months for a big hop in the general vicinity, mostly in fact, for old time's sake. Warm greetings of former friends, many of whom danced to our music in their days of romance, were abundant compensation for our efforts and mileage. The money received scarcely paid expenses.

Fiddlers' Contest

After leaving the Forest Service in January 1930, I was employed by the Arizona Game Department to make special field surveys of wildlife and its environment. Returning to Phoenix in February of 1931 from an extensive examination of the Kaibab National Game Preserve, I found a note on my desk to call Mrs. Viola Ruth (Mom Ruth), a lady fiddler of some note and an old acquaintance. She said the annual fiddlers' contest of Radio Station KOY was to be held on a certain date and she wanted me to enter "and take first place." I thanked her for the compliment but reminded her of the old adage about counting chickens before they are hatched. There was nothing to lose, however, and it might be an interesting experience.

The Ruths lived on a ranch near Tolleson, west of Phoenix, where we ran over a dozen or more hoedowns and decided on "Billy in the Low Ground," in the key of C, for the big event. Viola's daughter, Marie, played good pat-your-foot piano, having accompanied her mother since childhood, and a young family friend, whom I remember only as Johnny, played the guitar to round out a well-balanced trio. Both my fingering and bowing were faulty, since I had not played a note in several months, but by concentrating on the one piece for hours at a time, at the ranch and in my hotel room, sour notes and poor coordination began clearing up to my partial satisfaction. One piece only was allowed each contestant and it must be in 4/4, or square-dance time. Actually, by some misunderstanding, one or two waltzes were played, but ruled ineligible.

On the evening of the contest, all was abuzz at KOY headquarters. Forty fiddlers of all ages and descriptions were tuning their violins, accompanists their guitars and banjos. Cousin Marshall H. Flake, attending the legislature as representative from Navajo County, was present at my invitation and got quite a bang out of the whole affair. We drew for places, and mine came up fourth. John Green of Phoenix was among the first three, so I got to hear him play "Sally Goodin'," an excellent rendition of that fine old favorite. Scarcely had we finished "Billy in the Low Ground" when a long-distance call for me was announced. Another cousin, Hattye Hunt at Snowflake, wanted me to know the piece came in good and clear up there and to extend congratulations. Another call was waiting from Ed Gardner (mentioned elsewhere above) from Mesa, followed by one from Tolleson—someone I had known in McGaffy, New Mexico—and several locals, all of which kept me from hearing the remaining numbers.

Walking up front from the telephone booth, I caught the judge's verdict that: "First place goes to John Green playing "Sally Goodin'." Taking second is Kenner C. Kartchner playing "Billy in the Low Ground." Third place goes to (?) McLaughlin playing "(?)." I cannot recall the latter's first name or what tune he played. Among several honorable mentions was H. Cooper of Payson, I believe. He wound up the performance by leading all contestants playing "Casey Jones" together. Incidentally, Cooper was an outstanding fiddler of his time and had taken first in a previous KOY contest.

As we left the building Mom Ruth was furious. She, too, had placed first in previous competition but preferred not to enter this one. Instead, she had her heart set on my entry taking first place, which after all, was a big order among forty participants. She tearfully denounced the temerity of any judge who would relegate our number to second place. She disagreed with my own conviction that John Green had rightfully earned first honors, that his rendition was superb, on a good instrument, with excellent accompaniment, and I felt highly honored in taking second to such a musician. At any rate, the whole thing was fun. It constituted another unique experience, among many through the years, based upon the ability to play roughneck violin music reasonably well. I trust Mrs. Ruth's disappointment has long since worn off, for I shall never regret entering KOY fiddlers contest of 1931 nor begrudge John Green his prize. He reportedly died of tuberculosis not many years later.

The Importance of Harmony

Mention was made of our earlier guitar accompanists, Antolino Tafoya in particular, of the immediate 1900s. Just as he excelled in that era, so have two pianists who came on later. In July 1911, upon our return to Snowflake after three years in Utah, I was amazed at how well our baby-sister Leone could play the piano at fifteen years of age. Aside from her studies of the written note, she displayed natural talents for harmony, superior touch, and rhythm that inspired co-performers and audience alike. Nor was she alone among the other two sisters, Jennie and Thalia, with their guitars, and brother Lafe at seventeen, on his tuba horn, of all things.

How we loved to gather around the piano and spend an evening with this instrumental quintet, interspersed with family songs in quartet form, in which Mother and Dad joined in. And to round out the program, either at home, a party, or in public, Jennie would play her own guitar solo compositions to which Leone had fashioned lyric accompaniments with a high degree of skill. To music lovers this duo combination was most impressive. Lafe added spice by occasionally carrying the melody on his bass horn, a difficult procedure. With such an array of harmony support, hoedown fiddle tunes were restored to their proper significance, by contrast with their absence for three years while I laboriously drew the "long bow" under Professor Nebeker.

The years went by and the family scattered. In the meantime, Leone, with her early start, developed into one of the best of the all-around pianists. Her studies included a summer hitch at the Conservatory of Music in New York City to round out a rare ability to execute any type of music from hoedowns through the popular and to the classics. She has now retired as a school and music teacher, has raised a family, and at age sixty-six is still a noteworthy musician contributing her talents to church and community. We played together last on December 11, 1961, at the Phoenix home of Don F. and Marie Riggs, where relatives and old-time friends were gathered for an evening of music, singing, and readings in honor of our Aunt Lois Hunt West's eighty-sixth birthday. True to form, Leone's delightful piano parts for a dozen requested fiddle tunes were largely responsible for the generous applause.

Of equal ability is the other pianist mentioned above. Our daughter Merle, born July 30, 1909, while we were in Salt Lake City, was two years old when we returned to Arizona. During my first year with the Forest Service in 1913 we attended the Twenty-fourth of July celebration, commonly known as Mormon Pioneer Day, in the little town of Heber, Arizona. For a musical number on the afternoon program, we stood Merle, then six days short of her fourth birthday, up on a table to sing the tenor part of "Sweet Adeline," two verses and chorus, with her mother singing the melody and myself the bass. Before learning to talk, Merle was able to carry simple melodies and with special coaching for this occasion had mastered the words and learned to carry the separate part by herself, including difficult half-tones and minor sevenths that have made this old song a favorite for over half a century.

The open-air bowery shook with applause, not so much for the song itself as the novelty of a four-year-old tot singing tenor like a veteran. Encores brought us back for several chorus repeats, and Merle was enjoying the excitement. She could not fully understand its significance but knew we must be pleasing our listeners. With a degree of showmanship, she looked them over with a broad smile in obvious appreciation of their plaudits.

Her first piano was a Hamilton, purchased at Flagstaff in 1919. She was ten years old and made rapid progress with her lessons. We moved to Alamogordo, New Mexico, then to Albuquerque, where in 1923, at fourteen, she took the annual gold-medal award of the Robinson School of Music for having made the greatest advancement that year among a host of piano students. Albuquerque High

School auditorium was packed for the testimonial program on which Merle's thesis solo was the beautiful, but difficult, "Whispering Wind," by Wallenhaupt. We had anticipated her being among the leaders but were hardly prepared for the pleasant shock when Albuquerque's young mayor, Allen Bruce, announced the winner and pinned on the medal.

Of course, parents have a right to be proud of their children, particularly so when they stand out in achievements. The other five in the family have equal talents, musical and otherwise, but we are dealing here with outstanding piano accompanists and the harmony they must master to attain that rating.

Merle kept on at school, with additional piano studies under private teachers. At Tempe State Teachers' College, now Arizona State University, she was under the noted Mrs. Quaid, to whom many students of music give credit for their accomplishments. Going on to the University of Arizona, she majored in advanced piano, composition, arrangement, and harmony under Professor Otto Luening, of whom she speaks with great admiration. In the final phase toward a degree, each advanced student was required to present at class a new and complete composition of his own, with manuscript copy of the written assignment. Again, we were thrilled when her score received high acclaim.

Of great interest to me was the following sidelight. Professor Luening asked her where she obtained such unique themes as were used in her compositions. She replied that her dad was an old-time fiddler and they were taken largely from his various cow-country hoedowns. Mr. Luening was curious and wanted to know if her father could possibly visit the university for a demonstration of hoedown lore. She wrote me an urgent letter, but circumstances at the time prevented my acceptance. The invitation was left open even after Merle's graduation and departure from Tucson. We fully intended making a special trip at some convenient time, but for one reason or another, it never materialized. Looking back now, this is a matter of regret. Professor Luening had evinced a more than casual interest in folklore music of the American South and West, and was in a position of influence toward its deserved recognition, more nearly equal to those of the British, German, Scandinavian, and other similar cultures.

With no sorority membership, and by nature averse to swank, Merle was practically ignored by contemporary students until she passed highest in a natural talent test and was selected as a substitute to play on sight a difficult piano role for a Swedish opera star. Following these events were performances for various celebrities, including the venerable poet and historian Carl Sandburg, all of which brought showers of acclaim at school and in the press. She appreciated the genuine but resented palaver such as being called "our little sweetheart of the mountains" by certain obviously insincere social climbers. If these backgrounds seem top-heavy with detail, it is to emphasize a significant point. Although both pianists are products of scientific training, with the classical as its goal, each enjoys nothing better than to sit down for a series of harmony accompaniments to hoedown fiddle tunes. There is something about the latter that must be recognized when they inspire the musically elite—by no means all due to memories of childhood—and cause average audiences to twist on their seats in rhythmic cadence. But in any case, high-quality performance depends in large measure upon good accompaniment, just as do the songs of Bing Crosby, or as did the inimitable violin of Fritz Kreisler. That is why the two-subject pianists are outstanding. They not only play the classical, much of it at sight, but top accompaniment by ear as well—a rarity in the annals of music.

Had it not been for these two pianists over a twenty-year period, 1936 to retirement in October 1956, my violin playing would have ended for lack of practice. About twice a year, however, I played with one or the other while on vacation, which was enough to stimulate some practice between trips. Meanwhile, the old Stainer was given special care and seems to improve in tone with the years. Moving from New Mexico back to Phoenix to retire, and having more leisure time, we play together more often now, mostly in home groups. Public appearances are confined to church programs and celebrations, with the one stipulation that either Mrs. Merle K. Shumway or Mrs. Leone K. Decker be available for the piano parts.

Fritz Kreisler Note

It seems uncanny that within the hour of writing the above reference to Fritz Kreisler, this January 29, 1962, news of his death at eighty-seven in New York City of a heart attack has just flashed over the air. Never was it my privilege to hear him play in person, but by comparing albums of violin greats, he stands out in my mind as the greatest. His recording of "Humoresque" back in the twenties, among many others, would be my choice of all the music ever listened to. Although he succumbs to the inevitable, his mark on the pages of musical history will stand forever. Everyone must wonder who will fall heir to his famous violin, rated as one of the most valuable in the world—the Josef Guarnerius del Gesu of 1737. Let us hope it falls into the hands of a noteworthy violinist, or at least one of the large museums, to be kept strung at standard pitch and played by authorized persons for the benefit of students or general public. Better still would be that it hang alongside a statue of the master himself in perpetuity. Incidentally, I cannot help itching to play "Billy in the Low Ground" or "Snowbird in the Ash Bank" on such an instrument. Or would the indignity be too great?

Navajo-Apache Reunion

One exception to requiring the presence of one of the above accompanists is the Navajo-Apache County reunion and dance held each year at Mesa on the last Saturday in February. In 1957, sickness at home prevented my joining Claude Youngblood and his pianist, Mrs. Nellie Merrill, who furnished the dance music. (Mrs. Merrill is a younger sister of the late Ed Gardner who played guitar with us in the early 1900s). Beginning in 1958, however, we got together for these and other occasions, mostly for old-time's sake, and the bygone Youngblood and Kartchner combination was reborn. As in days of yore, I played harmony to many of the tunes [listed in Appendix A], excluding hoedowns, a two-violin combination quite popular for dance music in Navajo and Apache counties from 1902 to the fall of 1908, when we moved to Utah.

The great bulk of those who attend this reunion are residents, now aged sixty-five or over, or former residents, of Navajo or Apache counties, who comprised the younger set in that area during our active years as a dance orchestra. Thus, we fit into the occasion with double significance. To be sure some of the zip and rhythm of our youth is lacking, but in like measure, the dancers are older now and quite satisfied with the slower pace. I must say it has been a pleasant annual experience playing for these affairs. While we all look forward to many more of these fine occasions, Claude and I played our last together for this reunion and dance at Mesa, February 1962. He died March 28, 1965, at age eighty-five.

My Violins

I still have the old Stainer violin, acquired in 1904 at age eighteen. It has a rich tone, even better through the years, although only "a copy of Stainer models" can be claimed for it. It receives much less use now, but it will be kept as a family souvenir.

For the past four years, in June, I have entered the Weiser, Idaho, Old-time Fiddlers Contest, mostly to hear the best fiddlers in the nation and Canada. Merle went along and played piano twice; otherwise local accompanists were used. In the senior division, age seventy or over, my ratings ran as follows: In 1965, seventh place; in 1966, sixth; in 1967, seventh; and in 1968, fifth, with a nice trophy for making the top five. In the first three I used the old Stainer, but for the 1968 contest I used a new violin I had recently acquired, the Moore No. 5. At age eighty-two, some of the seventy-year-olds are hard to cope with. They are good.

All my life I have wanted an extra-good violin. Accordingly, the wife and I attended the annual convention and contest, in October 1967, of the Violin and Guitar Maker's Association at Miami, Arizona, where over a hundred violins were on display for ratings. Earl

L. Smith of Florida was there with four handmade violins of his own, all of which rated above average. I paid him $150.00 for his second-best fiddle, completed in January 1967. It is a wonderful instrument, both in workmanship and tone.

On Christmas Day 1967, Floyd Dees and I spent the evening with Howard L. Moore in his violin shop at Wilmington, California. The purpose was to have certain repairs made to the Stainer, on which Moore had done a fine job. Meanwhile, I played a dozen of his handmade fiddles for sale and compared them with the Smith model I had taken along. Outstanding above all the rest, including mine, was the Moore No. 5, 1963 model, which took the grand award at the above convention that year, and which he was holding at four hundred dollars. It is the finest instrument I ever played, in tone quality, volume, reverberation, and resonance. Seeing how I enjoyed it, Floyd (the wife's son) offered to buy it and make me a present of it. A nice gesture, but I told him I had planned to spend five hundred dollars for any violin that suited my ideal such as this one. Finally, I gave Moore the Smith fiddle and two hundred dollars for the Moore 5, which I shall never regret. The more it is played, the better it sounds, which is quite a satisfaction to me in my leisure hours. And, no doubt, it had to do with the fifth place rating at Weiser in 1968. I will keep it from now on, probably use it again at the 1969 contest.

In Retrospect

There are probably few exceptions to the belief that if one could live his life over again he would shape it differently in many respects. Of course, I am not one of the few. But what would I have done about becoming a fiddler-violinist? It threw me into bad company during formative years, but so it did in good society as well. As a virtual kid-hobo in 1903, it was the means of getting by when jobs were scarce, yet without it I probably would have been "home" where I belonged. It was largely responsible for my not going to college, although it might have been the means by which to make my own way. A certain stigma accompanies the title of "fiddler," implying a shiftless, ne'er-do-well existence. Speaking from experience, however, this applies only to individuals who are shiftless by nature, regardless of occupation.

Yes, if I had it to do over again, there would be many changes, but abandoning the violin would *not* be one of them. I would learn the same hoedowns, perhaps compose a few from the composite whole, run down case histories of old pieces that are now lacking, spend more time on the classical—especially double-stop harmony— but never at the expense of the hoedown. The goal would be to master "Humoresque," "Meditation from Thais," and so forth, a la Kreisler, or [Mischa] Elman on the one hand, and the diametrically opposite bowing for "Waggoner," "Billy in the Low Ground," or "Leather Breeches" on the other. To my knowledge, the combination is nonexistent, but need not be if leisure time were apportioned in early youth and followed through with diligent practice in both fields.

Enough has been said about the violin and its effect upon the life I have led. In conclusion, let me state that playing the fiddle, or violin as one prefers, has brought zest and satisfaction over the years, not so much as a vocation as a challenging hobby that sharpens the intellect and stirs the soul. Classical violin music will continue at the top in world appeal, but never should the cow-country hoedown vanish from the American scene.

Principal Fiddle Tunes Played by Kenner C. Kartchner

Hoedowns, Reels, and Hornpipes

"Alexander" (D-A) Good harmony part, played with Youngblood 1902 to 1908.

"Angus Campbell" (A)

"Arkansas Traveler" (D) Very popular and one of the oldest hoedowns.

"Billy in the Low Ground" (C) Comes from the South. A good one.

"Bob-tailed Mule" (A) A favorite in cross-tuning (EAEA).

"Buffalo Gals" (G)

"Cackling Hen" (G) Learned from Mr. Nagler, Williams, Arizona, in 1903.

"Cackling Hen (No. 2)" (G) Some call it Old Hen She Cackles.

"Chicken Reel" (D)

"Cotton-Eyed Joe" (G) Youngblood brought it from Mississippi, 1890.

"Devil's Dream" (A) Plenty old and difficult to play properly.

"Durang's Hornpipe" (D) An old stand-by.

"Eighth of January" (D) Tune known later as "Battle of New Orleans."

"Fisher's Hornpipe" (D) Played often at Weiser annual contest.

"Flowers of Edinburgh" (G) No doubt brought from Scotland long ago.

"Forgotten Hornpipe" (D) Good piece recalled from 1900, but no name.

"Girl I Left Behind Me" (G) Probably one hundred years old.

"Great Big 'Taters in Sandy Land" (C) Tune from Frank Pruitt, about 1900.

"Gray Eagle" (A) One of the best. Played by Mormon fiddlers crossing the Plains.

"Hell Amongst the Yearlin's" (D) Learned in 1966, but piece is old.

"John Whetton Quadrille" (G) First tune I ever played, 1898.

"Leather Britches" (G) Great favorite in early Texas cattle country.

"Long Ways to Holbrook" (C) Played by Frank Pruitt, 1900.

"Miss McLeod's Reel" (G) Was playing around Flagstaff-Williams in 1903.

"Mississippi Sawyer" (D) These are all very old, handed down by ear.

"Old Gray Mare" (D) ("She ain't what she used to be"). Rather simple melody.

"Pick 'em Up Joe" (C) Learned from bartender Jim Wheeler, Williams, Arizona, 1903.

"Rabbit Where's Yo' Mammy" (A) (Or "Walk Along John to Kansas") From the South. Can be played with cross-tuning EAEA or C#AEA.

"Ragtime Annie" (D) Thirty to forty years old. Most fiddlers play it.

"Rattle Snake" (A) Very old, from the South, in EAEA cross-tuning.

"Sally Goodin'" (A) Old Texas tune. Only a few play it well. All try it.

"Sally Johnson" (G) Same. Buddy Durham, Ft. Worth, plays it best of all.

"Snowbird in the Ash Bank" (G) Jumping bow in second change is popular, as it emulates a misguided snowbird flitting in ash bank, thinking it's snow.

"Soldier's Joy" (D) Every fiddler plays this. Some not so good.

"Sweets O'Weaver" (D) A good one, from Old Texas.

"The Buckin' Dun" (A) Dun horse threw rider at Magdalena, New Mexico, show about 1900. A fiddler took the hint with this result.

"Tom & Jerry" (A) Old South cross-tune EAEA. Hard to play in standard tuning.

"Tom Wagner" (or Waggoner) (C) Son of Dan, a wealthy Texas cowman and banker. They held rodeos, with the best fiddlers extant. One of them composed this hoedown in honor of Tom.

"Wagner" ("Waggoner") (C) In honor of Dan Wagner years earlier, maybe one hundred years ago. Some call it Tennessee Wagonner. Reason not known.

"Turkey in the Straw" (G) Old Edison record song hoedown time, around 1902.

Fox Trots, One-steps, Two-steps, and Polkas

"Alexander's Ragtime Band" (D) A great dance tune around 1904.

"Chaser Two-Step" (G) Tune from same period, in 6/8 time.

"D & G Two-Step" In 6/8 time. From sheet music 1911.

"Darkey's Dream" (G) Clog dance. Sometimes played for a schottische.

"G Polka" (G) Old as the hills. Original not known.

"Golden Slippers" (F) Good harmony one-step as per Youngblood and Kartchner.

"Haste to the Wedding" (D) In 6/8 time.

"Heel-Toe Polka" (G) Origin unknown. Popular with Mexican people.

"Irish Washer Woman" (G) In 6/8 time.

"Johnny Blevins Tune" (two-step) (D) In 6/8 time. Learned from Johnny Blevins, who used to spell us at Holbrook dances, 1902–8.

"Let the Women Do the Work" (or "Hiawatha") (G) An old Edison record.

"Little Brown Jug" (D) Many an amateur plays this simple old song.

"Mocking Bird" (D) With variations can be a classic. Mother sang this.

"Moonlight and Roses" (C) All the go in 1920. Good harmony.

"Nellie Gray, (My Darling)" (G) Old song, one-step or march.

"Old Spinning Wheel" (F) Harmony with Youngblood made a good fox trot in 1930.

"Pop Goes the Weasel" (G) In 6/8 time. Rather simple but real old.

"Rancho Grande" (D) Played with Youngblood in the thirties on occasion.

"Red Wing" (G) Old song. Good harmony.

"Ribs Henderson Two-Step" (C-A minor) Learned from Frank Dawson at Globe in fall of 1907. Named for cattle foreman near Pleasant Valley.

"San Antony Antonio" (B minor-D) Jack Mankins sang this in Globe 1907.

"Silver Bells" (G or C) Good harmony dance tune of the 1930s.

"Snow Deer" (D) Pioneer song of long ago.

"Spanish Polka" (D) Concho Mexicans loved this with the two violins, 1904.

"Spanish Wedding March" (D) Same. Youngblood and I walked in lead of several wedding marches one-fourth mile from downtown Concho north to old coffin-shaped church playing the two violins with blind Antolino Tafoya on guitar. There were many dances in between. They loved two-violin combination.

"Utah Trail" (F) Good two-step of later vintage.

"When the Bloom Is on the Sage" (F) Fox trot of the thirties.

"When You and I Were Young Maggie" (C) Same.

"Whistling Rufus" (G with third part in C) Good two-step around 1900.

Additional third-rate tunes come to mind in this category, but are considered not worth listing.

Schottisches

"Birds in the Brook" (F & D minor) Four sections, third is D minor. Best of them all. Learned from sheet music summer of 1911 when we moved back to Snowflake from three years in Salt Lake City.

"Blue Bird" (C & G) One of the first tunes I remember.

"Flop-Eared Mule" (G & D) Very old. Played at Weiser as fast hoedown.

"Goose Hangs High" (D) ("Everything is lovely when the... ") Century old.

"Jim Wheeler" (C) In three sections. Learned from Jim in Williams 1903. Good one.

"O'Brien" (E minor & G) From old Edison record in Holbrook 1903.

"Old South" (G-D-C) Name implies origin. Old as the hills.

"Pete Marker" (D & G) Pete and his son Solon played for dances in Snowflake–Holbrook vicinity about 1893. Local fiddlers learned some of their tunes.

"Rain Barrel" (D) Fictitious name. Origin unknown. Marker played it.

"Wagon Train" (G) Same category. Real name lost to antiquity.

Waltzes

"After the Ball" (C) I remember this back to 1893. Guess it is much older.

"All Alone, I'm So All Alone" Popular at Albuquerque in 1921.

"Black Hills Waltz (A) Cross-tune EAEA, goes at least back to 1890.

"Beautiful Ohio" (C-A minor) All the go 1915. Likely dates to before that.

"C Waltz, Old" (C) From the Old South out through the West before 1890.

"Chamois [Shamus?] O'Brien" (G) May have been brought from Ireland in 1890s.

"Diddle Do" (or "Epitacio") (D) The latter a cattle foreman for Huning, Show Low.

"Dream of Heaven" (F with third section in B flat) Very best. Learned in 1911.

"Drunkard's Hiccups" (A) Cross-tune (C#AEA). Favorite from the South.

"Dying Child's Request" (C-A minor) Good two-violin harmony. Learned in 1905.

"Frolic of the Frogs" (C) From Frank Wattron's Edison record, 1902.

"Garden of Roses" (A minor-C) Song hit 1908. Learned in Salt Lake City.

"Good-Night Waltz" (C & F) Nice, old tune. Learned in 1930s.

"Home Sweet Home" (G) Used as closing dance waltz since 1900.

"I'm Forever Blowing Bubbles" (G) Was rage in 1920s.

"In the Shade of the Old Apple Tree" (C) Edison record about 1902.

"Let Me Call You Sweetheart" (F) Came out prior to 1921.

"Mansion of Aching Hearts" (C) Learned 1902. New to Globe December 1907 where I borrowed a fiddle and played for several dances.

"Meet Me Tonight in Dreamland" (F) Salt Lake City hit in 1908.

"Memories" (C) Popular in 1920. Heard first in Albuquerque.

"Merry Widow" (G) Seventy-five years old perhaps. Not as popular as some.

"Missouri Waltz" (G-E minor) Old standby. Truman played at White House.

"Over the Waves" (G & C) One of my first memories about 1893.

"Peek-a-Boo Waltz" (F) Another old relic. Its history would be interesting.

"Pete Marker Waltz" (D) Another tune played by Pete Marker in 1893.

"Pinedale Waltz" (D) Named for the town, circa 1900, maybe by Frank Pruitt.

"Roses" (C) Another Pete Marker tune, one of my first in 1898.

"Rye Waltz" (D) First section in 2/4 time, second in waltz time.

"Rye Whiskey" (A) Old southern cross-tune (EAEA), converted to standard tuning.

"Smile the While You Kiss Me Sad Adieu" (F) World War I product.

"Soldier His Eyes Were Blue" (There Was A) (G) 1890s.

"Springtime in the Rockies" (F) Rage in 1930s.

"Strawberry Roan" (G) Favorite at rodeos as far back as 1920.

"Sweet Bunch of Daisies" (G) One of my first tunes in 1898.

"The Lost Goose" (G) Harmonics in second strain emulate the sound of the wild goose, which prompts the name. Old Texas.

"Three O'Clock in the Morning" (G) Came about 1910.

"Varsovienne" ("Put Your Little Foot") Popular dance for over seventy-five years.

"Wednesday Night Waltz" (D) Excellent piece, 1920s?
"When I Grow Too Old to Dream" (C) Song. Good waltz. Thirty to forty
    years old.
"When It's Moonlight on the Colorado" (C) Same.
"When the Moon Comes Over the Mountain" (C) Two-violin harmony in
    1930s.
"Whistler's Waltz" (D) Another good tune by Lloyd Wanzer, Weiser, 1966.
"You Tell Me Your Dream, I'll Tell You Mine" (C) Nice song, 1900.

Brief Analysis of Kartchner's Playing Style

The growth of Fiddling Contests at both the local and national level indicates the great appeal fiddle music still has for numerous people, though granted the contest atmosphere is, at best perhaps, an artificial environment. And the fiddling, while keeping something of the form, often lacks much of the essence of its former self. Many efforts have been made to preserve and study old-time fiddle music. Study to the present has focused primarily on the notation and analysis of melody (fingered by the left hand) and little has been said about the use of the bow (right hand). This is understandable, of course, because the melody is so easily apprehended. It is very unfortunate, however, because the essence of the music style is found primarily in the bowing and not so much in the melody line. The way the bow sits on the string determines the tone quality, and the way it moves determines the rhythmic vitality of the music. The following brief analysis is an attempt to outline the major elements of Kartchner's playing style, many of which he shares, of course, with other fiddlers. It is based on his recordings, particularly the early ones (1943) which show an excellent bow control as well as fingering technique.

Two of the most notable stylistic elements of fiddling are related to bowing technique, sawing on open strings (droning) and a driving rhythm characterized by off-beat accents, both of which pervade Kartchner's music. These two elements may derive in part from the fact that in early fiddling there was often no other instrument to provide harmony or a rhythm and the fiddler had to get along without them or provide his own on the fiddle.

Droning is what gives fiddle music its basic sonority. It is produced by drawing the bow simultaneously across two strings, one of which is fingered, the other usually played open. But it is not just the playing of two strings together, but rather the pervasive presence in the music of unisons (also octaves) and open fourth and fifth intervals. The music doesn't just move from one chord to the next, but often from one unison, fourth, or fifth to another unison, fourth, or fifth, with sawing on open strings in between. This is seen clearly in the opening phrase of "The Grey Eagle" (Example 1) where these intervals all appear on strong beats, and in the opening phrase of "The Buckin' Dun" (Example 2).

Example 1

Example 2

Of course, the intervals of a third and sixth are also to be found everywhere present in the music, as may be seen in any of the transcriptions in
Appendix IV. Generally, these are considered to be more "consonant," or
"harmonious" than the unisons, fourths and fifths. However, it is the strong
presence of these latter intervals which give fiddling its particular tone
color.

Another element related to droning, and therefore to the sonority of fiddling, is "tuning down," or "cross tuning," where the strings are tuned to
pitches different from the regular *EADG*. Tuning down is known more pre-
cisely by the musical term "scordatura."[1] It is interesting that the Arizona
fiddlers, according to Kartchner, referred to pieces played in these tunings
as being in the "Italian key." For him this Italian key actually encompassed
two tunings. The first one raised the two lower strings of the violin from *G*
and *D* to *A* and *E* (Example 3), and the second one, in addition to this, low-
ered the top *E* string down to *C#* (Example 4).

Example 3

Example 4

While there are a number of other nonregular tunings to be found in
American fiddling, Kartchner seems to have used only these two.

Though fairly widespread in traditional fiddling, such tunings have often
been banned in fiddle contests, being perceived as something akin to trick
fiddling. This is an unfortunate perception, for cross-tuning is very func-
tional in producing the fiddle "sound." In effect it does at least three things:
a) increases the resonance and sonority of the fiddle because the re-tuned

---

1. The terms "cross-tuning," "tuning down," and "scordatura" are more or less in-
terchangeable, though, as Thede points out, some fiddlers make finer distinctions.
They all mean an unusual tuning of a stringed instrument for a special effect. In fiddling, the practice seems to be primarily for the purpose of enhancing the sonorities
of droning, although in many cases it does make a fingering pattern easier to do or it
produces a particular aural effect. See Marion Thede, *The Fiddle Book*, New York:
Oak Publications, 1967, pp. 12, 17–22.

strings often function also as sympathetic strings; b) allows more possibilities or makes it easier for sawing on open strings, thus increasing the drone and/or harmonic effect; and c) in many cases it allows a tune also to be played an octave lower thus expanding the tone color range of a given piece. The latter may be seen in the excerpts from the first phrase of "The Rattlesnake" (Example 5).

Example 5  becomes

Besides droning, bowing technique can also enhance the rhythm inherent in a melody line by the way the bow stops and starts. Rhythmic vitality comes from the bowing, not just the way the bow sits on the strings, but from subtle pressure changes at the beginning, middle, or end of a stroke. In Kartchner's music the basic bowing style was similar to that of the Baroque era, in which the bow stops briefly between strokes. Holding the bow loosely between the thumb, middle, and index fingers, Kartchner used what he called the "rolling elbow" or "lazy arm" stroke. The wrist was very loose, but the arm itself was somewhat stiff with much of the driving power coming from the upper arm and shoulder. With the loose wrist and fingers, the bow was very sensitive to a change of direction or a pulse in the same direction. On up-bow strokes, in particular, the weight of the arm would put pressure on the bow to make it bite into the string, thus giving an accent. Since most up-bows occurred somewhere in the middle of a beat, or on a weak beat, such bowing produced a pervasive off-beat, or weak beat, accent in the music. This is what created the driving rhythm that was so much a part of this old-time music. The first phrase of the second part of "Tom Wagner" illustrates the various places the off-beat accent may occur (Example 6).

Example 6

The above are part and parcel of the fiddling aesthetic that shaped Kartchner's music. They pervade all of his tunes, whether hoedown, waltz, or two-step. They even appear in one form or another in his attempts at "classical" pieces. However, as in other oral-aural traditions, his "stylistics" were not limited by these but rather continued to evolve, most particularly as may be seen in the duet harmony he produced with Youngblood. To many of the tunes named in Appendix A, excluding hoedowns, he played a harmony part, which, as noted above, was very attractive to his listeners. This may have had some influence on his solo playing, for we see him doing a double-stop[2] harmony in some of the waltzes, which exceeds substantially the double-stops of the musical transcriptions found in standard studies of fiddle music. A good example is "Wednesday Night Waltz," (see Appendix D) where double-stop harmony exists virtually throughout the whole piece.[3]

2. Double-stop means playing two strings together, which are both "stopped" (fingered). This is in contrast to playing two strings together where one is stopped and the other open.

3. Compare this with Thede, *The Fiddle Book*, p. 145; see also R. P. Christeson, *The Old-Time Fiddler's Repertory*, Columbia, Missouri: University of Missouri Press, 1976, pp. 199–201.

Dance Descriptions

The following is a listing of dances done to the accompaniment of Kartchner's music, followed by a short description of each dance as it was done in Arizona in the early 1900s. The dances fall into three general categories: solo, formation couple, and couple round dance. Most of these dances were to be found across America, but there were certain adaptations that were unique to Arizona.

Kartchner mentions step dancing in several places. This was a solo-type dance done to hoedown rhythm but was usually unaccompanied. Nearly everyone could do it, but some were better than others. It features a light step, but no heel-work, and, as described by Kartchner's daughter, Merle, the interest was in the foot movement and not the body or arms. Step dancing could be done anywhere, outside, in the home, or on a stage. While the setting could be anywhere, it was often done for some kind of an audience, ranging from an informal just-for-the-heck-of-it show of exuberance to a showpiece as a formal part of a program.

The quadrille was the most common form of dance, a probable version of the square dance since it features four couples facing each other in a set. The term used by all, however, was "quadrille." It was in hoedown rhythm, and the sets of dancers were guided through the formations by a caller who stood near the musicians. The footwork was a sort of graceful running step, not the clogging step so closely associated with the square dancing of today. Another popular dance was the Virginia reel, which could be done with an indeterminate number of couples to a set, though six to ten was an ideal number. Not used as often as the quadrille, several reels were done in the course of an evening.

Dancing was not limited to the dance hall but also figured in home entertainment. If there were enough people to form a set, quadrilles were often done as after-dinner entertainment. Kartchner always carried his violin with him on his rounds by buggy, and many were the times that he played a couple of quadrilles for his hosts after dinner. At the ranch dances, the furniture was moved outside and sets were formed in each room. The fiddler positioned himself at a place where all could hear. Sometimes, in smaller houses, dancers might light a bonfire and dance outside.

In early Arizona pioneer times, couple dancing was restricted to the quadrille (square dance) or to dances that had little body contact other than arms or hands. In the mid-1890s, however, the waltz began making its appearance. It, and like dances which put the couple facing each other in closed position, were called "round dances." The younger set accepted the waltz readily, but the older generation thought such an intimate dancing position was scandalous. At first it was prohibited, but later it was grudgingly and only slowly accepted in the community at large.

The waltz is alleged to have been introduced to Snowflake by Solon and Pete Marker, two early dance fiddlers from Holbrook. Some years later, after a gradual social acceptance, the waltz became very popular and was interspersed between the quadrilles and schottisches. Not only was it popular, it came to be considered an elegant dance and an occasion to express chivalry. A person, particularly a male, was not thought to be all he ought to be if he could not waltz well. The dance tempo was somewhat fast, particularly when contrasted with the slower, "dreamy" waltz that became popular in the 1920s. It also featured a slight dip or hitch on the first beat. In a ranch dance setting, the people would dance from one room to the next. The waltz paved the way for other types of round dancing, most of which were variations of the waltz, such as the Rye waltz, or of another already existing dance, such as the schottische. In the Rye waltz, the first part was done with the partners holding hands, the second part with partners holding each other in closed dance position.

The schottische was an early dance on the Arizona frontier, first done with the couple holding hands but later in semi-closed dance position (side by side with the man's arm around the woman's waist and her arm on his shoulder) for the first phrase and closed dance position for the second. A variation of the earlier version was for two couples to get together, one behind the other, but facing the same direction and holding hands. There were several formations through which they could move, some improvised on the spot. The basic foot movement was step-step-step-hop for the first phrase and step-hop-step-hop-step-hop-step-hop for the second.

The varsovienne was an older dance, probably descending from the court dances of Europe. It was often given the nickname, "Put Your Little Foot," which described the first few steps. A popular variation was the circle varsovienne, which could be done only in a larger hall. Couples formed a large circle around the hall and the ladies moved forward to the next partner at the end of each section rather than remaining with one partner to the end of the set.

Another round dance which became popular was the two-step. It featured a step-quick step-step foot pattern which may be construed by some as a simplification of the polka. It was at quite a fast tempo and the couple did not seem to dance as close together as in the waltz, which made it somewhat more acceptable. Like the varsovienne, it also had a circle version, called the circle two-step, which featured a set of calls in the middle of a regular two-step directing the dancers to do different formations. Some of these had a mixer function that made the people change partners, including the familiar grand right and left. The final call, "Paul Jones," directed them to find their original partners, with whom to finish the dance.

The polka does not seem to have been a part of the Arizona dancing scene, although there was a dance called "the heel-toe polka." The adult version seems to have had some polkalike steps in it, but the kids' version had instead some sliding and stamping type steps.

Two somewhat complex dances that became very popular were the Rye waltz and the very elegant Chicago Glide. Both were something of a variation on the waltz with a preliminary section in 2/4 time. The name "Chicago Glide" is a mystery, though you do run across glides named after other cities. The elegance of these dances grew out of the grace of the waltz,[1] and with the movement of the long-flowing dresses of the ladies, the Chicago Glide in particular was perceived by the people as a thing of great beauty, perhaps even as a crowning symbol of civilization having reached their community.

Other activities at the dances served as mixers. Grand marches were popular, with one couple leading out first to march music. After marching up and down the hall for a short time, each marcher would pick up a new partner, repeating the process until everyone in the hall had joined in the procession. Marching was not random. People fit into set formations, which created columns with first two abreast, then four, then eight, and so forth, limited in numbers across only by the size of the hall. Another example of a mixer was often part of the circle two-step. The ladies would each take a shoe off and throw it in a pile in the center of the room. The men would then rush to retrieve a shoe and try to match it with its owner for the next dance. Such activities brought variety to the dance and also gave the musicians some valuable rest time.

---

1. See Christeson, *Old-Time Fiddler's Repertory*, p. 160, for a piece entitled, "Baltimore Glide." See also references to the "glide" for more modern uses of the dance in F. J. Mainey, *The Old Time Dancers' Handbook*, London: Jenkins, 1953, p. 53, for the "Coronation Glide," and p. 36 for the "Olympia Glide." It also gives the following description of the term "glide" on p. 9.

Term of interest when studying some of the older dances, as without knowledge of its meaning, some dance descriptions must be misunderstood. It denoted a sliding step for *as far as the foot could reach*, without transferring weight.

Though in the Arizona version of the Chicago Glide there is no such "sliding step," there is a step pattern of extending the leg out front and touching the floor three times with the toe, center, right, and left, without transferring weight.

Seventeen Fiddle-Tune Transcriptions

The following transcriptions are of tunes for which Kartchner left recordings. Since so much of the style depends on bowing, it seemed appropriate to be as prescriptive as possible in indicating bow direction and slurring. Of course, it is impossible to show everything in absolute detail and accuracy, but for one somewhat familiar with fiddle style, these bowing indications will be a big help in re-creating his tunes.

Black Hills Waltz

Bobtailed Mule

Buckin' Dun

Old "C" Waltz

Cacklin' Hen

Chicago Glide

The Drunkard's Hiccups

Grey Eagle

Johnny Blevin's Tune

Leather Britches

Pinedale Waltz

Rattlesnake

D.S. at lower octave

Schottische

Sally Johnson

Sweets O'Weaver

Tom Wagner

Walk Along John to Kansas

INDEX

A. & B. Schuster, 4, 164
A. L. & T. (Arizona Lumber and Timber Company), 45–47, 50, 55
A.C.M.I. (Arizona Cooperative Merchantile Institution), 4, 164
accompaniment, fiddling, xv, 38, 83, 86, 234, 241, 242, 244, 247
Adair, Port (Porter), 25–27, 30
Adair, Tom, 97
Alamogordo, N.M., move to, 233
Albuquerque, N.M., move to, 236, 240, 245
"Alexander Tell Me Don't You Love Yo Baby No Mo," 104
alfalfa, harvesting, 9, 17
Allen, Florrie, 23
Apache tribe, 5, 181, 182
Apache Forest, move to, 241
Armijo, (Jaramillo) Jake, 99, 156
Arthur, O. Fred, 233, 235, 236
asbestos mining, 67–68
assistant forest ranger, work as, 205, 206, 214
Aztec Land and Cattle Company (Hash Knife outfit), xiv, 167

Baca, Lorenzo, 84; family, 88
baile (Mexican dance), 86, 89
Bailey, George, 223
Bailey, Mrs. George, 11
Ballard, Charlie, 100
Ballinger, Richard, 197
banjo, accompanying the fiddle, xv, 158, 241, 242
barbershop singing, 123, 156, 179
Barclay, George, 111
Barrett, Elizabeth, 113
baseball, 89, 96–101
Basque sheepmen, 127, 128
Bazan, Ignacio, 89, 90, 93, 114

Bennett, Norman, 130, 150, 151, 153, 166
Berry, Pete, 62, 68, 69, 71
betting on horse and foot races, 92–96, 178
Bill Williams Mountain, 51, 52
"Billy in the Low Ground," 242, 243, 248, 251
bishops, dealings with, 39–43, 158–160, 201–202
"Black Hills Waltz," Appendix D
Blevins, Andy (Cooper), 112, 225–226
Blevins, Charlie, 227
Blevins gang, 224–225, 228
Blevins, Hamp, 227
Blevins, Johnny, 112, 227–228, 230
Blevins, Mart, 227
Blevins, Sam Houston, 112–113
Blue Dog (horse), 25–27
"Bobtailed Mule," Appendix D
bookkeeper, work as, 189–190
bowing, fiddle, 235, 242, 251, 258, 260
breakdowns (Texas hoedowns), 38
Brown, Frank, 235
Brown, Tom, 75, 78
Bruce, Allen, 246
Bucket of Blood Saloon, 105, 164
Buglan, Martin, 69, 70
Burk, Foul (File), 5, 6, 25–27, 29
Bursum Addition, 238, 240
Bursum, H. O., 238
Butler, David A., 3
Button, Charlie, 60

"Cacklin' Hen," Appendix D
Calkins, Hugh, 197, 198
campaign, election of 1904, fiddling for, 101

Campbell, Frank, 107, 108, 111–113, 200
Candelaria, Juan and Rosalie, 84
Cannon House, apartment in, 193
"Carry Me Back to Old Virginny," 179
"Casey Jones," 243
Casteel, Margaret Jane (Kartchner), 1, 187
Cedar Ranch, 60, 61
Chalender Junction, 50
chaps, 148
Chevalon Canyon, 24, 114, 118
"Chicago Glide," xvii, 49, 263, Appendix D
Chinaman Charlie, 45, 55
Chisholm, Alex, 54, 73
Chupadera Mesa Division, 236
Church of Jesus Christ of Latter-Day Saints (Mormon), colonization, 2, 15–17; Kartchner's troubles with, 39–43, 58; Pioneer Day, 245; Sunday School, 201–204; and Woodruff dance, 157–160
Clark Valley, 46, 48, 233
Clayton, Donny Jr., 191
Clayton, Marinda, 191
Cody, Archie, 45, 47
Coleman, O. L., 233, 234, 235
Collett, John, 189
colonization, Mormon, xiii, 15, 39
Concho, fiesta, 83–87
contests, fiddling, 242–243, 258, 259
Cooley, Col. C. E., family ranch, 182
Cooper, Andy (Blevins), 112, 225–226
Cooper, Harbert, 39–41
Cooper, Jimmie, 236–238
Cooper, Joseph, 40
copper mining, at the Grand Canyon, 65–68
cotillion (Spanish quadrille), 86
cowboys, 167–170. See also

wrangling
Crosby, B. B., 107, 114, 200, 241
Cross, Bill, 165
Custer, George Armstrong, battle site, 128
Customeyer, John, 44
cylinder records, 104–106

dancing, 82–83, 261–263
Dawson, Frank, 178
Day, Charlie, xxiii, 104, 106
Day, Sam, xxiii, 104
Decker, Leone (nee Kartchner), 3, 80, 244, 247
Decker, Silas, 3, 222, 226
Decker, Zechariah B., 222–227
Deer Spring Lookout, 210
Dees, Floyd, 250
DeWitt, Alex, 175
DeWolf, Billy, 122, 123, 125
Donahue, Johnnie, 46
Donahue, Sandy, 44, 45, 50, 54, 55
droning, on fiddle, 258–260
"Drunkard's Hiccups," Appendix D
duet style, fiddling, xviii, 37, 86, 260
Duke, Pat, 181

Edison phonograph, 104–106, 165
education, Kartchner's, 10–15
Edwards, Buff, 176, 177
Eggleston, W. W., 217
elections of 1904, fiddling for, 101–102
Ellison, Duett, 173
Ellison, J. W., and Ellison Ranch, 173–174
Elman, Mischa, 251
examination, Forest Service, 196–199

feud, Graham-Tewksbury (Pleasant Valley War), 174, 227
"Fiddlin' Forest Ranger," known as, 233–236
fiddling: contests, 242–243, 258,

259; for dance circuit, 82–84;
early years, 37–39; in Globe,
178–180; for 1904 election
campaign, 101; and public
relations, 231–240; recording on
cylinders, 104; technique and
tuning, 258–260
fiesta, Concho, 84
Flagstaff, living in, 44, 48, 233
Flake, Belle (nee Hunt), 7, 8
Flake, Charles, 6–8
Flake, James M., 7, 40, 41
Flake, Joel, 226
Flake, John T., 25, 196, 197
Flake, Lucy, 8
Flake, Marion, 6, 36
Flake, Marshall, 202, 204, 243
Flake, Osmer, 206, 208, 210, 211,
214
Flake, Samuel D., 40, 42, 43
Flake, William Jordan, 15, 17, 23,
25, 29, 32, 39, 40
Flake Brothers Hall, xvi, xvii, 37,
82, 166, 186
Flake ranch, 25
Flash, the (horseman), 91–93
Ford, Model-T, purchase of, 221
Forest Service, U.S.: examination
for, 196–197; years in, 205–230
Forrest, Earle, 112
Fort Valley logging camp, 50
four-up (Fresno scraper), 107
Freeman, Bill, 101
freighting, by farmers, 4–5
Fresnal Ranger Station, meeting
and dance, 233, 235
Frost, Al, 118–122, 131, 132, 157,
158, 166, 172, 175, 178
Fulton, Jack, 3

gambling, 46, 74, 78
Gardner, Ed (Edgar), 104, 241, 243,
248
Gardner, Gene, 100
Geronimo, 5

Gibbons, Andy, 99
Gibbons, Marion V. ("M.V."),
97–100
Gibson, Billy, 30, 36
Gillespie, Charlie, 130, 132, 156, 166
Globe, selling horses in, 175–176
Gov (Old Gov, horse), 21, 22, 29, 30,
32–36
Graham-Tewksbury feud (Pleasant
Valley War), 173–174, 225–228
Grand Canyon, working at, 62–73
Green, John, 233, 234
Greenhalgh, Pete, 122–125, 195
Greer, Dick, 93
"Grey Eagle," 258, Appendix D
Grover, E. P., 118
guitar, accompanying the fiddle, 83,
87, 104, 156, 158, 231, 234, 242,
244
gun battle, Owens and Blevins
family, 112

Hamilton family, xvi, xxiii
Hance, John, 71–73
Harvey, Fred, 71, 72
Hash Knife outfit, 155, 167, 228
Hatch family, Farmington, N.M.,
95, 96
Heber-Reno driveway (for sheep),
88
"Heel-Toe Polka," 263
Henderson, "Ribs," 178
Henderson, Lynn, 210, 218
Hills, Guy, 238
hoedown, xvii, 38, 234–235
Holbrook: gun battle at, 112–113;
trail's end at, 164–165
Holcomb, Red, 228, 229
"Home Waltz," 86
Hopkins, Dick, (and wife Birdie),
54, 73, 75, 77, 78
horses: wild, 23–25, 27–35; work,
18–22. See also Long H Ranch
Hosteen John, 63, 66
"Humoresque," 248, 251

Hunt, Annella (Kartchner) xvi, 2, 16, 19
Hunt, Belle (Flake), xvi, 7
Hunt, Celia Mounts, 187
Hunt, George W. P., 173
Hunt, Gilbert, 187
Hunt, Hattye, 243
Hunt, Ida, xvi
Hunt, Jefferson, 2, 187
Hunt, John, xvi, 2, 16, 29, 39, 41, 42, 137, 186, 187
Hunt, John Addison, 8, 37, 223
Hunt, Lewis, 18
Hunt, Lois (West), xvi, 189, 245
Hunt, Lois Pratt, 2
Hunt, Marshall, 187
Hunt, Martha, 166
Hunt, Taylor, 29, 30, 32, 33, 35, 36, 100
hunting, waterfowl, 109

Idaho, fiddlers' contest, 249
Isaacson, "Little Ike," 131, 142–147, 152, 163, 166
Italian key, 259

Jack's Canyon, sheep shearing at, 121, 122
Jarvis, C. R. "Rue," 130
Jenkins, Bill, 122–126, 195
Jenkins, Pearl, 126
Jennings, Charles H., 205, 214, 221, 222
Jensen, Len, 97, 118–121
Jenson, George, 130, 132, 156, 164, 166
"Johnny Blevins Tune," Appendix D
Johnson, Neph (Nephi), 59, 60, 62, 63, 69, 71
Jones, Ada, 104, 165
Jones, Jonnie, 54, 78
Joseph City (St. Joseph), 2, 18, 44, 105, 171, 172, 177, 183
julian (Hoolyan) rope catch, 134, 151

Kartchner family, migrates to Arizona, 2
Kartchner, Kenner Casteel. See specific entries: education, fiddling, forest service, Long H Ranch, marriage, etc.
Kartchner, Lafayette Shepherd (Lafe), 3, 80, 99, 100, 186, 195, 244
Kartchner, Lindsey Vernon, 206
Kartchner, Minda, xvi
Kartchner, Nowlin, xvi
Kartchner, Orin, xvi, 1
Kartchner, Thalia, 3, 80, 244
Kartchner, William Decatur, xv, 1, 2, 15–17, 187
Kartchner, Celia, 2
Kartchner, Prudence, xvi
Kaufman, Jake, 52, 53, 107
Kay, Orson, 26
Kay, Phile, 197
Kearns, Johnny, 65, 68, 69
Kissam, Charles H., 210
Knight, Hyrum Jerome ("Noche"), 118, 122, 130–136, 138, 142–144, 150, 153, 160, 162, 163, 167, 168, 227
Knight, Joe, 80, 131, 134, 139, 151, 152, 160–166
KOY radio station, fiddlers' contest, 242–244

lambing, 119–121
Laney, Louis, 237–240
Last Chance Copper Mine, 63, 65
Lathrop, Judd, 105
Latter-Day Saints. See Church of Jesus Christ of Latter-Day Saints
"Leather Britches" (or "Leather Breeches"), xx, 238, Appendix D
Lee, Joe, 95, 96
Lewis, Bill, 102, 103
Lincoln Forest, ranger for, 233
Lincoln Guard Station, 210, 211
Lindsey, Electa Adlee (Kartchner),

xx, 11, 13, 107, 186, 196, 231
Lindsey, Elizabeth Fair, 186–189, 196
Lindsey family, xvi, xxiii, 96
lineman, telephone, as part of ranger job, 210, 212–213
Linstrom, Fred, 51
lobo wolf, 173
logger, working as, 46–51
Long H Ranch, working for, 130–170
Lopez, Benigno, 84
"Lost Goose," 178
Luening, Otto, 246
Lundquist, Peter, 196

Mack, Willard, 191
Mankins, Jack, 179
"Mansion of Aching Hearts," 180
Manzano forest, 88, 216, 236–238, 240
Marker, Pete, xvii, 262
Marker, Solon, xvii, 262
marriage, to Electa Adlee Lindsey, 186
Martinez, Lorenzo, 84
Mason, Billy, 6, 7
Maxwell, Curt, 241
"Meditation from Thais," 251
Merrill, Loren, 127
Merrill, Nellie, 248
Mexican Americans, 89–94
Milford, Utah, 122, 123, 125, 195
Miller, John, 197
Miller, Sarah, 6, 187
mining, at the Grand Canyon, 63–65, 68
"Miss McCleod's Reel," 45
Monson, Gale, 111
Moore, Howard L., 249, 250
Morgan, William, 114
Mormon. See Church of Jesus Christ of Latter-Day Saints
Morris, Jennie (nee Kartchner), 3, 6, 8, 80, 244

Morris, William Ammon, 3
Morrow, Clarence, 116
mule skinner, work as, 52–53, 107–108
Murray, Billy, 165
music. See fiddling; accompaniment
musical transcriptions, xiii, 259, 260, Appendix D

Navajo (town), cowboy dances in, 104–105
Navajo Juan, 63, 66
Nave, Claude, 237
Nave, Judge Frederick S., 176, 177
Nebeker, Professor, xx, 232, 244
Neil (work horse), 18–22
Nelson, John, 119, 120
Nelson, Mollie (nee Baca), 119
Nichols, Don, 19, 131, 141, 142, 151
Noakes, George, 63, 65, 66, 69
Noche. See Knight, Hyrum Jerome
Nuanez, Jose, 94

Old Gov (horse), 21, 22, 29, 30, 32–36
"Old 'C' Waltz," 178, Appendix D
Ortega, David, 84
Ortega, Louis, 94
Ortega, Tom, 84, 94, 95
Osbourne, Charlie, 99
outlaws, 5–7, 113, 169, 222, 226, 229
"Over the Waves," 178
overgrazing, 207, 217
Owens, Clark, 218, 219
Owens, Commodore Perry, 111–114, 225, 228
oysters, mountain, 131, 168

packing mules, 63–69, 198
Padilla, Juan, 20, 21
Palace Saloon, 54, 73, 76–79
Palmer, Alma Z., 15
Palmer Farm, 8, 10
Panguitch, Utah, xvi, 2, 16
Park District. See Phoenix Park

District
Penrod, Eph, 182, 183
Perkins Farm, 2, 25
Perrin, Lila, 75
Perrin, Lilo, 76
Perrin, Robert, 75, 76
Perrin Ranch, 75–78
Peterson, Joseph ("Professor
    Pete"), 11–15
Phoenix, 118, 242–243, 247
Phoenix Park District, ranger at,
    206–230
phonograph, Edison cylinder,
    104–106, 165
piano, accompanying the fiddle, 45,
    54, 73, 78, 242, 244–247
Pickens, Red, 239, 240
Pinchot, Gifford, 196
"Pinedale Waltz," Appendix D
Pitchlynn, Paul P., 222
playback, on cylinder record, 104
Pleasant Valley War (Graham-
    Tewksbury feud), 173–174,
    225–228
poker, 74
Pooler, Frank, 236
Pratt, Addison, 2
Pratt, Louisa Barnes, 2
Pruitt, Frank, xvii, xxiii, 37, 38
Puerco River, 161–162

quadrilles, xvii, xviii, xxii, 38, 49,
    86, 227, 261, 262
Quaid, Hazel, 246
quartet, 128, 179, 244
Queen Creek, sheep shearing at,
    121

racing, horse and foot, 89–96
Radford, Charlie, 178
railroad, 2; at the Grand Canyon,
    61, 62; half-fare deal, 124–126;
    loading cattle, 162; and logging,
    50–51; travel by, 107, 125
Ramsey, Joe, 14

Ramsey, John, 206
ranger. See Forest Service
"Rattlesnake," Appendix D
ranch dances, 262
recordings, cylinders, 104–106;
    modern, xxii–xxiv
reunions, fiddling, xx, xxii, 241,
    248, 249
Rice Seeps campsite, 24–25
Richards, George Elmer, 44, 45, 79,
    171, 175–181, 183
Richards, Hi, 93
Richards, Joseph H., 171
Riggs, Don F. and Marie, 245
Rio de la Plata, Mexican dance at,
    87–93
Roberts, Mose, 112
Robinson, Joseph A. (Joe), 46,
    48–51, 53–57, 59, 62, 69, 71, 73,
    80, 233
rodeos, 89, 136, 182, 190
Rogers, Chase, 98
Rogers, George, 46, 48, 49, 51, 56,
    68, 69, 71, 233
Rogers, Ida, 46, 48, 69
Rogers, Sam, 40, 41
Rogers, Smith D., 14
rolling elbow (bowing style), 260
Roosevelt, Theodore, 77, 175
roundups: of cattle, 209, 214; of wild
    horses, 23–25, 27–35
Ruth, Arch, 90–93
Ruth, Marie, 242
Ruth, Viola ("Mom"), 242, 243
"Rye Waltz," 49, 86, 262, 263

Sacramento Division, 233, 235, 236
Saginaw and Manistee Lumber
    Company, work at, 49–51, 54
"Sally Goodin'," 243
"Sally Johnson," Appendix D
Salt Lake City, 122, 186–190, 192,
    194, 232
Sam Chinaman, 79, 103, 164, 166
Sandberg, Carl, 247

Sanders, Lon, 176
Sanders, Red, 176
Sanders Saloon, 176, 178
Sandoval, Fredrico, 85, 86
Savage, Levi M., 158
Schlee, Harry, 70, 71
schottische, xviii, 49, 178, 235, 262
"Schottische," Appendix D
Schuster, Adolph and Ben, 164
scordatura (tuning down), 259
Scorse, Harry, 94, 164
Scott, George, 119, 121
Scott, James, 223
Seiber, Al, 6
Shane, Oscar, 179
shearing sheep, xii, 114–120,
    122–129, 185, 186, 195, 200
sheet music orchestra, 232–233
Shumway, Charles, 4, 6–8
Shumway, Charlie, 118, 119, 121
Shumway, Dow, 100
Shumway, Ernest, 100
Shumway, James J., 100
Shumway, Lester, 100
Shumway, Merle (nee Kartchner),
    xii, 124, 192, 195, 196, 206, 215,
    223, 233, 245–247, 261
Shumway (town), 4, 87, 95
Silver Creek, 4, 8, 21
Silver Kid (racehorse), 89–96
Sitgreaves National Forest, 88, 197,
    205, 207, 223
Smith & Smith Livery, 103, 105
Smith, Alice 3
Smith and Page, 62, 63, 69
Smith, Basha, 10, 11
Smith, Burton R., 204
Smith, Earl L., 249
Smith, George, 100
Smith, H. B., 105
Smith, Janette Johnson, 61
Smith, Joseph F., 188
Smith, Samuel F., 201, 202
Smithson Effie, 158–160
Smithson, James D., 159

Snow, Erastus, 15
Snowflake, xiv–xxi, xxiii, 1–7, 232
Snowflake Stake Academy, 15
Snowflake Valley, 4, 15, 20
Snyder (Grand Canyon mule), 72
Sorenson, Jim, 130
square dance, xvii, xviii, 234–235,
    261, 262
St. Johns, baseball game at, 97–101
Stainer violin, 247, 249
stampede, 141, 142
Standifird, Bill, 127
Standifird, Lon, 118–120
step-dancing, 45, 121, 261
Stott, James W., 223, 224
Stratton, Cal, 185
Stratton, Ellis, 197
Stratton, Laura, 186
Sunday School superintendent,
    appointed as, 201–204
surveying, by horse, 217–218
"Sweet Adeline," 123, 157, 179, 245
"Sweets O'Weaver," Appendix D

Tafoya, Antolino, xviii, 83–87, 94,
    244
Tanner, Joe, 56, 59–61
technique, fiddling, 237, 240,
    258–260
telephone, xxi, 210–213, 231
Tewksburys, 174, 225
Texas ranchers, in "Little Texas,"
    233–239
Thomas, Joe, 130
"Tom Wagner" ("Waggoner"), 234,
    260, Appendix D
Tonto Basin, and Pleasant Valley
    War, 173, 174, 227
Topock Marsh, 109–111
Torres, Fermin, 119
Torres, Juan, 119
tourists, 62–63, 69–73
tower, at Deer Spring Lookout, 210
train. See railroad
transportation, buggy, 42, 83, 102,

215, 221, 226
Tsegini, 59, 60, 62
tunings, 242, 259
Tusayan National Forest, 205
two-step, 37, 49, 86, 104, 178, 179, 235, 260, 262, 263
two-violin style, 82, 86, 158, 184, 248

U.S. Mail, farmers carrying for, 5, 102
Udall, David K., 200
Udall, Levi S., 101
Uncle Josh, 165
Utah, grandparents migrate from, 1, 2, 16

Vail, Jim, 56
"Valley of Custer," 128
Van Gunten, Gottlieb, 189
varsovienne, xvii, 49, 235, 262,
violin. *See* fiddling
violins, Kartchner's, 249–250
Virginia Reel, 262

"Waggoner" ("Tom Wagner"), 234, Appendix D
Waha, A. O., 219, 220
"Walk Along John to Kansas," Appendix D
Walker, Ez, 89–91, 94–96
waltz, xvii, xviii, 49, 260, 262, 263
waterfowl, at Topock Marsh, 109, 110
Wattron, Frank, xxiii, 105, 106, 164, 165

Webb farm, 9, 10, 17, 196
"Wednesday Night Waltz," 260, Appendix D
Weiser, Idaho, Old-time Fiddlers Contest, 249–250
West, Joseph (Joe), 122, 189, 193, 194
westerns, cowboys in, 168
Wilbur, George, 119, 121
Williams (town), 50–52, 75–79
Willis, Hugh, 99, 100
Willis, Ira, 202
Willis, John Henry, 39
Willow Wash ranger station, xx, 206, 210, 213–216, 219
Wilson, Billy (Jeff), 223
Winslow, George, 52
wolves, lobo, 173
Woodruff, dance at, 157–160
Woods, Joe, 93, 94, 103, 121, 131, 164
wrangling: in 1901, 23–36; with Long H, 130–170
Wright, James H., 228

Young, Brigham, 2, 4, 188
Young, Mrs. Jack, 234, 235
Youngblood, Claude, as Kartchner's fiddling partner: on the dance circuit, 82–87, 101–102; first recording, 104–105; reunions, 240–241, 248–249; starting out, 37–38, 42; Woodruff dance, 157–158

Zulick, Governor, 228